Kathryn
Woodyatt

APPRAISAL

FIFTH EDITION

D1609772

In this revised and updated text, Fletcher and Williams take an evidence-based approach to analysing the key elements of the appraisal process and its place in performance management. Drawing on the academic literature and examples of best practice, the authors explain how performance appraisal can motivate and develop staff, foster commitment and positivity, and ultimately improve an organisation's performance.

Key topics covered include:

- designing an appraisal system
- identifying and developing talent
- multi-level and multi-source feedback
- appraising professionals
- cultural challenges
- evaluating and maintaining appraisal systems.

Appraisal: Improving Performance and Developing the Individual, 5th Edition, is a standard in the field and essential reading for all students of HRM and occupational psychology, and for any HRM professional looking to develop more effective performance appraisal systems.

Clive Fletcher is Professor Emeritus in Occupational Psychology at Goldsmiths, University of London, UK. He has authored more than 200 books, articles and conference papers on appraisal and assessment, and has been a consultant on appraisal to a wide range of organisations in both the public and private sectors.

Richard Williams has had a career that has spanned the academic world and the public sector as an occupational psychologist. Previous posts include Programme Director for MSc courses in the Organizational Psychology Department at Birkbeck, University of London, and Chief Occupational Psychologist in a UK government department.

APPRAISAL

Improving performance and developing the individual

FIFTH EDITION

Clive Fletcher and Richard Williams

Routledge
Taylor & Francis Group

LONDON AND NEW YORK

Fifth edition published 2016
by Routledge
2 Park Square, Milton Park, Abingdon, Oxon OX14 4RN

and by Routledge
711 Third Avenue, New York, NY 10017

Routledge is an imprint of the Taylor & Francis Group, an informa business

© 2016 Clive Fletcher and Richard Williams

The right of Clive Fletcher and Richard Williams to be identified as the authors of this work has been asserted by them in accordance with sections 77 and 78 of the Copyright, Designs and Patents Act 1988.

All rights reserved. No part of this book may be reprinted or reproduced or utilised in any form or by any electronic, mechanical, or other means, now known or hereafter invented, including photocopying and recording, or in any information storage or retrieval system, without permission in writing from the publishers.

Every effort has been made to contact copyright holders for their permission to reprint material in this book. The publishers would be grateful to hear from any copyright holder who is not here acknowledged and will undertake to rectify any errors or omissions in future editions of this book.

Trademark notice: Product or corporate names may be trademarks or registered trademarks, and are used only for identification and explanation without intent to infringe.

First published by the Chartered Institute of Personnel and Development 2004
Fourth edition published by Routledge 2008

British Library Cataloguing in Publication Data
A catalogue record for this book is available from the British Library.

Library of Congress Cataloging in Publication Data

Names: Fletcher, Clive, author. | Fletcher, Clive. Appraisal, feedback and development.
Title: Appraisal : improving performance and developing the individual/Clive Fletcher and Richard Williams.
Description: Fifth Edition. | New York : Routledge, 2016. | Revised edition of Appraisal, 2008. | Includes bibliographical references and index.
Identifiers: LCCN 2015046990| ISBN 9781138936096 (hardback) | ISBN 9781138936102 (pbk.) | ISBN 9781315677040 (ebook)
Subjects: LCSH: Employees--Rating of. | Performance standards.
Classification: LCC HF5549.5.R3 F556 2016 | DDC 658.3/125–dc23
LC record available at http://lccn.loc.gov/2015046990

ISBN: 978-1-138-93609-6 (hbk)
ISBN: 978-1-138-93610-2 (pbk)
ISBN: 978-1-315-67704-0 (ebk)

Typeset in Times New Roman
by Sunrise Setting Ltd
Printed by Ashford Colour Press Ltd.

CONTENTS

BOXES

CHAPTER 10

CHAPTER 11

APPENDIX A

PREFACE

This is intended to be a book on appraisal that gives the reader a sound grasp of both the academic theory and research base that underpin performance appraisal (PA), and the practical issues that arise in motivating, developing and assessing employee performance in the context of such systems. As such, it is aimed both at students studying formal courses and programmes which include or specifically focus on the subject of appraisal, and at human resource (HR) professionals, consultants and line managers who have the responsibility for setting up appraisal systems or revising existing ones. There is always a danger of falling between two stools in trying to meet the needs of student and practitioner audiences, but this is a risk we are happy to take because we strongly believe in evidence-based practice, and that students who are studying topics in this area should be given a good grasp of the practical realities and not just the theory.

The vast majority of organisations already have some kind of appraisal arrangements in place, so most practitioner readers are probably seeking to build on previous appraisal work in their organisation. It would be nice to think that this new building will be on sound foundations rather than on the ruins of an appraisal system that has become discredited, but experience suggests that this is not always going to be the case. Indeed, in the midst of writing this edition, the media were awash with reports of how a number of leading companies, notably Accenture and Deloitte, but many others also (see Pulakos *et al.*, 2015) were abandoning PA and much of performance management (PM) generally. Actually, what they were planning to cease to do was (a) to have a forced distribution of employee ratings or rankings; or (b) to hold a once-a-year discussion of performance between line managers and their staff. Perhaps the most astonishing thing is that organisations of this calibre were still following these practices, which many others had long since dropped and swapped for more effective strategies, and which had in most instances been found wanting by academic research over literally decades. And this is perhaps one of the biggest problems in PA and PM – the failure of some organisations to avail themselves of the relevant academic research. Or indeed simply to learn from experience – there has been a tendency to apply the same discredited solutions to PM problems over and over again. Fortunately, we are witnessing the demise of the 'one-size-fits-all' monolithic appraisal system. Doubtless the idea of a universally applied, ratings-driven, standard procedure that stays rigidly in place for years (perhaps kept there by the weight of its own paperwork) will lumber on in some quarters for a while yet, but its days are certainly numbered, and not a minute too soon. In keeping with that, the reader will *not* find in these pages copies of umpteen varieties of appraisal forms and documentation. This is not a book that places great emphasis on this aspect of appraisal, chiefly because there is little reason to believe that the forms themselves are all that important. Rather, the book will present a series of key issues in developing and implementing appraisal, review the relevant theory, give a description of some of the ways taken in dealing with these issues and, where possible, offer an evaluation of these approaches based on research. And as that research shows, PA and PM *can* be highly effective in generating positive attitudes, fostering commitment and impacting on organisational performance and the delivery of services (see Chapter 11).

Such is the remit of PA that a book on it has to cover a very wide range of complex topics and techniques – job analysis, management competencies, assessment centres, interview methods and so on. Many of these topics merit a book in themselves, so wherever relevant, the reader will be given references to more specialised texts. The evaluation of the varying approaches to appraisal looked at here will be based on organisational experience and on research findings. It would be less than honest to pretend that such an evaluation could be totally objective, any more than appraisal itself. The authors' own views and personal experience will surface from time to time. Arising out of the material reviewed, the lessons for good practice will be distilled and identified (see Chapter 11), which will, it is hoped, help students and practitioners to build future performance appraisal schemes better suited to the needs of both themselves and their organisations.

This is the fifth edition of this book, and the context of PA and PM has changed considerably from the last edition (2008). We have just been through a major economic recession, which impacted the priorities given to PA and thus how it was applied. Emerging from that recession, one would hope for a more positive emphasis on the developmental function of PA in the years ahead. Quite apart from economic circumstances and pressures, however, other changes have continued at a considerable pace. These include the ever-increasing globalisation of business – with the cultural diversity challenges it brings – and the relentlessly expanding knowledge base that runs all the way from advances in information technology (IT) to developments in brain sciences. The book will touch on all these points in one context or another. The wider application of PA and PM generally to public-sector bodies and to a broader range of organisational levels, which was noted in the last edition, has continued – perhaps somewhat ironically, given all the criticism of such systems. Finally, in terms of change, many organisations have gone through even more radical restructuring in response to the economic pressures of recent years. This has led to more flexible modes of operating. Managers have to build and manage virtual teams that cross organisational – and sometimes international – boundaries and which may exist only for the duration of the immediate task. These changes have far-reaching implications for appraisal practice, and have fuelled the application of methods such as multi-source, multi-level approaches to assessment and development, use of which seems still to be expanding. At various points we will address all these issues, and in doing so, we will draw on a wide range of sources and literature. This new edition of the book not only has an updated research literature, but is considerably longer than its predecessor, not least because we have devoted more space to consideration of the wider HR context and to the positioning of PA within PM. In this respect, we have included more material on the underlying psychological theories and constructs relevant to this domain. This is a very deliberate change as we feel that the knowledge base provided by occupational and organisational psychology is the most relevant and helpful in understanding and improving the nature and application of PA and PM.

REFERENCE

Pulakos, E. D., Hansen, R. M., Arad, S. and Moye, N. (2015) Performance management can be fixed: An on-the-job experiential learning approach for complex behavior change. *Industrial and Organizational Psychology*, **8**(1), 51–76.

DISCLAIMER

The publishers have made every effort to contact authors/copyright holders of works reprinted in this new edition of *Appraisal*. This has not been possible in every case, however, and we would welcome correspondence from those individuals/companies whom we have been unable to trace.

APPRAISAL AND ITS PLACE IN PERFORMANCE MANAGEMENT

1

There are few more persistent topics of dissatisfaction in organisations than the appraisal scheme. Over the years there have been numerous reports of one sort or another recording discontent with performance appraisal. Indeed, the shift from performance apppraisal (PA) to performance management (PM) can be attributed, in part, to concern that appraisal, as a backward-looking activity, is an insufficient tool for managing employee performance. But, as we will see, performance management seems to have fared little better: the view that performance management is broken is readily to be found (e.g. Pulakos and O'Leary, 2011; Deloitte, 2014).

Undoubtedly, appraisal has become an emotive word. This is partly because it tends to be done rather poorly, and partly because organisations persist in ignoring the clear messages that academic research provides about what will and won't work, and why. Perhaps as a result of this unpopularity, many organisations have displayed considerable ingenuity in thinking up alternative titles for what is often much the same process: 'Performance Review', 'Performance and Development Review', 'Work Planning and Review' and the like. The drift of these changes has been to emphasise the more forward-looking aspects of appraisal, and to play down the retrospective assessment element. This is particularly evident in the shift of terminology from performance appraisal to performance management. But it takes more than a change of name to shift people's perceptions, and staff still commonly refer to it as 'the appraisal' irrespective of any new label it has been given. Nor is it the case that the replacement terminology has improved things. So, for example, PM has come to take on negative connotations, particularly in the recent recessionary years (since 2008) with PM being seen as very much about the management of poor or underperformance.

No matter how difficult it is to devise satisfactory performance appraisal arrangements, the need for them is hard to avoid. Appraisal will take place in an unstructured and perhaps highly subjective form wherever and whenever people work together. They will automatically form judgements about their own abilities and performance and those of their colleagues. To try to deny this is foolish. Have you ever talked to employees who had no opinions about their bosses, their peers, their subordinates or themselves? Organisations which try to avoid the issue by not having appraisal arrangements will simply end up having the same processes occurring without them being open to scrutiny or to control, with all the potential for bias and unfairness that this holds. So, appraisal is here to stay. But over the years we have seen changes in thinking about appraisal, and both the nature of appraisal practice and the wider context in which it is set have changed.

FROM PERFORMANCE APPRAISAL TO PERFORMANCE MANAGEMENT

It is probably fair to say that since the mid-1960s the shift from PA to PM has been more evolution than revolution. And throughout that evolution there have been enduring problems. McGregor (1957) pinpointed the reluctance of managers to give critical feedback to their people. In his view, much of this stemmed from their having to make judgements about personality traits (which were the focus of appraisal at that time) – appraisers felt uncomfortable doing this. Empirical studies by Meyer *et al.* (1965) lent support for McGregor's analysis. They found that criticism in the interview seemed particularly damaging and unhelpful, especially if the appraisal was linked to rewards (chiefly pay). They advocated, on the basis of their studies, that pay should be separated from the appraisal as far as possible – it simply promoted more defensiveness on the appraisee's part. The appraisal–pay linkage continues to be a major area of difficulty, as we will explore later.

Like McGregor, Maier (1958) advocated a participative, problem-solving approach, on the grounds that self-generated action plans were more likely to be implemented than anything manager-imposed. The role of the appraiser was more that of 'helper' than that of 'judge' – in other words, to assist the individual in the formulation of their own goals and in assessing the extent to which they had been reached. Appraisal thus became more future-orientated than had previously been the case.

However, in the 1970s, particularly in the United States but also elsewhere, legal perspectives on appraisal turned the focus back on assessment more than development. Various equal opportunities provisions placed appraisal schemes under scrutiny in the courts and the public eye more broadly, resulting in numerous cases where the courts rejected the fairness of organisations' appraisal schemes. This equal opportunities interest in appraisal practice reinforced the psychometric perspective on appraisal, central to which was the use of performance ratings. From the inception of appraisal practice, such ratings have featured prominently. As noted above, there was some shift in *what* is rated (away from personality to performance, variously defined) and there have been different rating formats, but ratings have by no means disappeared, most particularly in the USA, where the psychometric tradition that views appraisal as a rational measurement process continues to hold considerable influence. Decades of research investigated rating-scale formats with the aim of increasing the accuracy of ratings – but with very limited success. In an extremely important review paper, Landy and Farr (1980) called for a moratorium on research on rating formats, arguing that attention should shift to a better understanding of the rating process as an information-processing activity. As such, appraisal may be seen as:

> [A] complex memory task in which the assessors must:
> - acquire performance information about an employee
> - encode and store that information in their memory
> - retrieve that information at a later date when asked to assess the employee's performance
> - weigh and combine the information into an overall performance judgment.
>
> (Fisher *et al.*, 1993)

Here again, little resulted in terms of greater rating accuracy – if anything, the information-processing perspective added to the reasons why we should *not* expect accurate ratings. And still more reasons for this were highlighted by the work of Longenecker *et al.* (1987) – inflated ratings were the likely consequence of the political factors they identified as a reality of organisational life:

> Politics played a role in the evaluation process because:
> - executives took into consideration the daily interpersonal dynamics between them and their subordinates;
> - the formal appraisal results in a permanent written document;
> - the formal appraisal can have considerable impact on the subordinate's career and advancement.
>
> (Longenecker *et al.*, 1987: 185)

Round about the same time, Cleveland and Murphy (1992) were approaching appraisal from the perspective of the goals of the parties most closely involved (appraiser and appraised). In doing so, they too questioned the rationalist, psychometric perspective and argued for viewing appraisal as a social and communication process. In these terms, appraisal takes place within a social context that involves two parties (at least) – the appraiser and appraisee. As a communication process, appraisal involves these two parties in, for example, agreeing performance requirements and giving and receiving feedback on performance – very much the stance adopted by McGregor, Maier, Meyer and others. Similar questioning of the rational, psychometric perspective (and of the political perspective) came from Folger *et al.* (1992: 164), who called for a more flexible approach to appraisal on the grounds that "No single PA approach will be consistently the best across all situations and different PA approaches will have strengths and weaknesses in relation to the type of job being assessed." Generally speaking, however – and unfortunately – these shifts in thinking failed to have as much impact in practice as they deserved, even to the present day.

What did happen, though, was that the need to embed appraisal in a wider context of human resource management (HRM) strategies – instead of it being a kind of stand-alone procedure that had a life of its own – was recognised. Specifically, it became a key element in PM. The origin of this concept and term dates back to the 1970s (Warren, 1972; Beer and Ruh, 1976), but it was only in the late 1980s and early 1990s that it became widely adopted – and still is. Initially, the nature of PM in practice was far from clear. In the first substantial report on PM in the UK the then Institute of Personnel Management (1992: 5) concluded, "There was no consistent definition of performance management among those professing to operate it." That said, it nonetheless became possible to discern three main perspectives on PM:

1. a system for managing organisational performance;
2. a system for managing employee performance;
3. a system for integrating the management of organisational and employee performance – these vary in the extent to which they place emphasis on the management of organisational or employee performance.

The first of these perspectives is very much about matters to do with formulating the organisation's mission and strategy and implementing that strategy through the organisation's technology, structure, business systems and processes, etc. All of these things are likely to impinge on employees and their performance, but it shouldn't be assumed that such impact necessarily is a primary concern or indeed recognised at all. It is hard to see the second perspective as anything other than a change in terminology – that is, the term 'performance management' replaced 'performance appraisal', reflecting the broader-ranging approach to appraisal that had come into being (and which we focus on in this book): in other words, a process having a forward-looking element, a backward-looking assessment element and a feedback-giving element, with all of this operating (supposedly) on an ongoing basis. In some organisations, this might be referred to as PM.

One way of looking at the third model is to view it simply as setting the second in the context of the first. In an integrative model that places the greater emphasis on employee performance, the broader organisational strategy, business processes, etc. are the context within which employee-focused PM fits. This model views employee performance management as an HR process and a central theme in this perspective on PM is alignment or congruence – in particular, the alignment of individuals' performance goals (and those of teams) with those of the organisation as a whole. A fair degree of consensus emerged as to the elements found within this conception of PM – essentially a cycle of activity (as illustrated in Box 1.1) incorporating policies and practices focusing on some or all of the following aspects of employee performance:

• directing/planning
• managing/supporting
• reviewing/appraising
• developing/rewarding.

So, in this model, appraisal is viewed narrowly as a backward-looking assessment activity. The four PM-related elements are set within the broader organisational context, with particular emphasis being placed on two aspects:

1. the organisation's mission, objectives and business plan; and
2. communication about that mission, etc.

BOX 1.1

ILLUSTRATIVE PERFORMANCE MANAGEMENT CYCLE

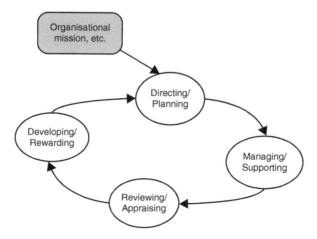

What this has meant in practical terms has varied widely, as one would expect. And what was intended by the developers of PM processes – typically the HR function – very often was not what came to be implemented in practice by line managers, even though line managers were cast as the 'owners' of PM. Nor, for that matter, was the employee experience as envisaged by HR – employee involvement and participation may have been advocated, but were not necessarily experienced.

As well as alignment/congruence, another central theme in the consensus about PM as an HR process was *integration* – specifically, integration with other HR processes and procedures. According to den Hartog *et al.* (2004: 559): "The performance management perspective stresses the need to align HRM practices with the aim of affecting employee and organisational performance. Thus, an integrated set of HRM practices is central to performance management."

APPRAISAL IN CONTEXT

There is no single context for PA. We have referred to several already – the immediate social context, the broader organisational context and the context of other HR policies. An illustration of the HR context is the conceptual model of PM put forward by den Hartog *et al.* (2004) shown in Box 1.2. So, in these terms, PA may be viewed as one of a number of PM-related HRM practices. Exactly what these HRM practices are will vary from organisation to organisation, of course.

A question of considerable practical interest has to do with the impact that HR practices have on performance. This is far from clear. Part of the difficulty here has to do with defining and measuring performance. We consider this at the level of the individual employee in Chapter 3. At more aggregated levels – a particular function, department, business unit, the whole organisation – it may be possible to identify a range of performance indicators (both subjective and objective), but this still leaves open to question what kind of a relationship one would expect to find between particular HR practices and particular indicators of performance. For example, Purcell and Kinnie (2007: 6) make this point with reference to financial indicators of organisational performance: "The problem with published financial measures is that no convincing explanation can be provided as to why, or indeed how, HR practices have an influence." They also make the point (2007: 6) that financial performance indicators are "far removed from HRM influence"; the model in Box 1.2 illustrates this well. So it is hardly surprising that many studies have failed to show a strong association between HRM practices and organisational-level performance measures. But some association has been established, and Paauwe (2009: 133) concludes that "HR practices, be it individually or bundled in a system, are at least weakly related to firm performance." Is this a disappointing finding? Well, it may be nothing other than a reflection of what is a still developing field of research that is being pursued under various banners; for example, strategic HRM (Snow and Snell, 2012), high-performance work practices (Belt and Giles, 2009; Belt and Rüdiger, 2010), high-involvement work processes (Wood and de Menezes, 2011) and employee voice (Wilkinson and Fay, 2011). The difficulties are threefold: it isn't clear what practices should be counted as high-performance/high-involvement (nor how they should be operationalised); it isn't clear what should be measured as the criteria (financial indicators, output measures, customer satisfaction, etc.?); and, as indicated above, the rationale for expecting a relationship between the two (whatever they might be) is lacking. We return to this theme in Chapter 11 in the more specific context of appraisal for which there is more promising evidence of impact.

Inside the 'black box'

Much happens between the HR function launching, say, performance management on unsuspecting managers and employees, and outcomes at the organisational level. It is understandable that HR should want to demonstrate

BOX 1.2

MANAGING PERFORMANCE IN ORGANISATIONS – A CONCEPTUAL MODEL OF THE HRM AND PERFORMANCE RELATIONSHIP FROM A PM PERSPECTIVE

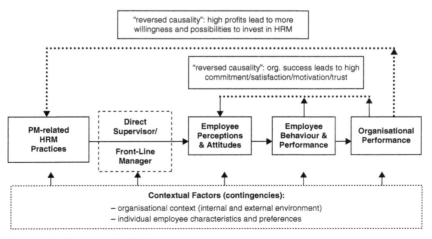

Source: den Hartog *et al.* (2004)

its worth and the value of the policies and practices that it develops. From this perspective, trying to show a relationship between an HR practice (or 'bundles' of practices) and some measure(s) of organisational performance makes sense. But this tells us nothing about the thoughts and feelings that managers and employees have about the policies that HR implements. Understanding these psychological aspects is referred to as unlocking the 'black box' of HRM. For example, there is likely to be an expectation on the part of HR managers that HRM processes will be implemented by line managers as intended by the HR department. But evidence (Truss, 2001) and experience suggest that many do not implement them as intended. It is quite likely that there are many reasons for this. The findings we referred to earlier in this chapter on the 'politics' of appraisal give some examples. Another example comes from a Belgian study which found, not surprisingly, that managers' perceptions of "the usefulness of PM activities are an important determinant of a successful implementation of PM policies" (Dewettinck and Vroonen, 2013: 21).

In similar vein, individual employees vary in their enactment of appraisal practices, regardless of what part in the process HR may have written for them. They will have thoughts and feelings (attitudes) about why the appraisal process is being introduced, about the nature of the process as it is expressed on paper, and about their actual experience of that process. So, for example, Nishii *et al.* (2008) have shown that employees make attributions about the 'why' of HR practices and these attributions bear on the attitudes that employees hold. Their study showed that an "attribution that HR practices are motivated by the organization's concern for enhancing service quality and employee well-being was positively related to employee attitudes [and an] attribution focused on reducing costs and exploiting employees was negatively associated with attitudes" (2008: 527). The attitudes that they measured were affective commitment (that is, the individual's feeling of attachment to the organisation) and overall satisfaction. Moreover, these positive attitudes were associated with aspects of organisational citizenship (see Chapter 3, pages 43–4) – specifically, helping behaviours and displays of conscientiousness (e.g. following rules); and, in turn, helping behaviours were positively associated with customer satisfaction.

As Boxall and Macky (2009) have argued:

> [I]f management wants to bring about valued organizational outcomes, it needs to influence employee beliefs, attitudes and behavior. Employee behavior is critical to whether the desired organizational outcomes will be achieved, and is influenced by employee perceptions of, and their cognitive and affective responses to, HR practices.
>
> (Boxall and Macky, 2009: 267)

This is as true for PA/PM practices as it is for any other HR practice. And there is no shortage of employee attitudes and responses that have been studied over the years. For example, there is a long history of studying employee job satisfaction and employees' commitment to their organisation. In more recent years, attention has shifted towards employee well-being and, most recently, something called 'employee engagement'. It is likely that a performer's experience of appraisal will have some impact on all of these.

So far as *job satisfaction* is concerned, much of the interest has been in seeking to establish that it leads to employee job performance – the so-called 'happy–productive worker' hypothesis. The balance of opinion (Judge and Kammeyer-Mueller, 2012; Bowling, 2013; Burt, 2014) concludes that the evidence supports the idea that a happy worker is indeed a productive worker. But the strength of the association is of a relatively modest order. This is probably because the relationship between job satisfaction and performance is more complex than ordinarily thought. There are many facets to satisfaction and many facets to job performance – we will expand on the latter in Chapter 3. And many influences bear on satisfaction – characteristics of the job itself, as one would expect, along with others such as the social environment (e.g. relationships with co-workers and supervisors) and leadership, leader consideration behaviours (e.g. showing concern, expressing appreciation) being particularly significant (Judge and Kammeyer-Mueller, 2012).

Turning to the concept of *organisational commitment*, interest in this arose at a time when there was considerable concern about high levels of employee turnover and the associated costs. So, the core idea here is that a committed employee will be a loyal employee, as this early definition makes clear:

> [T]he strength of an individual's identification with and involvement in a particular organization. Conceptually, it can be characterized by at least three factors:
> a. a strong belief in and acceptance of an organization's goals and values;
> b. a willingness to exert considerable effort on behalf of the organization;
> c. a strong desire to maintain membership of the organization.
> (Mowday *et al.*, 1982: 267)

As with job satisfaction, here also the implication is that a committed employee will be a better performer – "exert considerable effort". Theorising about the nature of commitment has recognised different forms of commitment, labelled by Meyer (2014) as "*affective* (want to), *normative* (ought to), and *continuance* (have to) commitment". And any one individual is likely to vary in the extent of each of these commitments, leading to the idea of a commitment profile. So, someone may feel a low level of affective commitment (they don't want to stay), not feel any sense of obligation (low normative commitment), but feel that they have to stay (high continuance commitment) because of the high costs of leaving or lack of other job opportunities.

Is an organisationally committed employee a loyal employee? Well, generally speaking, the evidence supports this relationship. But does an organisationally committed employee "exert considerable effort"? Possibly not: "those with a strong affective commitment are more likely to exert discretionary effort on behalf of the organization than are those with other mindsets, particularly continuance commitment" (Meyer, 2014). But, as is the case with job satisfaction, the strength of the association between a given form of commitment and a particular outcome is of a low order. So, here again, we have a phenomenon that is less straightforward than it might appear at first sight.

What about well-being? What's the evidence for a relationship between employee well-being and performance? Well-being is a more complex concept than either satisfaction or commitment. Indeed, some models of well-being incorporate these two concepts along with several other facets – Box 1.3 gives an illustration. There's broad consensus on three main aspects of well-being: a *happiness* dimension (sometimes referred to as *psychological*), a *health* dimension (sometimes referred to as *physical*) and a *relationships* dimension (sometimes referred to as *social*) (Grant *et al.*, 2007; Van De Voorde *et al.*, 2012).

BOX 1.3

WORK-RELATED WELL-BEING

- *Affective well-being:* e.g., job satisfaction, organizational commitment, emotional exhaustion/fatigue
- *Professional well-being:* e.g., aspiration and competence at work, autonomy
- *Social well-being:* e.g., depersonalization towards colleagues, quality of social functioning at work
- *Cognitive well-being:* e.g., the capacity to take up new information at work, ability to concentrate at work
- *Psychosomatic well-being:* e.g., health complaints such as headaches, stomach aches and symptoms of possible cardiovascular issues.

Source: Van Horn *et al.* (2004)

Systematic review findings about the relationship between HRM, well-being and performance report a preponderance of evidence supporting the view that HRM policies and practices are positively associated with happiness well-being and organisational performance, and this was found to be the case for relationships well-being too (Van De Voorde *et al.*, 2012; Peccei *et al.*, 2013). There was less evidence for health-related well-being and it was consistent with the so-called 'pessimistic' (Peccei, 2004) view of the HRM–well-being–performance relationship: "The pessimistic view of employee well-being and organizational performance as conflicting outcomes holds that there is a trade-off between employee well-being and organizational performance: enhancements in organizational performance are achieved at the cost of reduced employee well-being" (Van De Voorde *et al.*, 2012: 393).

That there are different dimensions to well-being gives rise to the possibility that a given HR practice (or set of practices) may have different impacts. Grant *et al.* (2007) provide some illustrations of this. So, for example, job enrichment may promote job satisfaction, but with potential risks to health – increased strain, fatigue and possible overload. Likewise, forms of incentive compensation may promote job satisfaction, but at the risk of harm to social well-being – for example, through the use of individual rewards in team settings.

Finally, in our exploration of the black box, let's consider employee engagement. In recent years, bold claims have been made for the performance benefits of employee engagement. For example, here's a selection of statements revealed by an Internet search in mid-June 2015:

- Engaged employees deliver greater productivity, better customer service, superior-quality products and services, and more innovative solutions. (www.aon.com/unitedkingdom/employee-engagement.jsp)
- Every disengaged employee, on the other hand, can cost an organisation more than £5,000 in annual profits. (www.aon.com/unitedkingdom/employee-engagement.jsp)
- It is no secret that engaged employees perform better, are more productive and are more likely to stick around. Most modern studies now show a direct link between engagement level and business profitability and financial performance. (http://hr-engagement.com/)
- Employee engagement is a win–win situation. (http://peopleinsight.co.uk/about-employee-engagement/)
- Employers get a more productive workforce who go that extra mile for the company and deliver better customer service. Employees get a job that they believe has real value, one which interests them and develops their talents, with fair recognition and reward. They are your best

advocates and usually want to stick around. Employee engagement benefits the health of employers and their employees alike. (http:// peopleinsight.co.uk/about-employee-engagement/)

While there is a lot of seemingly positive evidence about the outcomes of engagement, this cannot be accepted uncritically. As Briner (2014: 66) notes, "many of the claims made by proponents of employee engagement appear to be exaggerated and use supporting evidence which seems to be about something else". We concur with Briner and think that the sorts of claims commonly seen should be viewed with a high degree of caution, for several reasons.

First, there is no consensus as to the nature of employee engagement. Multiple interpretations are to be found, as Box 1.4 illustrates. The first few definitions come from the consultancy world: they are intended to be illustrative rather than necessarily representative. You might find yourself thinking that a couple of the definitions remind you of the Mowday *et al.* (1982) definition of organisational commitment that we referred earlier (see 'Inside the "black box"'). Do you work in an organisation that uses items like the following to measure employee engagement?

- I am willing to put in a great deal of effort beyond that normally expected in order to help this organisation be successful.
- I talk up this organisation to my friends as a great organisation to work for.
- I am proud to tell others that I am part of this organisation.
- This organisation really inspires the very best in me in the way of job performance.

Well, these are all items used by Mowday *et al.* (1979) in their Organizational Commitment Questionnaire, one of the measures that goes back to the early days in the study of the concept. So, is employee engagement really a new idea at all?

The last three definitions in Box 1.4 are from academics, again intended to be illustrative. And the main point being illustrated across the definitions is that they are more different than similar; but in order to draw general conclusions from different studies, those different studies need to be measuring the same thing. Yet when it comes to employee engagement, it often isn't clear at all what has been measured. Second, the studies need to be of a nature that allows causality to be inferred. This is a general problem with studies of the relationship between a work attitude and performance, but it seems to be particularly acute with engagement, notably because of an apparent readiness to make extravagant claims without any qualification.

BOX 1.4

PERSPECTIVES ON ENGAGEMENT

- Employee Engagement is defined as the extent to which employees are motivated to contribute to organisational success, and are willing to apply discretionary effort to accomplishing tasks important to the achievement of organisational goals. An engaged employee has pride in, advocates for, and is loyal to his/her employer and exerts discretionary effort toward achieving employer goals. (Kenexa, 2010: 2)
- We define engagement as employees' willingness and ability to contribute to company success. Put another way, engagement is the extent to which employees 'go the extra mile' and put discretionary effort into their work – contributing more of their energy, creativity and passion on the job. (Towers Perrin, n.d.: 3)
- We define engagement as a psychological state in which employees feel a vested interest in the company's success and are both willing and motivated to perform to levels that exceed the stated job requirements. It reflects how employees feel about the overall work experience – the organisation, its leaders, the work environment, and the recognition they receive for their efforts. (Mercer, 2007: 1)
- ORC International defines an engaged employee as one who "says", "stays" and "strives". They say – they are positive advocates of the company. They stay – they are committed to the company and want to stay as an employee. Last, but not least, they strive – they are willing to put in discretionary effort to excel in their job and help their company succeed. (ORC International, n.d.: 3)
- *Personal engagement*: "harnessing of organization members' selves to their work roles: in engagement, people employ and express themselves physically, cognitively, emotionally and mentally during role performances". (Kahn, 1990: 694)
- *Self-engagement/job engagement*: "feeling responsible for and committed to superior job performance, so that job performance 'matters' to the individual. . . . Because employees who are engaged in their work feel a sense of personal responsibility for their job performance, the outcomes that occur at work have greater implications for their identity. Therefore, to be engaged in work is also to care about and be committed to performing well." (Britt *et al.*, 2007: 144)
- *Work engagement*: "a positive, fulfilling, work-related state of mind that is characterised by vigour, dedication, and absorption.

- **Vigour** is characterised by high levels of energy and mental resilience while working, the willingness to invest effort in one's work, and persistence even in the face of difficulties.
- **Dedication** refers to being strongly involved in one's work, and experiencing a sense of significance, enthusiasm, inspiration, pride, and challenge.
- **Absorption** is characterised by being fully concentrated and happily engrossed in one's work, whereby time passes quickly and one has difficulties with detaching oneself from work." (Schaufeli and Salanova, 2007: 381)

As we've tried to show in these past few pages, understanding what is happening in the black box is highly complex. Several constructs describing employee thoughts and feelings are clearly implicated as important factors in the relationship between HR practices and performance. The reader will encounter them again at various points during the course of this book. But quite how much impact PM-related HR practices have on performance (individual, team, unit or whatever level, up to the organisation as a whole) continues to be a matter of great debate. Indeed, it probably is impossible to quantify the impact with any great precision, especially given that it is difficult enough even to demonstrate a causal relationship between HR practices and performance. Still more difficult is demonstrating reverse causality, but it is important to acknowledge this possibility, and den Hartog *et al.* represent it in their model. They suggest (2004: 565): "Organisational success (e.g. high profits or growth of market share) could increase (a) the willingness of top management to invest in HR practices, and (b) the employees' commitment, trust, and motivation."

IS PERFORMANCE MANAGEMENT WORKING?

This is by no means an easy question to answer, but as we noted at the outset, there is no shortage of opinions that it isn't. To the extent that traditional appraisal practice remains at the heart of performance management, it seems likely that the criticisms levelled against PA will continue to apply to PM. Stereotypes and prejudice still are a risk, managers continue to attach insufficient weight to factors in the workplace when they make their judgements (that is, failures of attribution), and some of the long-established areas of difficulty may have been exacerbated by changes that have taken place in some organisations. So, for example, flatter hierarchies will have increased spans of control, thereby adding to the manager's appraisal challenge (Dewettinck and

Vroonen, 2013). More distributed forms of working represent another illustration of an organisational change that has made traditional top-down appraisal more difficult.

But a quick glance at the literature on PM reveals additional problems. For example, one concerns alignment, a central plank of PM practice. A common approach to bringing this about is a cascading process – organisational-level goals are progressively cascaded downwards until they are reflected in performance goals for the individual employee. By this means, a *performance logic* (Rummler and Brache, 1995) or clear *line of sight* is established. But this is one of the key features of contemporary PM practice that has been called into question. For example, Pulakos and O'Leary (2011) point to the mismatch between what is advocated by proponents of cascading and everyday reality (Box 1.5).

Given the perception that PM is not producing the results expected of it, not surprisingly it tends to get reviewed rather frequently. For example, the 2015 Deloitte *Global Human Capital Trends* survey reported that 89 per cent of organisations have either recently revised their PM process or are planning to do so.

BOX 1.5

CASCADING ORGANISATIONAL GOALS – THE GAP BETWEEN ADVOCACY AND PRACTICE

Proponents advocate	Reality
• Cascade goals so that each level supports goals relevant to the prior higher level	• Organisational goals can be lofty and difficult to cascade down to individuals
• Help employees gain an understanding of how their work relates to higher levels	• It is time consuming and difficult to cascade goals, especially the first time
• Align the employee's activities with the organisation's strategic direction and goals	• Considerable consultant or HR time is needed to facilitate the cascade
	• If employees do not attach a high value to cascaded goals, the burdensome process will be frustrating and yield negative attitudes
	• The advantages associated with cascading goals can be achieved through more informal and simpler communication processes

Source: Pulakos and O'Leary (2011)

Other surveys and reports much more explicitly state the view that performance management isn't working as well as is desired. So, in one Australian survey (Australian Human Resources Institute [AHRI], 2008) more than a third of respondents rated their organisations' PM processes as ineffective; less than half saw their processes as only somewhat effective. In the United States, fewer than half (43 per cent) of respondents to a WorldatWork (2010) survey viewed their organisation's PM systems as effective. And less than half (47 per cent) of the respondents to an earlier survey published in the USA by the Society for Human Resource Management (2000) said they were satisfied with their PM systems. It is hardly surprising, therefore, that the view has emerged that performance management is broken (Pulakos and O'Leary, 2011) – or, at least, not operating as well as organisations wish it to. Why might this be?

Well, surveys offer some possible answers. For example, in the eyes of 63 per cent of respondents to a WorldatWork (2010) survey, "managers lack courage to have difficult performance discussions". And in the AHRI (2008) survey, about half the respondents reported appraisal skills as being average, and a quarter as below average. To be sure, the explanation – or part of it – may lie with 'deficiencies' on the part of the line manager. But blaming line managers merely invites questions such as:

- Have the 'right' people been appointed as managers; that is, was selection made on the basis of skills in managing people?
- What training have they had?
- How have they been supported by managers more senior to them?

We will come back to training in Chapter 10; for now, we will conclude with another view as to why performance management isn't working – that performance management is just too big and too complex.

This view has been well articulated by the Institute of Employment Studies (Hirsh *et al.*, 2011):

> Performance management has become such a key process in the eyes of HR professionals that the function is tempted to put more and more things it would like to address into this process. The shift in terminology from performance appraisal to performance management was intended to make the process more relevant to the business. It has, however, also encouraged HR to put more and more ideas into that concept of 'performance management'. Each time HR adds in another idea to its own performance management story, it becomes a bit more complex and the list of purposes for this system tends to grow.
>
> (Hirsh *et al.*, 2011: 1)

One might add to this astute observation that with each increment in complexity, it has taken PA/PM further and further away from the priorities and needs of the people who have to make it work – the appraisee and the appraiser. Yet their buy-in is crucial. Throughout this book, we will advocate a participative approach to the design of appraisal, because we believe that such an approach increases the likelihood of appraisal being implemented as intended and achieving the aims set for it.

IN SUMMARY

Appraisal has a long history; as an HR practice, it hasn't gone away, nor is it likely to. It has multiple contexts and it is important to recognise all of these when designing an appraisal process. A key element in designing appraisal is accepting that appraisers might not enact appraisal as HR intends: in our view, the risk of this is heightened if HR fails to actively involve appraisers in the design process and embrace their views. A similar point applies to appraisees – in particular, that HR is able to demonstrate sincerity of intent when it comes to the purposes of appraisal. This is important if appraisal is to be effective as a high-performance work practice – appraisees need to see that appraisal is for them and that they have a voice in the way that it operates.

DISCUSSION POINTS AND QUESTIONS

1.1 How might appraisal foster employee engagement?

1.2 What impact would you expect PA to have on employee attitudes, and why?

1.3 Is there any point in studying the impact that HR practices have on organisational performance?

KEY REFERENCES

Belt, V. and Giles, L. (2009) *High Performance Working: A Synthesis of Key Literature.* London: UK Commission for Employment and Skills.

den Hartog, D. N., Boselie, P. and Paauwe, J. (2004) Performance management: A model and research agenda. *Applied Psychology: An International Review,* **53**(4), 556–569.

Pulakos, E. D. and O'Leary, R. S. (2011) Why is performance management broken? *Industrial and Organizational Psychology,* **4**(2), 146–164.

REFERENCES

Australian Human Resources Institute (2008) *Dangling the Carrot: Investigating Performance Management Practices*. Melbourne: Australian Human Resources Institute.

Beer, M. and Ruh, R. A. (1976) Employee growth through performance management. *Harvard Business Review*, July–August, 59–66.

Belt, V. and Giles, L. (2009) *High Performance Working: A Synthesis of Key Literature*. London: UK Commission for Employment and Skills.

Belt, V. and Rüdiger, K. (2010) *High Performance Working: Case Studies Analytical Report*. London: UK Commission for Employment and Skills.

Bowling, N. A. (2013) Is the job satisfaction–job performance relationship spurious? A meta-analytic examination. *Journal of Vocational Behavior*, **71**(2), 167–185.

Boxall, P. and Macky, K. (2009) Research and theory on high-performance work systems: Processing the high-involvement stream. *Human Resource Management Journal*, **19**(1), 3–23.

Briner, R. B. (2014) What is employee engagement and does it matter? An evidence-based approach. In D. Robinson and J. Gifford (Eds) *The Future of Engagement: Thought Piece Collection*. London: Chartered Institute of Personnel and Development, pp. 51–71.

Britt, T. W., Dickinson, J. M., Greene-Shortridge, T. M. and McKibben, E. S. (2007) Self-engagement at work. In D. L. Nelson and C. L. Cooper (Eds) *Positive Organizational Behaviour*. London: Sage, pp. 143–158.

Burt, C. D. B. (2014) Job satisfaction. In C. L. Cooper (Ed.) *Wiley Encyclopedia of Management*. New York: Wiley.

Cleveland, J. N. and Murphy, K. R. (1992) Analyzing performance appraisal as goal-directed behavior. *Research in Personnel and Human Resources Management*, **10**, 121–185.

Deloitte (2014) *Global Human Capital Trends 2014: Engaging the 21st-century Workforce*. Deloitte University Press.

Deloitte (2015) *Global Human Capital Trends 2015: Leading in the New World of Work*. Deloitte University Press.

den Hartog, D. N., Boselie, P. and Paauwe, J. (2004) Performance management: A model and research agenda. *Applied Psychology: An International Review*, **53**(4), 556–569.

Dewettinck, K. and Vroonen, W. (2013) Antecedents and consequences of performance management enactment by front line managers. Working Paper in Human Resource Management 2013/02. Vlerick Business School, Leuven, Belgium. https://public.vlerick.com/Publications/e6b61499-e7d7-e211-a8b9-005056a635ed.pdf (accessed 13 January 2016).

Fisher, C. D., Schoenfeldt, L. F. and Shaw, J. B. (1993) *Human Resource Management*. 2nd edn. Boston, MA: Houghton Mifflin.

Folger, R., Konovsky, M. A. and Cropanzano, R. (1992) A due process metaphor for performance appraisal. *Research in Organizational Behavior*, **14**, 129–177.

Grant, A. M., Christianson, M. K. and Price, R. H. (2007) Happiness, health, or relationships? Managerial practices and employee well-being trade-offs. *Academy of Management Perspectives*, **21**(3), 51–63.

Hirsh, W., Brown, D., Chubb, C. and Reilly, P. (2011) *Performance Management: The Implementation Challenge. Key Research Findings*. Brighton, UK: Institute for Employment Studies.

Institute of Personnel Management (1992) *Performance Management in the UK: An Analysis of the Issues*. London: Institute of Personnel Management.

Judge, T. A. and Kammeyer-Mueller, J. D. (2012) Job attitudes. *Annual Review of Psychology*, **63**, 341–367.

Kahn, W. A. (1990) Psychological conditions of personal engagement and disengagement at work. *Academy of Management Journal*, **33**(4), 692–724.

Kenexa (2010) *The Kenexa Research Institute Asks: Does an Organization's Leadership Team Really Affect Employee Satisfaction?* Kenexa Research Institute.

Landy, F. J. and Farr, J. L. (1980) Performance rating. *Psychological Bulletin*, **87**, 72–107.

Longenecker, C. O., Sims, H. P. and Gioia, D. A. (1987) Behind the mask: The politics of employee appraisal. *The Academy of Management Executive*, **1**(3), 183–193.

McGregor, D. M. (1957) The human side of enterprise. In *Adventures in Thought and Action. Proceedings of the Fifth Anniversary Convocation of the School of Industrial Management, Massachusetts Institute of Technology*. Cambridge, MA: MIT, pp. 23–30.

Maier, N. R. F. (1958) Three types of appraisal interview. *Personnel*, March/April, 27–40.

Mercer (2007) *Engaging Employees to Drive Global Business Success: Insights from Mercer's What's Working™ Research*. New York: Mercer.

Meyer, H. H., Kay, E. and French, J. R. P. (1965) Split roles in performance appraisal. *Harvard Business Review*, **43**(1), 123–129.

Meyer, J. P. (2014) Organizational commitment. In C. L. Cooper (Ed.) *Wiley Encyclopedia of Management*. New York: Wiley.

Meyer, J. P. and Allen, N. J. (1997) *Commitment in the Workplace: Theory, Research, and Application*. Newbury Park, CA: Sage.

Mowday, R. T., Porter, L. W. and Steers, R. M. (1982) *Employee–Organization Linkages: The Psychology of Commitment, Absenteeism, and Turnover*. New York: Academic Press.

Mowday, R. T., Steers, R. M. and Porter, L. W. (1979) The measurement of organizational commitment. *Journal of Vocational Behavior*, **14**, 224–247.

Nishii, L. H., Lepak, D. P. and Schneider, B. (2008) Employee attributions of the 'why' of HR practices: Their effects on employee attitudes and behaviors, and customer satisfaction. *Personnel Psychology*, **61**(3), 503–545.

ORC International (n.d.) *Measuring Employee Engagement – Intuitive Model, Robust Science*. ORC International.

Paauwe, J. (2009) HRM and performance: Achievements, methodological issues and prospects. *Journal of Management Studies*, **46**(1), 129–155.

Peccei, R. (2004) *Human Resource Management and the Search for the Happy Workplace*. Inaugural Address. Erasmus Research Institute of Management (ERIM), Erasmus University Rotterdam. http://repub.eur.nl/pub/1108/ (accessed 13 January 2016).

Peccei, R., Van De Voorde, K. and Van Veldhoven, M. (2013) HRM, well-being and performance: A theoretical and empirical review. In J. Paauwe, D. Guest and

P. M. Wright (Eds) *HRM and Performance: Achievements and Challenges*. Chichester, UK: Wiley, pp. 15–46.

Pulakos, E. D. and O'Leary, R. S. (2011). Why is performance management broken? *Industrial and Organizational Psychology*, 4(2), 146–164.

Purcell, J. and Kinnie, N. (2007) HRM and business performance. In P. Boxall, J. Purcell and P. Wright (Eds) *The Oxford Handbook of Human Resource Management*. Oxford: Oxford University Press, pp. 533–551.

Rummler, G. A. and Brache, A. P. (1995) *Improving Performance*. 2nd edn. San Francisco: Jossey-Bass.

Schaufeli, W. B. and Salanova, M. (2007) Enhancing work engagement through the management of human resources. In K. Näswall, J. Hellgren and M. Sverke (Eds) *The Individual in the Changing Working Life*. Cambridge, UK: Cambridge University Press, pp. 380–402.

Snow, C. C. and Snell, S. A. (2012) Strategic human resource management. In S. W. J. Kozlowski (Ed.) *The Oxford Handbook of Organizational Psychology. Vol. 2*. New York: Oxford University Press, pp. 993–1008.

Society for Human Resource Management (2000) *Performance Management Survey*. Society for Human Resource Management, pp. 1–43.

Towers Perrin (n.d.) *Closing the Engagement Gap: A Road Map for Driving Superior Business Performance*. Towers Perrin Global Workforce Survey 2007–2008. Towers Perrin.

Truss, C. (2001) Complexities and controversies in linking HRM with organizational outcomes. *Journal of Management Studies*, **38**(8), 1121–1149.

Van De Voorde, K., Paauwe, J. and Van Veldhoven, M. (2012) Employee well-being and the HRM–organizational performance relationship: A review of quantitative studies. *International Journal of Management Reviews*, **14**(4), 391–407.

Van Horn, J. E., Taris, T. W., Schaufeli, W. B. and Scheurs, P. J. G. (2004) The structure of occupational well-being. A study amongst Dutch teachers. *Journal of Occupational and Organizational Psychology*, **63**, 193–210.

Warren, M. (1972) Performance management: A substitute for supervision. *Management Review*, October, 28–42.

Wilkinson, A. and Fay, C. (2011) New times for employee voice? *Human Resource Management*, **50**(1), 65–74.

Wood, S. and de Menezes, L. (2011) High involvement management, high-performance work systems and well-being. *The International Journal of Human Resource Management*, **22**(7), 1586–1610.

WorldatWork/Sibson Consulting (2010) *2010 Study on the State of Performance Management*. WorldatWork/Sibson Consulting.

THE AIMS OF APPRAISAL

ORGANISATIONAL AND INDIVIDUAL PERSPECTIVES

2

The most fundamental question facing an organisation that is setting up appraisal is 'What's it for?'. Get this bit wrong, and you can bet that whatever else follows, the appraisal system will not run smoothly – if it runs at all. To be sure, it is not hard to think up a number of aims that appraisal may serve, but the main problem is setting up a realistic and achievable agenda. As we noted in Chapter 1, PM has been challenged on the grounds that it has become overly complex with HR adding ever more to the process. As well as what the organisation wants, it is important to recognise that performers and their managers also will have views about appraisal – what they want from it and what it should be doing for them. We explore these perspectives in this chapter.

THE ORGANISATIONAL PERSPECTIVE

Surveys of practice have long shown that organisations attempt to achieve multiple aims – quite commonly five or more (e.g. Institute of Personnel Management, 1977, 1986). The shift to PM brought with it no noticeable diminution in the number of aims – if anything, the reverse. But it did bring some change in language (at least to the extent that later surveys of practice asked about different and additional aims from those featuring in earlier surveys). And there was some shift in emphasis, greater importance being attached to improving organisational effectiveness and motivating employees (Institute of Personnel Management, 1992). More broadly, the alignment of employee goals with those of the organisation overall has come to be seen very much as a core purpose of performance management – perhaps *the* core purpose. And in the more recent recessionary years since 2008, there has been (not surprisingly) a very strong emphasis on performance improvement – in particular, on the management of employee underperformance.

A long-running tension has been that between the development versus reward purposes of appraisal. For example, as we mentioned in Chapter 1, an early study in the United States undertaken within General Electric by Meyer *et al.* (1965) highlighted the potential difficulty of a single system satisfying multiple needs – in particular, the high risk of consideration of pay interfering with performance improvement. And this tension has by no means disappeared. Going down the performance–pay path is as hazardous as it ever was and puts at risk the developmental and motivational aspects of appraisal.

Most people do, of course, need to work for the money that paid employment brings – at least to satisfy subsistence needs and very probably to satisfy modern-day consumerism. But the incentive role of pay as a motivator has long been a matter of some contention. Herzberg *et al.* (1959), for example, regarded pay as a 'hygiene' factor – lack of it leads to dissatisfaction, but having it doesn't motivate. Over the years, however, evidence has accumulated to cast doubt on many of Herzberg and colleagues' propositions. With respect to pay, it is now generally accepted that various forms of performance-related pay (PRP), individual and team-based, can and do have positive benefits for performance (e.g. Guthrie, 2007; Gerhart, 2009). But Gerhart and Fang (2014) add a cautionary note – that the body of evidence remains small. They note also that early meta-analytic evidence

> which shows that [pay for individual performance] has a strong positive impact on performance pertains to a narrow set of contexts. Specifically, the evidence comes from studies that use results-based (objective) measures of performance and from settings where work is simple, easy to measure, and not interdependent.
>
> (Gerhart and Fang, 2014: 42)

This last point is important because it alludes to the diverse range of pay-for-performance systems that exists. And there's a wide variety of terminology – merit pay, incentive pay, variable pay, such that "Despite the simplicity of the title 'PRP', it is extremely difficult to say what it is in a simple sentence given its many guises" (Wilkinson and Redman, 2013: 188). The table in Box 2.1 gives a sense of what those many guises are. To the extent that there is a common thread, it is that base pay is "the foundational component" (Shields, 2007: 33) and the performance/variable element "is usually an overlay to base pay, and it varies according to the level of measured or assessed performance" (Shields, 2007: 34): in some applications of PRP, the variable element is 'consolidated', in effect becoming part of base pay, but this is not inevitable, in which case the variable element is likely to be paid as a bonus. As Box 2.1 indicates, many approaches to PRP do not use "results-based (objective) measures of performance", nor is the work simple and easy

	BOX 2.1

PERFORMANCE-RELATED REWARD OPTIONS

Who (= performance entity or unit) and when (= time frame for payout)?	How? (= behaviour)	How much? (= results)

Individual	• Merit raises or increments
	 • Merit bonuses
	   • Discretionary bonuses
	   • Individual non-cash recognition awards
		• Piece rates
		 • Sales commissions
		 • Goal-based bonuses

Large group short-term incentives (STIs)		• Profitsharing • Gainsharing • Goalsharing
Small group STIs		• Team incentives • Team non-cash recognition awards
Organisation-wide long-term incentives (LTIs)		• Share bonus plans • Share purchase plans • Share option plans • Share appreciation and other rights plans

Source: Shields (2007)

to measure. For example, applications of merit pay commonly are individually based approaches to PRP that rely on subjective ratings of the performance of complex jobs.

Some broadening of the evidence base about PRP is to be found in a review by Garbers and Konradt (2014). They found an effect on performance for both individual- and team-based performance pay, the effect for teams being greater in smaller-sized teams. And contrary to Gerhart and Fang (2014), they also showed that the effect was greater for more complex tasks. In direct contrast, an earlier meta-analytic review of public-sector studies by Weibel et al. (2009) concluded that pay for performance reduced performance in the case of what they termed 'interesting' (that is, more challenging) tasks.

Confusing? Well, this whole area is riddled with contradictions and uncertainties. For example, in a comprehensive review of PRP in the public sector, Ray et al. (2014: 6) conclude that there is "[s]ome evidence of positive effects from PRP schemes on directly incentivised outcomes across education, health and the civil service", but note (2014: 6) that "findings are mixed, and often context- or outcome-specific" and that positive benefits found in health settings were (2014: 37) "often small and sometimes short lived". They note the risk of various unintended consequences; for example, 'effort displacement' in health settings – little or no improvement in unincentivised outcomes; as well as the possibility of 'positive spillovers' (that is, improvements in unincentivised outcomes). And they note both positive and negative impacts on employee attitudes. Also unclear is the impact on 'crowding out' – the idea that emphasising extrinsic reward diminishes intrinsic motivation (Weibel *et al.*, 2009) – which some (Perry *et al.*, 2009) suggest may be a heightened concern in the public sector stemming from the notion of public-sector motivation. Though this demotivating effect is challenged by Gerhart and Fang (2014), the evidence remains unclear. And herein lies a major difficulty for PRP. The evidence supporting it is far from compelling; and that evidence is inconclusive when it comes to identifying the conditions under which PRP is more likely to be effective.

So, moderately positive though some evidence seems to be, linking pay with performance via appraisal or PM remains controversial – and understandably so, because it is quite simply difficult to accomplish. Consider, for example, what expectancy theory implies for performance-related pay. This stresses the need for individuals to be able to see a clear and positive relationship between the amount of effort they put in, the performance improvement it brings about and the way that improvement leads to valued outcomes. Only if all these conditions are met is the individual likely to be fully motivated. Heneman and Werner (2005) have spelled out what this means for merit pay:

> In summary, expectancy theory suggests that merit pay is likely to motivate increased performance because performance is instrumental in the attainment of a pay increase. For merit pay to motivate increased performance, performance must be accurately measured, pay must be a valued outcome, pay must be made contingent on performance, and the employee must have the opportunity to have an impact on performance.
> (Heneman and Werner, 2005: 27)

Satisfying all these conditions is hard to accomplish. For example, is increased pay an outcome that the individual values? For some, perhaps many, it will be. But how large does the increase need to be? Too small and there is the risk of no incentivising effect. The failure of a PRP scheme in an Australian healthcare setting was attributed to insufficiency of the reward on offer (Greene, 2013). Is there a risk of financial reward being too high? How much of a risk is there of 'gaming' – 'fiddling' the performance data to give the appearance of improvement when in fact there is little or no actual change? And, finally, can the employer afford to pay? Perry *et al.* (2009) note that this is a particular concern in the public sector because of where the money comes from, but in the tighter recessionary climate since 2008, it is likely that many private-sector organisations will have struggled to afford PRP.

What about a development-orientated pathway: is that a more straightforward route? On balance it is likely to be so, but that does not necessarily mean that it is absolutely problem-free. At the very least, line managers will need to have a better understanding of what motivates people at work. We consider aspects of motivation in Chapter 3 and training for motivation in Chapter 10. Also, what is meant by taking a developmental perspective needs to be clear. Hirsh *et al.* (2011) note a number of possible development purposes that might be served:

- development needed linked to a specific work objective, often some new challenge
- development to improve more general performance in the current job, often associated with an area of competence or behaviour which even a good performer might need to improve
- career development, which usually involves clarifying career direction and accessing new work experiences as well as strengthening skills
- development to overcome particular aspects of poor performance.

(Hirsh *et al.*, 2011: 13)

If appraisal is to be constructive and useful, there has to be something in it for the participants – both the appraisers and appraisees (Fletcher, 2002). They, after all, are the people who have to make it work. What, then, does the appraisal situation look like from their viewpoint? Box 2.2 introduces manager and employee perspectives on appraisal which we explore in more depth in the remainder of this chapter.

BOX 2.2

LINE MANAGER AND EMPLOYEE GOALS FOR APPRAISAL

- **line managers**: an easy-to-use system; encouraging employee motivation; clarifying and communicating what is expected of employees (avoiding role ambiguity); increasing employee performance (and productivity); avoiding interpersonal conflict; building and maintaining good interpersonal and working relationships; enhancing one's own status within the organisation; managing impressions; developing employees' competence; enhancing employees' self-esteem and other aspects of well-being

- **employees:** feedback (especially if it is positive); avoiding interpersonal conflict; building and maintaining good interpersonal and working relationships; enhancing one's status within the organisation; managing impressions; identifying and meeting development needs; knowing where one stands for the future – discussing advancement opportunities; developing personal competence; enhancing self-esteem and other aspects of well-being; defending against criticism; conveying upward feedback; having interesting and satisfying work; seeking improvements to working conditions.

Source: Adapted from Dulewicz and Fletcher (1989), Balzer and Sulsky (1990), Murphy and Cleveland (1995)

PERFORMERS' PERSPECTIVES

Employees have thoughts and feelings about their jobs; they have perceptions of what their job is or might be – how broadly or narrowly they define its scope and how they should go about tackling the tasks facing them (Parker, 2007); and the properties or characteristics of jobs (such as the opportunities for skill use, extent of autonomy the job allows) – as well as actually performing them – have an impact on the performer. One might think, therefore, that employees would want matters of this sort to be part of appraisal. Some evidence bearing on this comes from a recent Chartered Institute of Personnel and Development (2015) survey, as shown in Box 2.3.

BOX 2.3

WHAT EMPLOYEES WANT FROM PERFORMANCE MANAGEMENT – AND WHAT THEY DON'T GET!

	should be	is
	part of the performance management process (%)	
Performance assessed as an individual	79	62
Performance feedback provides clear objectives	79	44
Balanced feedback	77	34
Performance looks at the WHAT and the HOW	67	48
Performance feedback explains my contribution to the wider organisation	51	19
Performance discussions are mainly focused on the future rather than past performance	46	15

	should be	is
	part of the performance management process (%)	
Performance assessed as part of a team	39	18
Performance feedback provided by people other than just manager	38	19
Performance feedback conveyed as a rating or a ranking	27	33
Performance discussed regularly	23	8

Source: CIPD (2015)

So, nothing too surprising in these findings for the most part, at least to the extent that there's a gap in the expected direction between what employees believe should be part of the process and what they say they actually experience. But some findings are puzzling. For example, only just more than half the respondents seem to agree that performance feedback *should* explain their contribution to the wider organisation; fewer than half believe that performance discussions *should* be mainly focused on the future rather than past performance; and less than a quarter believe that performance *should* be discussed regularly. Unfortunately, the survey report throws no light that may help us to understand these findings. In Chapter 5, we argue for taking a diagnostic approach to appraisal design. The findings that we've just quoted illustrate one reason why it is important to discover what employees and managers want from appraisal.

Notwithstanding these particular findings, it is hard to envisage appraisal that doesn't have a forward-looking element. As such, appraisal is a key vehicle for manager and managed to agree what the job is in terms of its tasks and duties, for both parties to be clear about what the role requires, ensure that there are no ambiguities and conflicts about those requirements, ensure that the job demands are reasonable and agree action on learning/development/training needs, all as part of a constructive dialogue or performance conversation between line manager and employee.

As to the backward-looking aspect of appraisal, then, it is likely that appraisees will want to know where they stand and they often do want feedback, albeit with some degree of ambivalence, particularly if less than favourable feedback is in the offing. They also usually believe in fair distribution of rewards, and in those organisations that operate pay-for-performance systems linked to appraisal, then this, too, might feature on the agenda.

At least some of the above might imply a correspondence of organisational and employee needs, especially when it comes to the forward-looking aspects. But when it comes to the backward-looking matters, much turns on:

- employees perceiving their assessment as accurate and fair;
- the quality of their existing relationship with the appraiser;
- the impact of the assessment on their rewards and well-being.

The first of these is a condition that often does not appear to be met. Perhaps it is because of all the biases that can creep into judgements about others, or the imperfections of memory, or lack of contact between appraisers and the appraised, but there is a lot of evidence that appraisees do not readily accept the more unfavourable aspects of their assessment (Fletcher, 2002). Even when there is sound evidence of poor performance, there can be a reluctance to accept it. Although some people are more objective about themselves than others are, and some are more resilient and able to take criticism without feeling wounded, in general, the capacity to take negative feedback without experiencing any threat to self-esteem is fairly low. When people do face threats to their self-esteem, the most frequent reaction is mentally to reject as worthless the message and/or the source.

This is not to say that it is impossible to have any meaningful review of the adequacy of performance in the appraisal discussion, but it does indicate that such discussion has to be handled with the greatest care and that it may lead to defensiveness rather than to heightened motivation. The chances of defensiveness are increased greatly if pay or promotion is affected by the assessment. It takes a remarkably dispassionate, honest and self-denying individual to remain completely objective when faced with an assessment that may have adverse financial consequences. If, on top of all this, the existing relationship with the appraiser is not a good one, then it is extremely unlikely that the assessment will be seen as fair and acceptable. The main purpose of the appraisal, for the appraisee, becomes one of fighting a defensive action. As Hirsh (2006: 2) remarks, appraisals marked by ratings and pay linked to performance shift the discussion between manager and subordinate onto "a more nervous and adversarial footing".

LINE MANAGERS' PERSPECTIVES

The appraiser's agenda for appraisal is also often far removed from what the organisation would like it to be (Fletcher, 2002). As already suggested, the person appraised will not always agree with the appraiser's views, irrespective of the objectivity and accuracy of the latter. Appraisers are all too aware of this; in addition, the more insightful of them realise that assessing others is

a tricky business, and that either they may lack the information and evidence
necessary to make a fair judgement, or they may have biases that affect the way
they interpret the information they do have. So they have ample reason to feel
apprehensive about the situation and the likely reaction they may get from
appraisees – particularly if they have had rather limited contact with them on
a day-to-day basis (a situation likely to have become more commonplace as a
consequence of de-layering, greater incidence of home-working and the like).
The appraisal interaction has to be seen for what it is in the eyes of most
appraisers – one isolated event in the year. It might not be so tricky to deal
with if the effects could be contained within that one event, but the truth for
many managers is that any adverse reactions from the person appraised can
make working relationships more problematic for a long while afterwards.
Small wonder, then, that managers are prone to avoid carrying out appraisals
if they can, and where they cannot, they tend to give overly favourable ratings
(Arvey and Murphy, 1998). Even this tactic – being generous in the
assessment – is not without problems, as it not surprisingly generates
unrealistic expectations about future rewards on the part of the appraisee, and
so simply stores up trouble for a later date.

In the case of genuinely high-performing subordinates, one might expect the
appraiser to be only too happy to sit down and have the pleasure of passing on
their satisfaction. After all, the appraisee's reaction will be no cause for concern,
apart from their reasonable expectation that the appraiser will be able to
accompany the words with some tangible reward (which is not always possible).
Unfortunately, it is not unknown for managers to be reluctant to identify high
performers to the personnel department, because they fear that they will lose
them through promotion or transfer. On top of all this, developing subordinates
hasn't always ranked highly in organisations' priorities, or been something that
is rewarded. Indeed, the evidence indicates quite the opposite – that managers
who are good at staff development are less likely to make rapid career progress.
The message is further reinforced in some organisations by the lack of central
action in response to recommendations that come out of appraisals, and the lack
of response to failure to carry out appraisals at all.

For all these reasons, the annual appraisal is, for many managers, a high-risk
activity with little immediate positive outcome or reward, even though line
managers want their people to perform well. Being in charge of a well-
performing group of employees is likely to reflect favourably on the manager,
and so line managers do have a degree of self-interest in making the PA
process work for them. But this doesn't necessarily correspond with what the
organisation has determined the purposes to be.

In Chapter 1, we noted research by Longenecker and his colleagues
(e.g. Longenecker *et al.*, 1987; Longenecker and Gioia, 1988; Gioia and

Longenecker, 1994) that has specifically focused on what they call the politics of appraisal. Among other things, this research identified the following reasons why managers inflate their ratings of subordinates:

1. believing that accurate ratings would have a damaging effect on subordinate motivation and performance;
2. desire to improve the subordinate's chances of getting a pay rise;
3. a wish to avoid others outside the department seeing evidence of internal problems and conflicts;
4. preventing a permanent written record of poor performance coming into being which might have longer-term implications for the subordinate;
5. need to protect subordinates whose performance had suffered from the effects of personal problems;
6. wanting to reward subordinates who had put in a lot of effort even if the end result was not so good;
7. avoiding confrontation and potential conflict with 'difficult' subordinates;
8. aiming to promote out of the department subordinates who were disliked or problem performers.

Though less frequently reported, some reasons for deliberately manipulating performance assessments in a downward direction were also uncovered:

1. scaring people into performing better;
2. punishing difficult or non-compliant subordinates;
3. encouraging unwanted subordinates to leave;
4. minimising the merit pay award(s);
5. complying with organisational restrictions on the number of higher ratings given.

The general observation from this research is that managers frequently allow their appraisal of staff to be influenced by non-performance issues. Indeed, Cleveland and Murphy (1992) suggest that arriving at an objective and accurate assessment of performance is usually not the highest priority for the appraiser. Moreover, the accumulated body of research about appraisal, particularly that on ratings, clearly indicates that a high degree of psychometric accuracy and objectivity in appraisal is not a realistic goal.

SETTING REALISTIC AIMS FOR APPRAISAL

If there is so much potential conflict amongst the different aims of appraisal, and if the participants frequently have differing objectives, what can we reasonably expect of the appraisal process? The answer is – quite a lot, though not perhaps as much as has traditionally been demanded. The failure to realise that appraisal cannot do all that has been asked of it, and that there has to be something in the process that will be seen to be of benefit to the participants, has probably been the root cause of the lack of success of so many appraisal systems. The evolution of performance appraisal into performance management hasn't particularly helped. As Mueller-Hanson and Pulakos (2015) have put it:

> Unfortunately, over time, PM processes have become increasingly over-engineered to the point that they have taken on a life of their own. Managers and employees alike complain that they spend an inordinate amount of time on PM documentation, forms and other administrative tasks that have nothing to do with managing performance.
> (Mueller-Hanson and Pulakos, 2015: 6)

This echoes a message that we have heard across the past decade here in the UK (Hirsh, 2006; Hirsh et al., 2011).

The question becomes one of priorities: what are the essential purposes of the appraisal system, and how are they to be identified? A common way of determining this is for the HR director and/or the HR department to dream the whole thing up themselves. Sometimes top management personnel take a direct interest, too. The likely outcome is an appraisal system that is all about the organisation's needs, with scant attention paid to the perspectives of the appraisers and appraisees. So, as Hirsh et al. (2011) put it:

> HR needs to change its own mindset to think less about PM as an HR system defined by a series of topics on a form and the administrative process of getting that form filled in and returned. HR needs to think more about how performance management systems can support managers and all employees to achieve individual and organisational performance.
> (Hirsh et al., 2011: 8)

As to purposes, our view is that the core purpose of performance appraisal has to be to enable employees to perform well – this means that appraisal has to embrace all the 'causes' of performance; in other words, not just employees' skills, abilities and knowledge, but also those factors external to the performer which facilitate or inhibit performance. The parties who are central to this endeavour are the performers – those doing the work – and their line managers. The appraisal process must therefore meet their needs. This places particular emphasis on appraisal as a shared, mutual and ongoing process.

And this implies a much more active role for appraisees than perhaps is commonly the case, the more so given that many of the changes that have taken place in the workplace have made appraisal more difficult for managers to carry out effectively. This shifts the emphasis away from appraisal as something that is done *to* the performer. A more employee-centred definition of appraisal has been put forward by Buchner (2007):

(1) a process for learning and clarifying what is to be achieved (at organization, work unit and key process levels), highlighting what *I* need to achieve to be a productive, contributing performer within this context; (2) a process for learning, clarifying, or verifying what *I* need to do to make that contribution – specifically, what behaviours describe how *I* am to achieve my goals; (3) a process for goal-setting and establishing feedback loops so that *I* can monitor my own progress and impact; and (4) a process for self-assessing performance capability and system support, surfacing any obstacles *I* recognise that will limit performance.

(Buchner, 2007: 66)

IN SUMMARY

The first and crucial question in designing an appraisal scheme is deciding what its primary aims are. Choosing to go down a motivational/developmental route or a reward route (which probably involves PRP) continues to be a fundamental dilemma. The PRP path is a risky route to take. There is evidence that some forms of PRP can work, but under what circumstances isn't clear. Though there also is evidence of unintended consequences, these perhaps are not necessarily inevitable. Moreover (at least in the public sector), there is a lack of evidence of cost-effectiveness (Ray *et al.*, 2014). So, proceed with caution if you take this route, if you proceed at all. Throughout the course of this book, we try to show that research and experience suggest that defining the function of appraisal in terms of employee development and motivation is preferable to a pay-for-performance ideology. Generally speaking, this definition is acceptable and welcome both to appraisees and most appraisers; and it represents what is generally the highest priority for the organisation – a strategy for improving performance. This does not mean that the needs of those involved – the organisation's senior management, HR, the appraiser and the person appraised – always coincide. But understanding the different perspectives is essential to establishing an effective appraisal system – one which sets realistic and achievable goals that offer something of value to all parties.

DISCUSSION POINTS AND QUESTIONS

2.1 If your performance was to be appraised tomorrow, what would you be aiming to get out of the appraisal session? How would you be feeling about it? Given more notice, how would you prepare for the session?

2.2 In what ways can we use performance appraisal to motivate people?

2.3 What do you see as the advantages and disadvantages of individual performance-related pay for school teachers? How effective would such a scheme be?

KEY REFERENCES

Buchner, T. W. (2007) Performance management theory: A look from the performer's perspective with implications for HRD. *Human Resource Development International*, **10**(1), 59–73.

Gerhart, B. and Fang, M. (2014) Pay for (individual) performance: Issues, claims, evidence and the role of sorting effects. *Human Resource Management Review*, **24**(1), 41–52.

Mueller-Hanson, R. A. and Pulakos, E. D. (2015) *Putting the "Performance" Back in Performance Management*. Society for Human Resource Management and Society for Industrial and Organizational Psychology.

Ray, K., Foley, B., Tsang, T., Walne, D. and Bajorek, Z. (2014) *A Review of the Evidence on the Impact, Effectiveness and Value for Money of Performance-related Pay in the Public Sector*. London: The Work Foundation.

REFERENCES

Arvey, R. D. and Murphy, K. R. (1998) Performance evaluation in work settings. *Annual Review of Psychology*, **49**, 141–168.

Balzer, W. K. and Sulsky, L. M. (1990) Performance appraisal effectiveness. In K. R. Murphy and F. E. Saal (Eds) *Psychology in Organizations*. Hillsdale, NJ: Erlbaum, pp. 133–156.

Buchner, T. W. (2007) Performance management theory: A look from the performer's perspective with implications for HRD. *Human Resource Development International*, **10**(1), 59–73.

Chartered Institute of Personnel and Development (2015) *Employee Outlook: Employee Views on Working Life*. London: Chartered Institute of Personnel and Development.

Cleveland, J. N. and Murphy, K. R. (1992) Analyzing performance appraisal as goal-directed behavior. *Research in Personnel and Human Resources Management*, **10**, 121–185.

Dulewicz, V. and Fletcher, C. (1989) The context and dynamics of performance appraisal. In P. Herriot (Ed.) *Assessment and Selection in Organisations*. Chichester, UK: Wiley, pp. 651–664.

Fletcher, C. (2002) Appraisal – an individual psychological analysis. In S. Sonnentag (Ed.) *The Psychological Management of Individual Performance: A Handbook in the Psychology of Management in Organizations*. Chichester, UK: Wiley, pp. 115–136.

Garbers, Y. and Konradt, U. (2014) The effect of financial incentives on performance: A quantitative review of individual and team-based financial incentives. *Journal of Occupational and Organizational Psychology*, **87**(1), 102–137.

Gerhart, B. (2009) Compensation. In J. Storey, P. M. Wright and D. Ulrich (Eds) *The Routledge Companion to Strategic Human Resource Management*. Abingdon, UK and New York: Routledge, pp. 224–244.

Gerhart, B. and Fang, M. (2014) Pay for (individual) performance: Issues, claims, evidence and the role of sorting effects. *Human Resource Management Review*, **24**(1), 41–52.

Gioia, D. A. and Longenecker, C. O. (1994). Delving into the dark side: The politics of executive appraisal. *Organizational Dynamics*, **22**(3), 47–58.

Greene, J. (2013) An examination of pay-for-performance in General Practice in Australia. *Health Services Research,* **48**(4), 1415–1432.

Guthrie, J. P. (2007) Remuneration: Pay effects at work. In P. Boxall, J. Purcell and P. Wright (Eds) *The Oxford Handbook of Human Resource Management*. Oxford: Oxford University Press, pp. 344–363.

Heneman, H. L. and Werner, J. M. (2005) *Merit Pay: Linking Pay to Performance in a Changing World*. 2nd edn. Greenwich, CT: Information Age Publishing.

Herzberg, F., Mausner, B. and Snyderman, B. (1959) *The Motivation to Work*. 2nd edn. New York: Wiley.

Hirsh, W. (2006) *Improving Performance through Appraisal Dialogues*. London: Corporate Research Forum.

Hirsh, W., Brown, D., Chubb, C. and Reilly, P. (2011) *Performance Management: The Implementation Challenge*. Brighton, UK: Institute for Employment Studies.

Institute of Personnel Management (1977) *Appraising Performance: Present Trends and the Next Decade*. London: Institute of Personnel Management.

Institute of Personnel Management (1986) *Performance Appraisal Revisited*. London: Institute of Personnel Management.

Institute of Personnel Management (1992) *Performance Management in the UK: An Analysis of the Issues*. London: Institute of Personnel Management.

Longenecker, C. O. and Gioia, D. A. (1988) Neglected at the top: Executives talk about executive appraisal. *Sloan Management Review*, Winter, 41–47.

Longenecker, C. O., Sims, H. P. and Gioia, D. A. (1987) Behind the mask: The politics of employee appraisal. *The Academy of Management Executive*, **1**(3), 183–193.

Meyer, H. H., Kay, E. and French, J. R. P. (1965) Split roles in performance appraisal. *Harvard Business Review*, **43**(1), 123–129.

Mueller-Hanson, R. A. and Pulakos, E. D. (2015) *Putting the "Performance" Back in Performance Management*. Society for Human Resource Management and Society for Industrial and Organizational Psychology.

Murphy, K. R. and Cleveland, J. N. (1995) *Understanding Performance Appraisal.* Thousand Oaks, CA: Sage.

Parker, S. K. (2007) "That *is* my job": How employees' role orientation affects their job performance. *Human Relations*, **60**(3), 403–434.

Perry, J., Engbers, T. and Jun, S. Y. (2009) Back to the future? Performance-related pay, empirical research, and the perils of persistence. *Public Administration Review*, **69**(1), 39–51.

Ray, K., Foley, B., Tsang, T., Walne, D. and Bajorek, Z. (2014) *A Review of the Evidence on the Impact, Effectiveness and Value for Money of Performance-related Pay in the Public Sector*. London: The Work Foundation.

Shields, J. (2007) *Managing Employee Performance and Reward: Concepts, Practices, Strategies*. Cambridge, UK: Cambridge University Press.

Weibel, A., Rost, K. and Osterloh, M. (2009) Pay for performance in the public sector – Benefits and (hidden) costs. *Journal of Public Administration Research and Theory*, **20**(2), 387–412.

Wilkinson, A. and Redman, T. (2013) *Contemporary Human Resource Management*. 4th edn. Harlow, UK: Pearson Education.

3 PERFORMANCE

Performance is a tricky term, not least because it applies to many different levels – the organisation as a whole, departments, establishments, teams, etc. In this chapter, we will be concerned with the performance of individual employees as they go about doing their jobs. As Campbell and Wiernik (2015: 48) note, "Without individual performance there is no team performance, no unit performance, no organizational performance, no economic sector performance, no GDP."

The first point that needs to be made is that 'doing their jobs' is only one interpretation of the term performance. Roe (1998: 11) indicated the distinction between "the activity shown by people when performing work roles, and the results of those activities": the former has been referred to as *process* performance, and the latter as *outcome* (or *results* or *output*) performance (Roe, 1999; Reijseger *et al.*, 2013). As described by Taris and Schaufeli (2015):

> *Process performance* refers to the actions or behaviours employees engage in to achieve the goals of their job, i.e., what they do at work. Conversely, *outcome performance* refers to the products or services that are produced and whether these are consistent with the overall strategic goals of the organisation.
>
> (Taris and Schaufeli, 2015: 21)

When it comes to appraisal, both are important.

Also important are the determinants and antecedents of performance – the causes, in other words. These commonly are thought of as individual factors within the performer – the employee's knowledge, skills, abilities, motivation, dispositions, attitudes, emotional states and the like. But there also are situational factors – that is, factors outside the individual, but within the context of their work (or possibly beyond) – which may facilitate or inhibit what the performer does. Box 3.1 shows a simplified model of employee job performance. We will explore this model in this chapter.

PROCESS PERFORMANCE

From the 1990s, particular attention focused on behavioural models of employee performance. Today, there is general consensus over three broad facets of process performance: task performance, citizenship performance and counterproductive work behaviour. In addition, some (e.g. Hesketh and Neal, 1999; Pulakos et al., 2000) have drawn attention to adaptive performance; and more recently, because of the tremendous popularity of employee engagement, the term engagement performance has come along (Macey et al., 2009). Box 3.2 introduces these concepts.

BOX 3.1

Determinants of job performance person and system factors

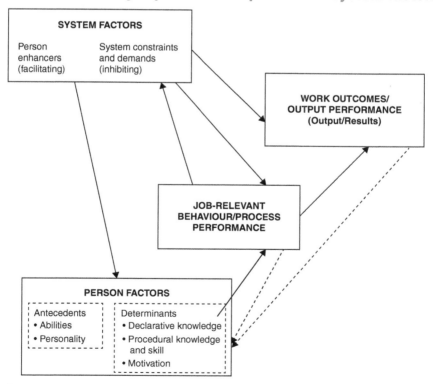

Source: Adapted from Campbell et al. (1993); Cardy and Dobbins (1994); Waldman (1994)

BOX 3.2

PROCESS PERFORMANCE

Task performance:

- "the set of behaviors that are relevant to the goals of the organization or the organizational unit in which a person works" (Murphy, 1990: 162);
- "Performance is . . . defined as synonymous with behavior. It is something that people actually do and can be observed. By definition, it includes only those actions or behaviors that are relevant to the organization's goals and that can be scaled (measured) in terms of each individual's proficiency (that is, level of contribution). Performance is what the organization hires one to do, and do well. Performance is *not* the consequence or result of action, it is the action itself. . . . performance consists of goal-relevant actions that are under the control of the individual, regardless of whether they are cognitive, psychomotor, or interpersonal" (Campbell *et al.*, 1993: 40);
- task performance might take either of two forms – "One involves activities that directly transform raw materials into the goods and services that are the organization's products. Such activities include selling merchandise in a retail store, operating a production machine in a manufacturing plant, teaching in a school, performing surgery in a hospital, and cashing cheques in a bank. The second form of task performance involves activities that service and maintain the technical core by replenishing its supply of raw materials, distributing its finished products or providing important planning, coordination, supervising or staff functions that enable it to function effectively and efficiently." (Motowidlo, 2003: 43).

Citizenship (contextual) performance:

- "individual behaviors that support the organizational, social, and psychological environment in which the technical core must function" (Koopmans *et al.*, 2011: 861);
- "behaviours or actions that help [in] bringing about the organisation's goals while at the same time not being part of a worker's formal job description" (Taris and Schaufeli, 2015: 22).
- Note that citizenship performance is today the preferred term that encapsulates a number of other overlapping terms, e.g. organisational citizenship behaviour, prosocial organisational behaviour.

Counterproductive work behaviour:

- "behavior that harms the well-being of the organisation" (Koopmans *et al.*, 2011: 862);

- "deliberate acts that are harmful to the organisation and impede achieving its goals" (Taris and Schaufeli, 2015: 22); "intentional behavior by employees that harms or intends to harm organizations and people in organizations, including customers/clients" (Rotundo and Spector, 2010: 489);
- "any intentional behaviour on the part of an organisation member viewed by the organisation as contrary to its legitimate interests" (Sackett and DeVore, 2001: 146).

Adaptive performance:

- "the extent to which an individual adapts to changes in a work system or work roles" (Koopmans et al., 2011: 862);
- "task-performance-directed behaviors individuals enact in response to or anticipation of changes relevant to job-related tasks. For the purposes of this definition, we consider task-relevant changes to include changes in the nature of job-related tasks, the methods (both individual and interpersonal) for accomplishing tasks, and the ways that effectiveness is evaluated" (Jundt et al., 2015: 55).

Engagement performance (engagement behaviour):

- "engaged employees:
- behave in more *persistent* ways;
- respond *proactively* to emerging threats and challenges;
- *expand their roles* at work; and
- *adapt* more readily to change" (Macey et al., 2009: 27–28).

Task performance

This is that behaviour which is thought of as traditionally falling within the ambit of what gets expressed in the job description: these are the sorts of behaviours that typically would be regarded as doing – that is, performing – the job. And, as one would expect, they are job-specific (albeit with varying degrees of similarity within job families). In other words, task performance for a train driver will be different from that for an accountant, which in turn is different from the performance of a hotel receptionist. This is obvious, of course, simply from looking at job descriptions for a range of different jobs. We mention job descriptions because they are one means of expressing performance requirements and as such they can have a part to play in appraisal.

For less complex jobs, the task list itself may give a clear enough indication of required behaviours. But for more complex jobs, specifying the behaviours needed is, well, more complex. Managerial jobs provide a good illustration, not least because there is a long history of describing in behavioural terms what managers (and leaders) do. Using various methods of study, this research has been carried out for many purposes – very often of a practical kind; for example, in selection, particularly using assessment centres, or for development purposes, as in the design of 360° feedback instruments. This commonly has been described as the identification of *dimensions* of performance, a dimension being "a cluster of behaviors that are specific, observable, and verifiable, and that can be reliably and logically classified together. . . . a *dimension* is defined in terms of specific behaviors the person carries out to accomplish the task" (Thornton and Byham, 1982: 117). A dimension of performance typically will have a label, a short narrative description and a number of more specific behavioural indicators. Box 3.3 illustrates this for *problem solving*, commonly identified as a behavioural dimension of management performance, but relevant for many other jobs too.

Looking at this example, you may be thinking that *problem solving* sits oddly with a behavioural view of performance. Surely, *problem solving* is a cognitive process that *isn't observable* whereas behaviour supposedly *is observable* – as in the Campbell *et al.* (1993) definition in Box 3.2. However, as Campbell *et al.* (1993: 40) note, "behavior is not always observable (for example, cognitive behavior, as in solving a math problem) and can be known only by its effects

---

BOX 3.3

AN EXAMPLE OF A DIMENSION OF PERFORMANCE

Problem Solving. The extent to which an individual gathers information; understands relevant technical and professional information; effectively analyses and uses data and information; generates viable options, ideas and solutions; selects supportable courses of action for problems and solutions; uses available resources in new ways; and generates and recognises imaginative solutions.

- Identifies underlying as well as surface problems;
- gathers available data;
- sifts relevant data from irrelevant data;
- develops alternatives;
- uses sound criteria to select or reject alternatives;
- makes unconventional or novel proposals or suggestions;
- redefines a problem so that new solutions/options can be considered.

(abbreviated from a longer list)

Source: Abbreviated from Arthur (2012)

(for instance, producing a solution after much 'thought')". This illustrates just one of the practical difficulties that arises with a behavioural approach. There are numerous others. For example, how many dimensions are needed? From numerous published and unpublished studies, Borman and Brush (1993) identified 187 managerial performance dimensions. They weren't all different from one another, of course, and Borman and Brush were able empirically to reduce the number to 18 'mega-dimensions', such as 'planning and organising', 'training, coaching, and developing subordinates' and 'decision making/problem solving'. You may be thinking that 18 still is rather a lot. So how about a smaller number of broader, more general factors? The "basic factors comprising leadership and management performance" put forward by Campbell (2012) are an illustration, as shown in Box 3.4. Campbell (2012: 172) describes these as "a distillation of all previous taxonomic, or taxonomic-appearing, research on the substantive performance content of leadership and management". If you already use a behavioural framework to set out what your leaders/managers are expected to do, you might care to compare it against the Campbell model. Though the

BOX 3.4

BASIC FACTORS COMPRISING LEADERSHIP AND MANAGEMENT PERFORMANCE

Leadership Performance Factors (*Supervisory, managerial, executive, i.e., hierarchical leadership*)

1. *Consideration, support, person-centeredness*: Providing recognition and encouragement, being supportive when people are under stress, giving constructive feedback, helping others with difficult tasks, and building networks with and among others.
2. *Initiating structure, guiding, directing*: Providing task assignments, explaining work methods, clarifying work roles, and providing tools, critical knowledge, and technical support.
3. *Goal emphasis*: Encouraging enthusiasm and commitment for the group/organisation goals and emphasizing the important missions to be accomplished.
4. *Empowerment, facilitation*: Delegating authority and responsibilities to others, encouraging participation, and allowing discretion in decision making.
5. *Training, coaching*: Providing one-on-one coaching and instruction regarding how to accomplish job tasks, how to interact with other people, and how to deal with obstacles and constraints.
6. *Serving as a model*: Modelling appropriate behaviour regarding interacting with others, acting unselfishly, working under adverse conditions, reacting to crisis or stress, working to achieve goals, showing confidence and enthusiasm, and exhibiting principled and ethical behaviour.

Management Performance Factors *(Hierarchical management performance)*

1. *Decision making, problem solving, and strategic innovation*: Making sound and timely decisions about major goals and strategies and forecasting future trends and formulating strategic and innovative goals (a.k.a. vision) to take advantage of them.
2. *Goal setting, planning, organising, and budgeting*: Formulating operative goals, determining how to use personnel and resources to accomplish goals, anticipating potential problems, and estimating costs.
3. *Coordination*: Actively coordinating the work of two or more units or the work of several work groups within a unit; this includes negotiating and cooperating with other units.
4. *Monitoring unit effectiveness*: Evaluating progress and effectiveness of units against goals, and monitoring costs and resource consumption.
5. *External representation*: Representing the organisation to those not in the organisation (e.g., customers, clients, government agencies, non-government organisations, the public).
6. *Staffing*: Procuring and providing for the development of human resources; this does not include one-on-one coaching, training, or guidance.
7. *Administration*: Performing day-to-day administrative tasks, documenting actions, and making information available in a timely manner.
8. *Commitment and compliance*: Complying with and showing commitment to the policies, procedures, and directives of the organisation, together with providing loyal constructive criticism.

Source: Campbell (2012), by permission of Oxford University Press, USA; Campbell and Wiernik (2015)

latter should not be regarded as some kind of definitive specification of required leader/manager behaviours, it nonetheless has great value as a kind of sounding board against which to assess what you have already.

Dimensions of performance – aren't these competencies? Possibly, but here is another conceptually (and practically) tricky area. So, do you mean *competence* or *competency*: or *a* competence/competency? In the former case, the term is being used as an uncountable noun – for example, sufficiency of qualification or being able to carry out a task in a satisfactory fashion. Used in this way, there is no plural to the term. But when used as a countable noun – that is, *a competence/competency* – there are plural forms (*competences/competencies*). In the HRM domain, both countable and uncountable interpretations are to be found – and this, of course, only reinforces the confusion. But when it comes to equating 'dimensions of performance' with 'competencies', then this means the countable noun. Bartram's (2005: 1187) definition provides an illustration: competencies are "sets of behaviors that are instrumental in the delivery of desired results or outcomes". In other words, behavioural competencies may be seen as synonymous with dimensions of performance. If you are familiar with this field, you will know that there are other interpretations of competencies. We will come on to those later. For the present, we continue our exploration of process performance.

Citizenship performance

Unlike task performance behaviours, which generally are job-specific, citizenship behaviours occur across jobs (and organisations) in a broadly similar way. To illustrate citizenship performance, we have adopted the framework set out by Borman *et al.* (2001) – shown in Box 3.5. While task behaviours typically are expressed formally as performance requirements, this is less likely to be the case when it comes to citizenship performance. But there is not a hard-and-fast separation here – the boundaries between task and citizenship performance are fuzzy to say the least. So, for example, 'cooperating with others' or 'putting team objectives ahead of personal interests' are behaviours that could be expressed formally as requirements for those engaged in roles involving team working. However, one of the difficulties with contextual performance is that managers may have implicit expectations that don't get expressed, not in any written way and not orally either, yet their personal theory of what constitutes a good performer is what gets used when the manager comes to assess performance.

BOX 3.5

CONCEPTUAL MODEL OF CITIZENSHIP PERFORMANCE

Dimension	Description
Personal Support	• Helping others by offering suggestions, teaching them useful knowledge or skills, directly performing some of their tasks, and providing emotional support for their personal problems. • Cooperating with others by accepting suggestions, informing them of events they should know about, and putting team objectives ahead of personal interests. • Showing consideration, courtesy, and tact in relations with others as well as motivating and showing confidence in them.
Organisational Support	• Favorably representing the organisation by defending and promoting it as well as expressing satisfaction and showing loyalty by staying with the organisation despite temporary hardships. • Supporting the organisation's mission and objectives, complying with organisational rules and procedures, and suggesting improvements.
Conscientious Initiative	• Persisting with extra effort despite difficult conditions. • Taking the initiative to do all that is necessary to accomplish objectives even if they are not normally a part of one's duties and finding additional productive work to perform when one's duties are completed. • Developing knowledge and skills by taking advantage of opportunities within the organisation and outside the organization through the use of one's own time and resources.

Source: Borman *et al.* (2001)

If you're thinking that some of what's in Box 3.5 reminds you of organisational values/valued behaviours, then don't be surprised, as this is precisely the way in which some organisations have embraced contextual performance in a formal way. 'Respecting the individual', 'being supportive and helpful', 'working together collaboratively' are just some of the labels that you will find.

Bear in mind that citizenship performance makes its contribution to organisational functioning in an indirect way: it "influences and supports the social and psychological environment of the organization, the environment in which the technical core operates" (Reilly and Aronson, 2009: 299). So, if an individual engages in citizenship behaviour, will there be any increase in the quality or quantity of what they do? Possibly not. Indeed, engaging in some citizenship behaviours could actually be to the detriment of what is accomplished by the performer who displays citizenship – helping another worker, for example, takes the performer away from their own work for a period of time. Nonetheless, helping behaviour is a kind of citizenship performance that has been shown to contribute to organisational effectiveness. Dorsey *et al.* (2010: 480) note, "This is especially true in cases in which work tasks are interdependent in nature as highly interdependent tasks are facilitated by helping behaviors and cooperation."

In other words, the benefits of citizenship performance are more likely to be seen at some aggregated level – a team, a work unit or the like. Much of what we know in this area comes from research that has studied organisational citizenship behavior (OCB). This has shown that OCBs are positively related to organisational effectiveness, as measured using a range of indicators, including measures of both quality and quantity. Organ *et al.* (2006) conclude:

> [T]he empirical evidence suggests that citizenship behaviors are . . . positively related to a variety of important organizational outcomes, such as the quantity and quality of work group productivity, sales team performance, customer satisfaction and complaints, sales revenue, profitability, and operating efficiency.
>
> (Organ *et al.*, 2006: 212)

Counterproductive work behaviour

This, of course, is what *isn't* wanted! Box 3.6 illustrates the wide range of behaviours: some are directed against the organisation and others against people. Appraisal arrangements may be the means through which such behaviours get dealt with, but probably only for relatively minor transgressions; for more serious infractions, it is likely that disciplinary procedures will be invoked, and the documentation about those procedures may be the means of formally communicating that these sorts of behaviours

BOX 3.6

COUNTERPRODUCTIVE WORK BEHAVIOURS

- Theft and related behavior
  - e.g., theft of cash or property, giving away of goods or services, misuse of employee discount
- Destruction of property
  - e.g., deface, damage, or destroy property; deliberate sabotage of production
- Misuse of information
  - e.g., reveal confidential information, destroy or falsify records
- Misuse of time and resources
  - e.g., waste time or resources, conduct personal business during work time, spend time on internet/use email for non-work reasons
- Unsafe behavior
  - e.g., fail to learn/follow safety procedures
- Poor attendance
  - e.g., unexcused absence or tardiness, misuse sick leave
- Poor quality work
  - e.g., intentionally slow or sloppy work
- Alcohol use
  - e.g., consumption of alcohol on the job, coming to work under the influence of alcohol
- Drug use
  - e.g., possess, use, or sell drugs at work, coming to work under the influence of drugs
- Inappropriate verbal actions
  - e.g., argue with customers, verbally harass co-workers
- Inappropriate physical actions
  - e.g., physically attack others (e.g., co-workers, customers), physical sexual advances towards others.

Source: Gruys and Sackett (2003)

are not expected. Or there may be codes of conduct of one sort or another – for example, about legitimate/illegitimate uses of the Internet, email, social media and the like.

Some of the behaviours shown in Box 3.6 look like underperformance – for example, poor-quality work. However, note that poor-quality work as underperformance could be caused by lack of knowledge, skill or ability, for example; whereas poor-quality work as counterproductive performance is volitional behaviour – that is, the performer chooses to go slow or be sloppy even though they are otherwise perfectly capable of doing what's required. This is an important point for appraisal because it signals the need to properly diagnose the causes of performance for each performer.

Adaptive performance

This is far from being a new idea (Hesketh and Neal, 1999), but is considered to be of particular importance these days because of the pace of change in organisations and the need to be responsive – a requirement not just for individuals, but for organisations too. An important first step in mapping the domain of adaptive performance was taken by Pulakos *et al.* (2000), who identified eight dimensions of such performance based on a large-scale critical incidents study across a range of different jobs. Their eight dimensions are set out in Box 3.7.

BOX 3.7

DIMENSIONS OF ADAPTIVE PERFORMANCE

Handling emergencies or crisis situations	Reacting with appropriate and proper urgency in life threatening, dangerous, or emergency situations; quickly analyzing options for dealing with danger or crises and their implications; making split-second decisions based on clear and focused thinking; maintaining emotional control and objectivity while keeping focused on the situation at hand; stepping up to take action and handle danger or emergencies as necessary and appropriate.
Handling work stress	Remaining composed and cool when faced with difficult circumstances or a highly demanding workload or schedule; not overreacting to unexpected news or situations; managing frustration well by directing effort to constructive solutions rather than blaming others; demonstrating resilience and the highest levels of professionalism in stressful circumstances; acting as a calming and settling influence to whom others look for guidance.
Solving problems creatively	Employing unique types of analyses and generating new, innovative ideas in complex areas; turning problems upside-down and inside-out to find fresh new approaches; integrating seemingly unrelated information and developing creative solutions; entertaining wide-ranging possibilities others may miss, thinking outside the given parameters to see if there is a more effective approach; developing innovative methods of obtaining or using resources when insufficient resources are available to do the job.

Dealing with uncertain and unpredictable work situations	Taking effective action when necessary without having to know the total picture or have all the facts at hand; readily and easily changing gears in response to unpredictable or unexpected events and circumstances; effectively adjusting plans, goals, actions, or priorities to deal with changing situations; imposing structures for self and others that provide as much focus as possible in dynamic situations; not needing things to be black and white; refusing to be paralysed by uncertainty or ambiguity.
Learning work tasks, technologies, and procedures	Demonstrating enthusiasm for learning new approaches and technologies for conducting work; doing what is necessary to keep knowledge and skills current; quickly and proficiently learning new methods or how to perform previously unlearned tasks; adjusting to new work processes and procedures; anticipating changes in the work demands and searching for and participating in assignments or training that will prepare self for these changes; taking action to improve work performance deficiencies.
Demonstrating interpersonal adaptability	Being flexible and open-minded when dealing with others; listening to and considering others' viewpoints and opinions and altering own opinion when it is appropriate to do so; being open and accepting of negative or developmental feedback regarding work; working well and developing effective relationships with highly diverse personalities; demonstrating keen insight of others' behavior and tailoring own behaviour to persuade, influence, or work more effectively with them.
Demonstrating cultural adaptability	Taking action to learn about and understand the climate, orientation, needs, and values of other groups, organisations, or cultures; integrating well into and being comfortable with different values, customs, and cultures; willingly adjusting behavior or appearance as necessary to comply with or show respect for others' values and customs; understanding the implications of one's actions and adjusting approach to maintain positive relationships with other groups, organisations, or cultures.
Demonstrating physically orientated adaptability	Adjusting to challenging environmental states such as extreme heat, humidity, cold, or dirtiness; frequently pushing self physically to complete strenuous or demanding tasks; adjusting weight and muscular strength or becoming proficient in performing physical tasks as necessary for the job.

Source: Pulakos *et al.* (2000)

Reflecting on this list, a number of thoughts may cross your mind. For example, the domain of adaptive performance seems very broad – broader than you thought, perhaps. Do a lot of the dimensions look simply like task performance? *Handling emergencies* – isn't this just part of the job for, say, a firefighter? Well, not necessarily every day of the week, but it nonetheless seems reasonable to take the view that for some jobs *handling emergencies* really is just part of the job. *Demonstrating cultural adaptability* – you work for a country's foreign/diplomatic service, or for an overseas aid agency or a big multinational business: wouldn't you take "action to learn about and understand the climate, orientation, needs, and values" of people in an overseas nation to which you find yourself posted? From the practical perspective of performance appraisal, it seems to us that there is value in signalling that performers are expected to behave in an adaptive way when the circumstances require it, but we're not sure that this has to involve a detailed specification such as that in Box 3.7. That said, adaptive performance and its determinants remain poorly understood; from a research perspective, therefore, treating adaptive performance as a separate category is likely to be of value as it enables studies to be more focused and potentially more informative.

Some of the dimensions shown in Box 3.7 raise a question about the reasonableness of performance expectations, in particular *handling work stress* and *demonstrating physically orientated adaptability*. Yes, jobs can be a source of stress; and some jobs exert substantial physical demands. But to expect *handling work stress* and *demonstrating physically orientated adaptability* as performance requirements seems to imply a fixedness to the work conditions that could be unhealthy – both for the individual, and ultimately, for the organisation more broadly. This is important from the perspective of an employer's duty of care, and the general principle to follow must surely be to organise jobs and work so that stress-inducing and physically hazardous conditions are designed out. When it comes to threats to physical well-being, various legislative provisions help to reduce the risks. Psychological well-being arguably is less well provided for so far as legislation is concerned, but there are clear lessons from research to help design healthier (and more productive) work – for example, the Management Standards for avoiding stress that have been developed by the UK's Health and Safety Executive (www.hse.gov.uk/stress/standards/), along with the accompanying competencies for managers (www.hse.gov.uk/stress/mcit.pdf).

A theme common to most of the dimensions identified in Box 3.7 is being responsive or reactive. To be adaptive requires the individual to recognise that there has been a change in their work environment that necessitates a change in their behaviour "that leads to more effective functioning [making] further adjustments, as needed, to achieve the desired result" (Dorsey *et al.*, 2010: 464). But a rather different kind of adaptive performance is implied by '*solving problems creatively*' – this suggests action by the performer to change the situation and this sometimes is referred to as '*proactivity*': "the extent to which individuals engage in self-starting, future-orientated behavior to change their individual work situations, their individual work roles, or themselves" (Griffin *et al.*, 2007: 332). In other words, proactivity involves change initiated by the performer.

Engagement performance

As with adaptive performance, we've included this as a category of performance not so much because we believe that it is a distinct category, but rather because of the bold claims that have been made about employee engagement, as we showed in Chapter 1. We also showed in Chapter 1 that it isn't clear what employee engagement actually is; equally unclear is what an engaged performer does that a typical performer doesn't do. Here is one view (NHS Employers, 2013: 8): "We all know what staff engagement is when we see it, be it in the way work colleagues act, or in the way staff act in other workplaces, for instance when you go shopping."

Well, perhaps the fruits of employee engagement are in the eye of the beholder. But taking such a view doesn't help. There is some hint of what might be expected in some of the consultants' definitions in Chapter 1, Box 1.4 — discretionary effort, willingness to 'go the extra mile'. The latter is a bit platitudinous, perhaps, but this is often interpreted as organisational citizenship and therefore embraces a wide range of behaviours, as we showed earlier in the section on citizenship performance. Another hint is in the Mercer definition in Chapter 1, Box 1.4: "perform to levels that exceed the stated job requirements". A bit ambiguous, perhaps, but this could be taken to mean producing more, delivering to a higher quality, working faster (while maintaining quality and quantity) and the like. And another possible interpretation is signalled by Kahn (1990) – physical expression. One study (May et al., 2004: 36) that sought to test Kahn's ideas operationalised the physical expression of engagement by using the following survey items:

- "I stay until the job is done."
- "I avoid working overtime whenever possible." (reverse scored)
- "I take work home to do."

Though much of what is claimed for employee engagement looks to be highly positive, a dark side to engagement is hinted at in these items. Is engagement necessarily a good thing if it leads to longer working hours and taking work home? This is likely to mean increasing demands being placed on the employee, possible disruption to work–life balance, risk of personal sacrifice and strain. So, is engagement always fun? When does it become work intensification and lead to overload? The possible downsides are rarely mentioned (see George, 2010, for one exception).

Yet another perspective, again one that emphasises the positives, is introduced in Box 3.2 – *persistence, proactivity, role expansion* and *adaptability* (Macey et al., 2009), and elaborated in Box 3.8. If engagement performance means all of these things being displayed by a performer, we think it is going to be a pretty tall order to build engagement across the whole of a workforce. In much

BOX 3.8

ENGAGEMENT PERFORMANCE

Persistence. "The most straightforward examples of this are employees working harder, for longer stretches of time without a break, and for longer hours during the day or week. . . . Persistence can also take the form of increased perseverance in the face of adversity and greater resilience when a setback occurs."

Proactivity. "In its simplest form, to be proactive means taking action when the need for action first becomes apparent to the individual, such as performing maintenance on a machine in a plant at the first sign of decreased efficiency, rather than waiting for a supervisor to authorise maintenance. . . . engaged employees not only take action immediately after a need becomes evident, but they are also more likely to *recognise* or *anticipate* the need or opportunity for action in the first place."

Role Expansion. "At times this can be simple and ordinary, such as helping a busy co-worker complete a task or fixing a mistake someone else made. At other times, role expansion involve assuming longer-term or even permanent changes to one's role."

Adaptability. "An adaptive employee will help his company anticipate and respond to changes in the competitive landscape more quickly, more successfully, and with lower costs. Adaptive employees are more likely to develop new skills as job demands change, reducing hiring needs. In addition, while many large-scale changes require formal training to facilitate skill development, adaptive employees can adjust to changes without the need for formal training, saving time and money."

Source: Macey *et al.* (2009): 28, 29, 31, 33–34

of what has been written about employee engagement, there seems to be an assumption that everyone in an organisation is willing to be engaged: this is open to question. Another questionable assumption has to do with the ease with which the conditions that foster engagement can be created – less, rather than more, straightforward must surely be the order of the day. This, then, takes us on to consider the antecedents and determinants of process performance.

WHAT ARE THE 'CAUSES' OF PROCESS PERFORMANCE?

As the diagram in Box 3.1 indicates, process performance is 'caused' by two sets of factors – characteristics of the person and system (or situational) factors. So far as person factors are concerned, an influential theory introduced by Campbell *et al.* (1993: 43–44) proposes that an employee's performance will be a function of three within-person determinants:

1. declarative knowledge: that is, knowledge about facts and things and oneself (knowing *what* to do);
2. procedural knowledge and skill (cognitive skill, psychomotor skill, physical skill, interpersonal skill, self-management skill);
3. motivation: that is, choice behaviour:
    *   the choice to perform (expend effort)
    *   the choice of level of effort to expend
    *   the choice to persist over time in the expenditure of that level of effort.

These determinants derive from underlying antecedents. These include attributes of the person – what psychologists refer to as *individual differences*, such as intelligence and personality. These are the characteristics of people that are developable (albeit within limits) as a consequence of the influence of education, training and other everyday learning experiences. According to the Campbell *et al.* (1993) model, antecedents have an *indirect* effect on performance (behaviour), whereas it is knowledge, skill and motivation as determinants that have the *direct* effect.

One key practical implication of this for employee performance is, of course, obvious: performers need to have the required knowledge and skill, and this applies across all the categories of performance that we have identified. But for some categories, it is possible that dispositional/motivational attributes have more weight. Take contextual performance, for example. Performers must *want* to volunteer to help out: they need to have the relevant knowledge and skill, but the desire must come first. Choice is an important determinant of counterproductive work behaviours, and likewise for proactive forms of adaptive performance – yes, the performer must see the need/opportunity (and have the requisite skill to do what's required), but the motivation to act is important too.

As an example we'll consider contextual performance. This category embraces a wide range of behaviours. Given the nature (particularly the volitional nature) of many of them, you may wonder what would lead workers to engage in them. Well, as one might expect, motivational factors are important. A study by Rioux and Penner (2001) showed that different people may have different motives for engaging in a particular citizenship behaviour. Moreover, any given instance of citizenship behaviour on a performer's part may have more than one underlying motivation. They developed a scale to measure three different citizenship motives: organisational concern (e.g. I care what happens to the company); prosocial values (e.g. I believe in being courteous to others); impression management (e.g. to avoid looking bad in front of others). They found, as hypothesised, two associations – one between prosocial values and altruistic citizenship performance, and one between organisational concern and conscientious citizenship performance. In other words, concern for other people is associated with citizenship performance directed at individuals; and concern for the organisation is associated with citizenship performance directed at organisations. No association was found between impression management and altruistic performance or conscientious performance.

How should performers' personal characteristics be taken into account in appraisal? Well, it all depends on what personal characteristics you mean. In Chapter 1, we noted that rating personality was a feature of early appraisal schemes, but this gradually died out due to its extreme unpopularity with appraisers and appraisees. Does this move away from appraising personality mean that personality is now viewed as irrelevant to work performance? Not at all; indeed, there is an enormous body of research on the relationship between facets of personality and aspects of job performance. Though there is evidence supporting the importance of conscientiousness across jobs generally, the view is increasingly being held that our understanding of personality–performance relationships will be improved by focusing attention on narrower personality traits and on compound personality variables. Bateman and Crant (1993), for example, developed a proactive personality scale and positive relationships have been demonstrated with a range of outcomes, such as individual job performance, leadership and team performance (Crant, 2000).

But much of what we know about personality–performance relationships is more helpful in a selection context (see Schmitt, 2014, for an overview if you have a particular interest in this area) than for appraisal. Bear in mind, though, that if you select people because they have, say, a proactive personality, this will only work as a strategy if those people then have the opportunity to be proactive. If you've appointed such people and they find themselves in jobs where they have little opportunity for autonomy and discretion, then frustration is likely to set in.

The key point to bear in mind about personality is that it is relatively stable. So, it is hard enough for people to deliberately change their personalities over a protracted period, let alone do it more or less overnight at the instigation of the appraiser. On the other hand, people's knowledge, skills and abilities are developable (albeit within limits), and so there is a strong case for these to feature in appraisal. We will return to this theme in Chapter 4.

Important though the person is, so too are system (or situational) factors – the design of the job itself, the organisation of the work more broadly, social/interpersonal relationships among co-workers, the quality of supervision and numerous others. The range is vast: an illustrative list (abbreviated from Schneider and Hough, 1995) is shown in Box 3.9. These factors may have a

BOX 3.9

POTENTIAL SYSTEM (SITUATIONAL) FACTORS

Task characteristics

- Consistency of task
- Stage of skill acquisition with respect to task
- Amount of task structure
- Amount of time pressure to complete task
- Skill variety, task identity, task significance, autonomy, and feedback

Goal characteristics

- Specificity
- Complexity
- Difficulty
- Rewards associated with goal attainment
- Conflict with other goals
- Performance versus mastery goal

Characteristics of the physical environment

- Ambient conditions (e.g., light, noise, heat)
- Danger of bodily harm
- Workplace layout (e.g., open-plan office versus non-open-plan office; amount of privacy at workstation)

Characteristics of work role

- Role ambiguity
- Role overload
- Role conflict

Characteristics of social environment

- Management style of immediate supervisor (e.g., autocratic versus democratic)
- Cohesiveness of work group
- Amount of social support from co-workers, friends and family

Characteristics of organisation

- Organisational values
- Organisational reward systems
- Organisational structure (e.g., matrix versus hierarchical)

Source: Abbreviated from Schneider and Hough (1995: 119)

facilitating (enabling) or inhibiting (constraining) effect on performance (Blumberg and Pringle, 1982; Guzzo and Gannett, 1988). Though it has long been held that performance is a function of *motivation* and *ability* (e.g. Maier, 1947), Blumberg and Pringle (1982: 563) should be credited with adding *opportunity* to the equation, defining opportunity as "facts in the person's objective environment". They go on to say (1982: 563) that "The most important of these facts affecting level of performance appear to be elements of the technical system, physical conditions, actions of co-workers, actions of supervisors, and organizational policies and procedures." So far as the forward-looking aspect of appraisal is concerned, the key principle is that jobs (and the wider conditions of work) should be designed and organised so as to remove constraining factors and include ones that are enabling/facilitating. We consider the backward-looking aspect of appraisal and system (or situational) factors in Chapter 4.

OUTCOME (OUTPUT/RESULTS) PERFORMANCE

What the employee produces, what they accomplish, the results they achieve, the goals, targets or objectives that are met – all these constitute what very often is thought of as job performance. Survey evidence has long shown results-orientated approaches to be a feature of appraisal schemes. For example, early surveys by the Institute of Personnel Management here in the UK showed (in 1973, 1977 and 1986, respectively) that 51 per cent, 57 per cent and 63 per cent of responding organisations were using results-based approaches. And more recently, the 2005 and 2009 CIPD surveys reported 62 per cent and 75 per cent of responding organisations to be using objective-setting.

Though the early interest arose from management by objectives, in more recent years the use of goals/objectives-based approaches has been much to do with a central plank of performance management practice; that is, the alignment of individual and organisational goals. For example, a survey by Hewitt Associates (2010) showed that almost three-quarters of responding organisations used performance management to "align employees' performance goals with the company's business strategies". But only 15 per cent reported a high degree of alignment.

Why is this aspect of performance management not working? One possible explanation is that it is too bureaucratic, too cumbersome. Pulakos and O'Leary (2010) note, for example, that at the topmost level, goals and objectives need to be set

in a thoughtful and realistic way to ensure that mistakes made in setting the highest level goals do not cascade down throughout the entire organisation.

For this reason, goals set by the top leadership of the organization need the most critical scrutiny and opportunities for correction or revision, things that do not always occur to the degree they should.

(Pulakos and O'Leary, 2010: 517)

Another practical difficulty is ensuring line of sight for support functions – for someone working in HR, for example, it can be genuinely difficult to specify work objectives that clearly relate to overall organisational goals. Moreover, the cascading process can all take a long time – quite possibly several months, particularly when it is being done for the first time. This should hardly come as a surprise: practical problems of one sort or another were experienced with management by objectives and, as Campbell (2014) notes, "firms have often found successful implementation difficult. . . . Common criticisms of MBO are that such systems generate too much paperwork and that they emphasise quantitative goals at the expense of more qualitative objectives."

Goals and goal-setting have been subject to considerable research and as a result we have one of the more robust theories in the domain of work psychology, particularly when it comes to throwing light on aspects of the motivation of work performance. The fundamental principles of goal-setting are long-established: "specific high goals lead to higher performance than vague goals such as urging people to do their best. Furthermore, the higher the goal, the higher the performance" (Latham and Locke, 2014).

Bear in mind, of course, that these principles assume that the performer has the necessary knowledge and skills (and other resources) required to achieve the goal. For a performer who lacks the required knowledge/skills, setting challenging *performance* goals may have deleterious effects:

Specific challenging goals can produce 'tunnel vision' in which existing strategies are activated in preference to a search for new strategies, which may be required as tasks become more complex and when a person lacks the knowledge and skills for the task.

(Wood *et al.*, 2013: 135)

In such circumstances, the performance goal can act as a distraction and get in the way of learning what's required in order to achieve the goal successfully. Where new learning is required, challenging *learning* goals are preferable so as to focus attention on knowledge/skill acquisition (Seijts *et al.*, 2013).

Also, though the two do not invariably go hand in hand, it is likely that those who do have the required knowledge/skills will also have a sufficiently positive view of their *self-efficacy* – that is, their belief that they have the capabilities to achieve what's required (Bandura, 2013). Where the individual has doubts, there is a role for the manager in fostering self-efficacy beliefs:

> If people are persuaded to believe in themselves they will exert more effort. This increases their chance of success. However, credible persuaders must be knowledgeable and practice what they preach. Effective efficacy builders do more than convey faith in others. They arrange situations for others in ways that bring success. They avoid placing them, prematurely, in situations where they are likely to fail.
>
> (Bandura, 2009: 185)

Tackling complex tasks may bring particular risks of failing. According to Heslin *et al.* (2009: 98), "Complex tasks are those on which the path to goal achievement is not immediately apparent or easily understood." In such circumstances, there is a place for learning goals, as noted above. As Bandura (2009: 194) puts it, "Difficult goal challenges are not achievable at once. Seemingly overwhelming activities are mastered by breaking them down into smaller manageable steps." This is particularly so in the case of long-range goals. Though they may provide a vision of the future, they are likely to be too far in the distance to serve much value as day-to-day motivators. So-called *proximal* goals – short-term, sub-goals – provide more attainable steps on the way (Bandura, 2009).

Performers who have the required knowledge and skill and who are self-efficacious have to accept and commit to the performance goal. However, goals that really are too hard to achieve will simply be seen as such and risk not being accepted. Or, if the performer does have a go, they "work harder and harder until they eventually conclude that the goals cannot be attained, whereupon they become demoralized and disengaged" (Kerr and LePelley, 2013: 39).

Commitment to the goal is essential because, without it, there isn't really a goal at all. In order to bring about commitment to goals, is employee participation necessary in the goal-setting process? Simply assigning goals can work, but this does not mean that goals should be set in some curt, authoritarian fashion – the rationale, etc. needs to be explained so that the importance of the goal is understood. Participation may offer added value as a means of increasing the personal importance that the performer attaches to the goal, may increase understanding, and may lead to a higher goal being set. This may particularly be so in the case of setting team goals (Heslin *et al.*, 2009).

When it comes to the practical application of goal-setting, it is quite commonplace to find the acronym SMART, of which there are several variations – Box 3.10. If you are going to use a version of the SMART acronym, be careful about the combination of words you use. For example, you

BOX 3.10

SMART GOALS

Perhaps the most common version of the SMART acronym refers to "goals that are *specific, measurable, attainable, relevant*, and have a *timeframe*" (Latham, 2009). But there are many other versions to be found based on combinations of the following:

Stretching or **S**ignificant or **S**imple or **S**ustainable

Meaningful or **M**otivational or **M**anageable

Achievable or **A**greed or **A**cceptable/**A**ccepted or **A**ssignable or **A**ctionable or **A**ction-orientated or **A**djustable or **A**mbitious or **A**ligned with corporate goals or **A**spirational or **A**ppropriate

Results-orientated or **R**esults-based or **R**ealistic or **R**esourced or **R**easonable

Time-bound or **T**ime-limited or **T**ime-orientated or **T**imed or **T**imetabled or **T**ime/Cost limited or **T**ime-sensitive or **T**ime-specific or **T**imely

A variation on this theme is **FRAME** (Whetten *et al.*, 1994):

Few

Realistic

Agreed

Measured

Explicit

probably don't want 'Significant' *and* 'Meaningful' or 'Appropriate' *and* 'Relevant'. Also, be sure that a goal-setting approach fits. Pulakos and O'Leary (2010: 522) note several practical difficulties with goals – for example, that they aren't relevant for all jobs, and that they tend to work best with jobs that "have relatively static performance requirements". So, heed Bevan's (2014: 20) caution against a "slavish obsession" with SMART objective setting.

Two final points to note about goal-setting concern feedback and merit pay. At the very least, feedback lets the performer know how she/he is getting on – the progress that is being made towards accomplishing the goal(s). Feedback may also encourage self-setting of goals (Ashford and DeStobbeleir, 2013). Moreover, goals *and* feedback are more effective than either alone. As to merit pay,)

Heneman and Werner (2005: 33) note that "goal-setting theory suggests that merit pay increases motivation because merit increases result in the setting of more goals, the setting of more difficult goals, and greater commitment to goals". They note also (2005: 33) that goal difficulty needs to be taken into account; otherwise "employees may be motivated to set lower goals because they are easier to accomplish and still rewarded".

IN SUMMARY

Performance is a complex, multi-faceted concept – as we've shown in this chapter. There are two primary interpretations – one that emphasises ends (results/output) and one that emphasises means (behaviours). Not all jobs lend themselves to the appraisal of performance by way of results, but as a general principle, both ends and means should feature in appraisal. This may be a substantial undertaking, particularly when it comes to incorporating the behavioural aspects. How many dimensions of task performance should be included? How will contextual performance feature? From a development perspective, there is a strong case for having regard for the skills and abilities that the performer brings to the job. And to be complete, appraisal should also acknowledge situational factors, those factors outside the performer which may inhibit or facilitate performance.

DISCUSSION POINTS AND QUESTIONS

3.1 What do you see as the challenges of incorporating process performance in appraisal?

3.2 What do you see as the drawbacks to goal-setting?

3.3 Is whistleblowing counterproductive work behaviour? Research some examples from the past few years.

KEY REFERENCES

Bevan, S. (2014) *Performance Management: HR Thoroughbred or Beast of Burden?* London: The Work Foundation.

Campbell, J. P. and Wiernik, B. M. (2015) The modeling and assessment of work performance. *Annual Review of Organizational Psychology and Organizational Behavior,* **2**(1), 47–74.

Pulakos, E. D., Mueller-Hanson, R. A., O'Leary, R. S. and Meyrowitz, M. M. (2012) *Building a High-Performance Culture: A Fresh Look at Performance Management.* Alexandria, VA: Society for Human Resource Management.

REFERENCES

Arthur, W. Jr (2012) Dimension-based assessment centres. In D. J. R. Jackson, C. E. Lance and B. J. Hoffman (Eds) *The Psychology of Assessment Centres*. New York: Routledge.

Ashford, S. J. and DeStobbeleir, K. E. M. (2013) Feedback, goal setting and task performance revisited. In E. A. Locke and G. P. Latham (Eds) *New Developments in Goal Setting and Task Performance*. New York: Routledge, pp. 88–93.

Bandura, A. (2009) Cultivate self-efficacy for personal and organizational effectiveness. In E. A. Locke (Ed.) *Handbook of Principles of Organizational Behavior: Indispensable Knowledge for Evidence-based Management*. 2nd edn. Chichester, UK: Wiley, pp. 179–200.

Bandura, A. (2013) The role of self-efficacy in goal-based motivation. In E. A. Locke and G. P. Latham (Eds) *New Developments in Goal Setting and Task Performance*. New York: Routledge, pp. 199–210.

Bartram, D. (2005) The great eight competencies: A criterion-centric approach to validation. *Journal of Applied Psychology, 90*(6), 1185–1203.

Bateman, T. S. and Crant, J. M. (1993) The proactive component of organizational behavior: A measure and correlates. *Journal of Organizational Behavior, 14*(2), 103–118.

Bevan, S. (2014) *Performance Management: HR Thoroughbred or Beast of Burden?* London: The Work Foundation.

Blumberg, M. and Pringle, C. C. (1982) The missing opportunity in organizational research: Some implications for a theory of work performance. *Academy of Management Review, 7*(4), 560–569.

Borman, W. C. and Brush, D. H. (1993). More progress toward a taxonomy of managerial performance requirements. *Human Performance, 6*(1), 1–21.

Borman, W. C., Buck, D. E., Hanson, M. A., Motowidlo, S. J., Stark, S. and Drasgow, F. (2001) An examination of the comparative reliability, validity, and accuracy of performance ratings made using computerized adaptive rating scales. *Journal of Applied Psychology, 86*(5), 965–973.

Campbell, D. J. (2014) Management by objectives. In C. L. Cooper (Ed.) *Wiley Encyclopedia of Management*. Chichester, UK: Wiley.

Campbell, J. P. (2012) Behaviour, performance, and effectiveness in the twenty-first century. In S. W. J. Kozlowski (Ed.) *The Oxford Handbook of Organizational Psychology*. Vol. 1. New York: Oxford University Press, pp. 159–194.

Campbell, J. P. and Wiernik, B. M. (2015) The modeling and assessment of work performance. *Annual Review of Organizational Psychology and Organizational Behavior, 2*(1), 47–74.

Campbell, J. P., McCloy, R. A., Oppler, S. H. and Sager, C. E. (1993) A theory of performance. In N. Schmitt, W. C. Borman and Associates (Eds) *Personnel Selection in Organizations*. San Francisco: Jossey-Bass, pp. 35–70.

Cardy, R. L. and Dobbins, G. H. (1994) *Performance Appraisal: Alternative Perspectives*. Cincinnati, OH: South-Western.

Chartered Institute of Personnel and Development (2005) *Performance Management*. London: Chartered Institute of Personnel and Development.

Chartered Institute of Personnel and Development (2009) *Performance Management in Action: Current Trends and Practice*. London: Chartered Institute of Personnel and Development.

Crant, J. M. (2000) Proactive behavior in organizations. *Journal of Management,* **26**(3), 435–462.

Dorsey, D. W., Cortina, J. M. and Luchman, J. (2010) Adaptive and citizenship-related behaviors at work. In J. L. Farr and N. T. Tippins (Eds) *Handbook of Employee Selection*. New York: Routledge, pp. 463–487.

George, J. M. (2010) More engagement is not necessarily better: The benefits of fluctuating levels of engagement. In S. L. Albrecht (Ed.) *Handbook of Employee Engagement*. Cheltenham, UK: Edward Elgar, pp. 253–263.

Griffin, M. A., Neal, A. and Parker, S. K. (2007) A new model of work role performance: Positive behavior in uncertain and interdependent contexts. *Academy of Management Journal,* **50**(2), 327–347.

Gruys, M. L. and Sackett, P. R. (2003) Investigating the dimensionality of counterproductive work behavior. *International Journal of Selection and Assessment,* **11**(1), 30–42.

Guzzo, R. A. and Gannett, B. A. (1988) The nature of facilitators and inhibitors of effective task performance. In F. D. Schoorman and B. Schneider (Eds) *Facilitating Work Effectiveness*. Lexington, MA: Lexington Books, pp. 21–41.

Heneman, H. L. and Werner, J. M. (2005) *Merit Pay: Linking Pay to Performance in a Changing World*. 2nd edn. Greenwich, CT: Information Age Publishing.

Hesketh, B. and Neal, A. (1999) Technology and performance. In D. R. Ilgen and E. D. Pulakos (Eds) *The Changing Nature of Performance*. San Francisco: Jossey-Bass, pp. 21–55.

Heslin, P. A., Carson, J. B. and VandeWalle, D. (2009) Practical applications of goal-setting theory to performance management. In J. W. Smither and M. London (Eds) *Performance Management: Putting Research into Action*. San Francisco: Jossey-Bass, pp. 89–114.

Hewitt Associates (2010) *The Current State of Performance Management and Career Development 2010*. www.aon.com/attachments/thought-leadership/Hewitt_Survey_Results_PerfMgmtCareerDevSV10.pdf (accessed 6 September 2015).

Institute of Personnel Management (1973) *Performance Appraisal in Perspective: A Survey of Current Practice*. London: Institute of Personnel Management.

Institute of Personnel Management (1977) *Appraising Performance: Present Trends and the Next Decade*. London: Institute of Personnel Management.

Institute of Personnel Management (1986) *Performance Appraisal Revisited*. London: Institute of Personnel Management.

Jundt, D. K., Shoss, M. K. and Huang, J. L. (2015) Individual adaptive performance in organizations: A review. *Journal of Organizational Behavior,* **36**(1), 53–71.

Kahn, W. A. (1990) Psychological conditions of personal engagement and disengagement at work. *Academy of Management Journal,* **33**(4), 692–724.

Kerr, S. and LePelley, D. (2013) Stretch goals: Risks, possibilities, and best practices. In E. A. Locke and G. P. Latham (Eds) *New Developments in Goal Setting and Task Performance*. New York: Routledge, pp. 52–65.

Koopmans, L., Bernaards, C. M., Hildebrandt, V. H., Schaufeli, W. B., de Vet, H. C. W. and van der Beek, A. J. (2011) Conceptual frameworks of individual work performance: A systematic review. *Journal of Occupational and Environmental Medicine,* **53**(8), 856–866.

Latham, G. P. (2009) Motivate employee performance through goal setting. In E. A. Locke (Ed.) *Handbook of Principles of Organizational Behavior: Indispensable Knowledge for Evidence-Based Management.* 2nd edn. Chichester, UK: Wiley, pp. 161–178.

Latham, G. P. and Locke, E. A. (2014) The science and practice of goal setting. In C. L. Cooper (Ed.) *Wiley Encyclopedia of Management.* Chichester, UK: Wiley.

Macey, W. H., Schneider, B., Barbera, K. M. and Young, S. A. (2009) *Employee Engagement: Tools for Analysis, Practice, and Competitive Advantage.* Chichester, UK: Wiley–Blackwell.

Maier, N. R. F. (1947) *Psychology in Industry: A Psychological Approach to Industrial Problems.* London: Harrap.

May, D. R., Gilson, R. L. and Harter, L. M. (2004) The psychological conditions of meaningfulness, safety and availability and the engagement of the human spirit at work. *Journal of Occupational and Organizational Psychology,* **77**(1), 11–37.

Motowidlo, S. J. (2003) Job performance. In W. C. Borman, D. R. Ilgen and R. J. Klimoski (Eds) *Handbook of Psychology. Vol. 12. Industrial and Organizational Psychology.* Hoboken, NJ: Wiley, pp. 39–54.

Murphy, K. R. (1990) Job performance and productivity. In K. R. Murphy and F. E. Saal (Eds) *Psychology in Organizations.* Hillsdale, NJ: Erlbaum, pp. 157–178.

NHS Employers (2013) The staff engagement toolkit. www.nhsemployers.org/~/media/Employers/Documents/SiteCollectionDocuments/staff-engagement-toolkit.pdf (accessed 12 January 2016).

Organ, D. W., Podsakoff, P. M. and MacKenzie, S. B. (2006) *Organizational Citizenship Behavior: Its Nature, Antecedents, and Consequences.* Thousand Oaks, CA: Sage.

Pulakos, E. D. and O'Leary, R. S. (2010) Defining and measuring results of workplace behavior. In J. L. Farr and N. T. Tippins (Eds) *Handbook of Employee Selection.* New York: Routledge, pp. 513–529.

Pulakos, E. D., Arad, S., Donovan, M. A. and Plumondon, K. E. (2000) Adaptability in the workplace: Development of a taxonomy of adaptive performance. *Journal of Applied Psychology,* **85**(4), 612–624.

Pulakos, E. D., Mueller-Hanson, R. A., O'Leary, R. S. and Meyrowitz, M. M. (2012) *Building a High-Performance Culture: A Fresh Look at Performance Management.* Alexandria, VA: Society for Human Resource Management.

Reijseger, G., Schaufeli, W. B., Peeters, C. W. and Taris, T. W. (2013) Ready, set, go! A model of the relation between work engagement and work performance. In S. P. Gonçalves and J. G. Neves (Eds) *Occupational Health Psychology: From Burnout to Well-being.* Rosemead, CA: Scientific and Academic Publishing, pp. 289–306.

Reilly, R. R. and Aronson, Z. H. (2009) Managing contextual performance. In J. W. Smither and M. London (Eds) *Performance Management: Putting Research into Action.* San Francisco: Jossey-Bass, pp. 297–328.

Rioux, S. M. and Penner, L. A. (2001) The causes of organizational citizenship behavior: A motivational analysis. *Journal of Applied Psychology,* **86**(6), 1306–1314.

Roe, R. A. (1998) Personnel selection: Principles, methods and techniques. In P. J. D. Drenth, Ch. J. de Wolff and Hk. Thierry (Eds) *Handbook of Work and Organizational Psychology. Vol. 3.* Hove, UK: Psychology Press, pp. 5–32.

Roe, R. A. (1999) Work performance: A multiple regulation perspective. In C. L. Cooper and I. T. Robertson (Eds) *International Review of Industrial and Organizational Psychology. Vol. 14.* Chichester, UK: Wiley, pp. 231–335.

Rotundo, M. and Spector, P. E. (2010) Counterproductive work behavior and withdrawal. In J. L. Farr and N. T. Tippins (Eds) *Handbook of Employee Selection.* New York: Routledge, pp. 489–511.

Sackett, P. R. and DeVore, C. J. (2001) Counterproductive behaviours at work. In N. Anderson, D. S. Ones, H. Kepir Sinangil and C. Viswesvaran (Eds) *Handbook of Industrial, Work and Organizational Psychology. Vol. 1. Personnel Psychology.* London: Sage, pp. 145–164.

Schmitt, N. (2014) Personality and cognitive ability as predictors of effective performance at work. *Annual Review of Organizational Psychology and Organizational Behavior,* 1, 45–65.

Schneider, R. J. and Hough, L. M. (1995) Personality and industrial/organizational psychology. In C. L. Cooper and I. T. Robertson (Eds) *International Review of Industrial and Organizational Psychology.* Chichester, UK: Wiley, pp. 75–129.

Seijts, G. H., Latham, G. P. and Woodwark, M. (2013) Learning goals: A qualitative and quantitative review. In E. A. Locke and G. P. Latham (Eds) *New Developments in Goal Setting and Task Performance.* New York: Routledge, pp. 260–276.

Taris, T. W. and Schaufeli, W. B. (2015) Individual well-being and performance at work: A conceptual and theoretical overview. In M. Van Veldhoven and R. Peccei (Eds) *Well-being and Performance at Work.* Hove, UK: Psychology Press, pp. 15–34.

Thornton, G. C. and Byham, W. C. (1982) *Assessment Centres and Managerial Performance.* New York: Academic Press.

Waldman, D. A. (1994) The contributions of total quality management to a theory of work performance. *Academy of Management Review,* **19**(3), 510–536.

Whetten, D., Cameron, K. and Woods, M. (1994) *Developing Management Skills for Europe.* London: HarperCollins.

Wood, R. E., Whelan, J., Sojo, V. and Wong, M. (2013) Goals, goal orientations, strategies, and performance. In E. A. Locke and G. P. Latham (Eds) *New Developments in Goal Setting and Task Performance.* New York: Routledge, pp. 134–159.

4 ASSESSING PERFORMANCE, THE PERSON AND THE SITUATION

There are multiple perspectives that can be taken on the reviewing/assessing elements of appraisal. From a measurement perspective, ratings are very much the focus of attention. From a social/communication perspective, it is the feedback that comes to the fore. From a justice perspective, it is the fairness of the appraisal arrangements and the way that they are enacted by line managers that come into play, along with the fairness of the assessment and any consequential outcomes. Though the evolution of PA into PM brought with it greater advocacy of more frequent interim reviews, a requirement for an annual review remains the foundation of the typical appraisal arrangements. This annual event is likely to include a conversation between appraiser and performer (traditionally called the appraisal interview) and the completion of a form that probably includes one or more ratings and provision for some narrative assessment of performance. Agreement on action on development needs and on performance objectives for the next review period may also be included within this discussion and form, or possibly as a separate event/document.

ASSESSING PERFORMANCE

Across several decades the major topic of interest in the appraisal field was accuracy in performance rating. When it comes to the mechanics of appraisal, that is, the 'how' of appraisal, the choice of methods is far from wide – basically, there are narratives or there are ratings. The larger (by far) body of research is that on ratings, much of it concerned with the psychometric properties of different rating formats. There are several rating formats, including various behavioural ones – examples of the latter are illustrated in Box 4.1. Behavioural formats represent the most sophisticated approach to improving the problems inherent in rating-scale use. Essentially, they try to put the appraiser into the role of an objective observer of behaviour rather than a judge, thereby seeking to minimise the scope for subjectivity. However, these formats are undoubtedly time-consuming to devise, which deters many organisations from using them, but bear in mind the process benefits that may arise from the development process that has to be undertaken – involvement of job holders, their managers and others may help to engender understanding and acceptance of the behaviours, for example, and there may be developmental value for performers in signalling to them the nature of desired behaviours. But from an assessment perspective, various problems do arise. For example, managers are not always able to identify where on the scale they should place the behaviours they see; the anchors, after all, are only indicative, not comprehensive, behavioural descriptions.

BOX 4.1

BEHAVIOURALLY BASED RATING SCALES

The basic concept and methodology for all these approaches stems from BARS (Behaviourally Anchored Rating Scales). The development of these scales goes through five stages:

1. Examples of behaviours reflecting effective and ineffective job performance are obtained from people who are knowledgeable about the job to be rated.
2. The examples are grouped into a series of separate performance dimensions by these experts.
3. Another expert group repeats the second stage, allocating the examples to dimensions. They provide an independent check on the relevance of the behavioural examples to their dimensions. Any that are allocated differently by the two groups are probably too ambiguous and should be discarded. Also as a result of this, the dimensions should be quite independent of each other.
4. Taking each dimension separately, the examples relating to it are rated by the experts in terms of effectiveness on a numerical scale. Where an example does not get rated similarly by different judges, then it will be deleted; a high level of agreement on how an example is rated on that dimension is required.
5. The resulting dimensions are each expressed as a scale, the points of which are anchored by the behavioural descriptions arrived at through the preceding stages. The number of dimensions can vary according to the job; anything from six to nine would be quite typical.

There is no single way of laying out a BARS. Here is one example:

BARS example: teamwork dimension

	50	
Consistently seeks to help others		
Tolerant and supportive of colleagues		
	40	Contributes ideas and takes full part in group meetings
Willing to change own plans to fit in		Listens to colleagues
	30	
Keeps colleagues in the picture about own activities		
		Mixes willingly enough
	20	
Is not very aware of what colleagues are doing		
		Inclined to alter arrangements to suit self
		Always criticising others
	10	
Lets everyone else do the more unpopular jobs		
Never goes out of way to help or cooperate		
	0	

A variation on this method is offered by the use of BOS (Behavioural Observation Scales). Here, again, the end result is a series of performance dimensions linked to behavioural descriptions. The way the rating task is structured is rather different, though. Each behavioural example relating to the dimension is given a separate rating, and the overall dimension rating is the sum or average of these.

BOS example: teamwork dimension

Teamwork

(a) Tolerant of others and shows patience with them

Almost Always 1 2 3 4 5 Almost Never

(b) Consistently seeks to offer help and support

Almost Always 1 2 3 4 5 Almost Never

(c) Plays full and balanced role in team discussions

Almost Always 1 2 3 4 5 Almost Never

(d) Keeps colleagues informed where necessary

Almost Always 1 2 3 4 5 Almost Never

(e) Volunteers for fair share of less popular duties

Almost Always 1 2 3 4 5 Almost Never

(f) Willing to change own plans to cooperate with others

Almost Always 1 2 3 4 5 Almost Never

Moreover, the extensive research on ratings did not yield a 'best' rating format so far as psychometric properties were concerned. A wide range of other considerations bears on the assessment process – like the political factors that we referred to in Chapters 1 and 2 – such that achieving accuracy in appraisal is very much against the odds. Why is appraisal likely to be inaccurate? We'll consider ratings first – some data are shown in Box 4.2.

The data shown in Box 4.2 come from a number of UK Government departments at two periods in time when the appraisal arrangements were largely uniform across the Civil Service. The scales shown here illustrate a very widely used format, one in which the scale points have brief verbal labels. (You will find more examples of rating scales in Pulakos, 2007.) Such labels aren't much to go on when it comes to deciding whether an individual is a good or very good performer, but documentation about how to apply the scale might include further guidance for the appraiser. Even so, distinguishing between levels still represents a problem for appraisal. And as the figures in the tables show, appraisers are not very good at spreading their ratings across the full width of the scales. Of course, a three-point scale inherently doesn't allow much spread. But as the figures in the first table show, a six-point scale doesn't necessarily help matters: the six-point scale is, in effect, a four-point scale. For all practical purposes, the middle box of the three-point scale conflates the 'very good' and 'good' categories. So, the figures illustrate two common findings – a central tendency in which most people get rated at the mid-point of the scale (inevitable with just three categories) and leniency, where most people are rated higher up the scale.

The figures show some variations across departments. The most straightforward explanation, of course, is that the ratings are genuine reflections of performance. However, it also is likely that across departments managers vary in their willingness and ability to appraise. Also, we can't help but wonder whether the language of the scale has some impact. Consider Department A, for example: about 90 per cent in the middle category in 2011

BOX 4.2

ILLUSTRATIVE APPRAISAL RATINGS

	Dept. 1 2nd level		Dept. 2 1st level		Dept. 3 2nd level		Dept. 3 1st level		Dept. 4 2nd level		Dept. 4 1st level	
	M	F	M	F	M	F	M	F	M	F	M	F
Outstanding	5	2	2	3	6	2	4	2	5	4	4	6
Very good	60	66	43	54	63	63	41	48	59	65	52	55
Good	32	29	40	37	31	30	43	44	30	28	37	34
Fair	3	4	13	7	0	4	12	6	5	3	6	5
Not quite adequate	0	0	2	0	0	0	1	0	0	0	1	0
Unsatisfactory	0	0	0	0	0	0	0	0	0	0	0	0

Source: Williams and Walker (1985)
Note: All figures shown are percentages. Performance appraisal ratings for 1st and 2nd levels of supervision.

		BAME*	White	F	M
Dept. A 2011	Wholly Exceptional	2.1	2.8	2.7	2.4
	Consistently Good	91.4	91.6	89.7	87.9
	Unsatisfactory	0.2	0.1	0.1	0.2
Dept. A 2013	Exceeded	16.0	20.5	20.5	17.7
	Achieved	74.7	73.3	73.7	72.7
	Must Improve	8.6	6.0	5.3	9.2
Dept. A 2014	Exceeded	17.2	21.6	21.7	18.9
	Achieved	72.9	71.0	71.8	70.5
	Must Improve	9.4	7.1	6.2	6.2
Dept. B 2012-13	Top	9.9	14.9	13.9	13.5
	Good	86.3	82.8	83.6	83.7
	Improvement Needed	2.0	1.3	1.1	1.9
Dept. B 2013-14	Exceeded	14.2	20.6	19.6	18.4
	Achieved	74.2	72.1	74.1	71.0
	Must Improve	11.5	7.3	6.2	10.6

Sources:
www.gov.uk/government/uploads/system/uploads/attachment_data/file/141742/equality-info-report-2011.pdf
www.gov.uk/government/publications/performance-markings-dwp-equality-information-2013-data
www.gov.uk/government/uploads/system/uploads/attachment_data/file/359612/Department_for_Work_and_Pensions_Equality_Information_2014_-_Employee_Data.pdf
www.gov.uk/government/uploads/system/uploads/attachment_data/file/275061/141010_HMRC_Workforce_Diversity_Data_2012-13_-_final.pdf
www.gov.uk/government/uploads/system/uploads/attachment_data/file/397093/Equality_Act_2010_Workforce_Diversity_Data_for_2013_to_2014.pdfNotes:

Notes: All figures shown are percentages. Where totals do not add up to 100 per cent, this is because annual appraisals were not required for some employees, e.g. new entrants.

* BAME = Black, Asian, minority ethnic.

and about three-quarters in 2013. Has the change from 'consistently good' to 'achieved' contributed to that shift?

Are there differences between the genders and by ethnicity? Visual inspection of data such as those shown in Box 4.2 should not be relied on. On the face of it, it looks as though consistently higher proportions of ethnic minorities get a 'must improve/improvement needed' rating, but when you carry out diversity monitoring on your appraisal data you should use appropriate statistical testing to check for significant effects. That said, it is well known that biases of various kinds do exist and they can affect our assessment of people. Box 4.3 gives some examples.

So, if you find differences in performance ratings between women and men, among different ethnic groups or on any of the characteristics protected by law, what might the explanations be? The differences might be real and genuine performance differences, of course, so that possibility shouldn't be ruled out. But then neither should racism, sexism or some other 'ism'. Line managers may have stereotyped views about women at work, older workers, younger workers, etc. and what to expect of them as performers; and they may have stereotyped views about jobs – nursing and secretarial work are for women, firefighting and repairing motor vehicles are for men. Such factors as these potentially affect not just performance assessments, but also the way in which people at work get treated (Roberson and Block, 2001). Negative stereotypes about, say, women or older workers (e.g. only working for the 'pin money') put them at risk of discriminatory treatment that devalues their contribution – such as not getting praise and recognition, not getting opportunities to develop their skills, which may lower motivation and performance. A mismatch between a stereotype about a particular group (women, say) and a particular job role (such as viewing leadership roles as male) may engender lowered performance expectations, and possibly lower performance assessments (Heilman and Eagly, 2008; Heilman, 2012).

Worryingly, the 'isms' aren't necessarily overt; indeed, it shouldn't be assumed that people are aware of the biases to which they are prone. There has been a growing recognition that biases can be implicit or unconscious (see the examples in Box 4.3) – they 'kick in' or activate automatically in, for example, situations like appraisal where judgements have to be made about people. It is possible to raise people's awareness of unconscious bias, but action to try to avoid or reduce such bias should be designed into the appraisal arrangements, as we suggest below.

Notwithstanding their limitations, ratings do have their advantages: they are easily understood; they offer a lot of flexibility; where multiple dimensions of process performance are rated, they encourage a more analytical view of performance by asking appraisers to think about the different aspects of the

BOX 4.3

SOURCES OF BIAS AND ERROR IN ASSESSMENT

Implicit bias (unconscious bias). This "refers to the attitudes or stereotypes that affect our understanding, actions, and decisions in an unconscious manner. These biases, which encompass both favorable and unfavorable assessments, are activated involuntarily and without an individual's awareness or intentional control" (Staats *et al.*, 2015: 62). We all have implicit biases, and they aren't necessarily in concert with our expressed beliefs. Nor are stereotypical beliefs necessarily correct. Implicit bias is a particular hazard in an appraisal context when making ratings and writing narrative assessments.

Faulty implicit personality theory. Most people, without being conscious of it, have some ideas about personality and how it is structured; they have an implicit personality theory that guides them, and which may not always be built on sound foundations. You can see this in how untrained assessors rate candidates in group exercises: the candidates who talk most easily are often judged as being the highest on emotional stability. Actually, there is no good reason for assuming that an articulate person is also a stable one, but although faulty, it is a common inference about personality. Another frequent error is to assume that an assertive individual is also more organised and more intellectually able than someone who is not. These kinds of ideas about personality traits and the relationship between them can be a source of distortion in the way appraisers assess their staff.

Implicit person theory. Do you think that people are able to develop and grow (you have a *growth mindset*) or do you think that people's abilities tend not to change much over time (a *fixed mindset*)? Holding the latter view may make you disinclined to modify whatever initial impressions you have formed of an employee's performance (Heslin and VandeWalle, 2008). You see someone as a poor performer or as a good performer; the risk of having a fixed mindset is that you won't change this view even if the employee improves their performance (in the case of a poor performer) or if their performance deteriorates (in the case of a good performer). So, performance improvements may get ignored and not reflected through appreciation or in the appraisal. Likewise, performance deterioration may not get tackled.

Attributional error. Before this is described, try a little exercise for yourself. Think of an incident recently where you did not perform as well as you would have hoped. Why did this happen? How would you explain it? When you have mulled that over, move on to another incident, this time one where one of your subordinates (or, if you do not have any, a peer) did not perform as well as you hoped. Again, why did this happen? How would you explain it? No cheating now; do not read on until you have analysed the two incidents!

Have you displayed 'fundamental attributional error' (to give it its full name)? This refers to a pervasive tendency we all have to take much more account of the situational circumstances in explaining our own behaviour – especially when we have been less than successful – than we do in explaining other people's behaviour. When it comes to understanding why others have acted the way they did, we are much more likely to make dispositional attributions. In other words, we see other people's actions as being caused by their personality and abilities and we play down the importance of the situation, the context of the behaviour. The implications of this for appraisal are clear: the danger is that the appraiser will be too ready to see a lack of goal achievement as being due to the appraisee's deficiencies and will not make enough allowances for other factors (of which the appraiser may well be one).

'Similar to me' effect (affinity bias). This is very common in interviews and can affect appraisals, too. It happens very quickly when we meet someone for the first time. We categorise the person either as 'one of us' (in-group) or as different from us (out-group). In this way, similarity in attitudes, preferences or background between the appraiser and appraisee influences the former to be positive in response to the latter, even to the extent of being unduly favourable in assessing performance. Good performance on the part of a 'like-me' (in-group) performer is likely to be attributed to ability and skill, whereas poor performance would probably be attributed to bad luck or some other factor external to the person. But in the case of a 'not-like-me' (out-group) performer, the reverse applies. Good performance is because of good luck; poor performance is the fault of the individual.

Biased sampling. There are two main forms of this. First, the tendency to base the appraisal on the last month or two of the period under review, because that is what dominates in the memory. Things that happened earlier, in what is the greater part of the appraisal period, are forgotten. The second form, which sometimes occurs in combination with the first, is to recall only the times when things have gone wrong, when the appraisee has not performed well. The extent to which this happens is demonstrated by the large number of people in organisations who work on the philosophy of 'no news is good news'.

Halo effect. This is the tendency to allow one or two favourable attributes of an individual to colour one's judgement of all their other attributes. The result is to produce an overall, rather un-discriminating positive assessment – a 'halo'. The opposite phenomenon is sometimes called the 'horns effect'; this is where some unfavourable attribute of the person appraised leads to a generally negative impression being formed. This kind of error is one of the most commonly encountered, in selection interviews as well as in appraisal.

job; and they have the potential to facilitate comparisons between people (but be wary of the hazards noted above). They can be applied to process performance and to output performance; for example, the extent to which goals/objectives are achieved. However, the whole point of *quantifiable* objectives is that it is easier to determine whether, or to what extent, they have been achieved. This means that such objectives ought to offer some prospect of a more reliable and valid measure of an individual's performance. This is obviously worth having in itself, but it has further and very significant knock-on effects. The greater objectivity serves to reduce some of the appraisees' concerns about the appraisal process, as well as those of appraisers. It therefore is easy to understand the attraction of expressing performance requirements in terms of goals/targets/objectives, and then appraising performance in terms of the extent to which those requirements are met.

Ratings may be accompanied by a narrative assessment – a statement describing what has been accomplished (ideally, with evidence), an explanation of any mitigating factors, commendation for particularly high achievement and the like. But which should come first: the rating or the narrative? In the typical 360° appraisal system, it is probable that the ratings come first with an opportunity to add narrative comments towards the end in answer to questions like 'What should this manager do more of?'. However, when it comes to appraisal, there is a case for saying that the narrative should come first. At the very least, there should be some means for the manager (and the appraisee) to reflect in a structured way on the past review period and note what has gone well and less well, if only to use this information as an aide-memoire. This is one way of helping to counteract the effect of implicit biases. Slowing down the process of making a judgement by gathering evidence of performance ought also to promote a more accurate assessment and, in turn, a greater sense of fairness on the part of the performer (see Box 4.4). The notes that manager and appraisee make from their respective reviews then become the basis of the appraisal interview, from which arise agreed ratings and an agreed narrative assessment. Although one would expect ratings and narrative comments to be consistent with one another, a study by Wilson (2010: 1925) showed that such consistency was lacking. In particular, "Supervisors systematically gave lower ratings to black staff relative to white staff that they did not explain in their written summaries."

Does all this sound a bit too bureaucratic? Managers do find the report-writing aspect of appraisal to be a chore but this could, of course, be done by the appraisee. Pulakos *et al.* (2012: 11) advocate reducing or eliminating requirements for narratives on the grounds that "The value of performance narratives in many situations is unclear." So, be clear about what (and how much) needs to be written down and why a written record is being kept. And, if a written record does need to be kept, another relevant consideration

BOX 4.4

FAIRNESS IN APPRAISAL

Research has identified four forms of fairness, all of which are relevant in an appraisal context.

- *Distributive justice* is to do with the perceived fairness of outcomes – in the appraisal context this principally means the perceived fairness of the assessments (narratives and ratings) made, but would also embrace any decisions about rewards (e.g. pay for performance) that are based on the performance assessment.
- *Procedural justice* is to do with the perceived fairness of the process that is followed in determining particular outcomes. So, does the appraisal process as it has been designed incorporate features that research has shown to promote perceptions of fairness? For example, does the procedure provide for the employee to have their say?
- *Interactional justice* is to do with how the process that exists on paper is enacted in practice and it is regarded as having two components:
  - *Interpersonal justice* is to do with the quality and nature of the interpersonal interaction between appraiser and appraisee. So, for example, the procedure on paper allows the appraisee to have their say, but in practice the manager in some way curtails this opportunity.
  - *Informational justice* is to do with the quality of the information/ evidence, given as explanation. For example, an appraisal is likely to be seen as unfair if the manager bases it on little or poor-quality evidence.

is how long – or how short! – the retention period should be. Be wary of simply retaining a written record because that's what has always been done in the past.

ASSESSING THE PERSON

Given what we've said about the assessment of personality having fallen out of favour, you might think it odd that we're including a section on assessing the person. Surely, appraisal is about assessing performance? This undoubtedly is true. But it is impossible to ignore what the individual brings to the job: this is especially the case for development- and motivation-orientated appraisal. Developing performance means developing the individual's knowledge, skills and abilities.

Though the terms knowledge, skills and abilities are used in the workplace, these concepts sometimes are subsumed under the label 'competencies' – but this is a very different interpretation of competencies from the one we set out in Chapter 3. That interpretation of competencies placed the emphasis on behaviour – *what the person does*; in other words, equating competencies with dimensions of performance. The interpretation that we move on to now places the emphasis on *what the person has* – that is, competencies are properties or characteristics of the performer.

Widely acknowledged as a starting point for the application of this interpretation of competencies within work settings was the work of David McClelland, George Klemp Jr and their colleagues associated with the McBer Company. Though their studies arose from recognition that traditional predictors used in selection settings were less than successful in doing what they were intended to do, this approach to competencies has come to have broader application across different fields of HR. As defined by Klemp and McClelland (1986), competencies (a 'competency' in the singular) are characteristics of outstanding performers:

> attributes of an individual that are necessary for effective performance in a job or life role. These attributes can include (1) general or specialized knowledge of use in an occupation; (2) abilities, both physical and intellectual; (3) traits, such as energy level and certain personality types; (4) motives, or need states that direct individuals toward desired behaviour patterns; and (5) self-images that reflect the roles people see themselves in and their concept of how effective they are in their roles.
>
> (Klemp and McClelland, 1986: 32)

A later version (e.g. Spencer and Spencer, 1993: 9) emphasised the causal relationship with performance: "A competency is an *underlying characteristic* of an individual that is *causally related* to *criterion-referenced effective and/or superior performance* in a job or situation."

So, according to this conception, competencies clearly are characteristics of the person – and a wide range of characteristics at that – and they are necessary for effective performance. The description of the method (the Job Competence Assessment Method – JCAM) used to define competencies makes clear what is meant by performance – output/outcome/results. For example, performance criteria that have been used have included measures of work output and ratings by supervisors – both 'hard' and 'soft' indicators, in other words, including unit-level criteria and not just those at the level of the individual performer. The JCAM involves comparing those who score higher on the various relevant performance indicators with those who are average performers and the process

leads to the identification of *differentiating competencies*. There also are
threshold competencies: "the essential characteristics (usually knowledge or
basic skills, such as the ability to read) that everyone in a job needs to be
minimally effective but that do not distinguish superior from average
performers" (Spencer and Spencer, 1993: 15). Both are important: Schippmann
(2010: 211) makes the point that undue emphasis on differentiating
competencies "may result in overlooking or undervaluing the basic
competencies that are foundational for success in the . . . job". Note an essential
practical implication of this model of competencies: if you want to adopt it,
then you need to undertake appropriate job analysis to establish the relationship
between competencies and job (that is, *outcome*) performance.

Though the McBer competencies manifest themselves in behaviour, this
approach fundamentally is about performers' *underlying characteristics*. So, if
you say that someone is adaptable, then you are making a statement about an
attribute of the person – that is, the quality of *adaptability* – and this is an
inference that you are drawing based on observations of behaviour. The range
of characteristics (or *person factors* to use the terminology from Chapter 3,
Box 3.1) is broad and includes what people have learned as well as the basic
raw material they are born with and which establishes boundaries on the extent
to which a person is able to develop. Relevant in this regard are competencies
for life-long learning. A programme of work carried out under the auspices of
the European Union has identified eight such competences (the preferred
term), one of which is '*learning to learn*', and is seen as particularly important
on the grounds that it supports all learning activities.

> Learning to learn is the ability to pursue and persist in learning, to
> organise one's own learning, including through effective management of
> time and information, both individually and in groups. This competence
> includes awareness of one's learning process and needs, identifying
> available opportunities, and the ability to overcome obstacles in order to
> learn successfully. This competence means gaining, processing and
> assimilating new knowledge and skills as well as seeking and making use
> of guidance.
>
> (European Communities, 2007: 8)

This definition is quoted here because it illustrates one very particular type of
competency, namely a meta-competency. This is a fuzzy area, not least because
you will encounter various terms – for example, 'meta-competences', 'meta-
skills', 'meta-qualities' or 'meta-abilities' – which may all basically be
synonyms. There's no agreed list of meta-competencies (-abilities/-qualities)
but, given their nature, one would expect only a small number – Box 4.5 shows
a number of examples. So, be suspicious if you come across long lists of

BOX 4.5

META-COMPETENCIES, META-QUALITIES AND META-ABILITIES

- Meta-competencies

Hall and Kahn (2002; also Briscoe and Hall, 1999) refer to these as higher-order qualities that enhance a person's ability to learn. They propose two, and associated learning behaviours:

- self-knowledge, which they define as "a clear sense of identity";
  - accurate self-assessment
  - seeking, hearing, and acting on feedback
  - exploring, communicating and acting on personal values
  - being open to diverse people and ideas
  - engaging in personal development activity
  - being able to modify one's self-perception as one's attributes change
- adaptability;
  - being able to identify for oneself the qualities that are critical for future performance and being able to make the changes needed to develop them
  - eagerness to accept new challenges
  - exploration of new territory
  - comfort with turbulent change.
- Meta-abilities (Butcher and Harvey, 1998)
  - cognitive skills: these include cognitive complexity, cognitive flexibility and interpersonal awareness. They make up the key thought processes which help individuals "read" situations and understand and resolve problems;
  - self-knowledge: this is a capability of seeing oneself as others do, being clear about one's own motivations and values, and distinguishing between one's own needs and those of others;
  - emotional resilience: this is effective self-management of emotions and impulses, including self-control and self-discipline, using emotion appropriately, coping with pressure and adversity, and keeping a balanced view of the self;
  - personal drive: refers to an attitude of personal achievement and self-motivation.
- Meta-qualities

  Burgoyne and Stuart (1976):
  - creativity;
  - mental agility;
  - balanced learning habits and skills;

  A fourth was added later (Pedler et al., 1986):
  - self-knowledge.

meta-competencies covering wide-ranging aspects of the person – such lists suggest that the essential nature of meta-competencies has not been grasped.

You may also come across other concepts and find yourself wondering where they fit in – *learning agility* (De Meuse *et al.*, 2010; Cavanaugh and Zelin, 2012), for example: is this a meta-competency or cluster of meta-competencies or 'ordinary' competencies (or something different altogether)? As defined by Lombardo and Eichinger (2000), learning agility comprises four factors:

1. *People Agility* – Describes people who know themselves well, learn from experience, treat others constructively, and are cool and resilient under the pressure of change.
2. *Results Agility* – Describes people who get results under tough conditions, inspire others to perform beyond normal, and exhibit the sort of presence that builds confidence in others.
3. *Mental Agility* – Describes people who think through problems from a fresh point of view and are comfortable with complexity, ambiguity, and explaining their thinking to others.
4. *Change Agility* – Describes people who are curious, have a passion for ideas, like to experiment with test cases, and engage in skill building activities.

(Lombardo and Eichinger, 2000: 324)

Though there are clear overlaps with some of the meta-characteristics shown in Box 4.5, learning agility would seem to be a much more wide-ranging notion than a meta-competency.

To the extent that there is a common thread in writing on meta-competencies it is the emphasis placed on learning and the idea that the ability to learn from experience may be more important than existing competency levels. As summarised by Winterton *et al.* (2006):

> [M]eta-competence is concerned with an individual's knowledge of their own intellectual strengths and weaknesses, how to apply skills and knowledge in various task situations and how to acquire missing competences. . . . The common theme with . . . lists of meta-competencies is they relate to the cognitive aspects of work, especially with the processes of learning and reflection that are critical to developing new mental models.

(Winterton *et al.*, 2006: 16)

This idea was set out by Brown and McCartney (1995: 47): "higher-order skills and abilities upon which competences are based and which have to do with being able to learn, adapt, anticipate and create, rather than with being able to demonstrate that one has the ability to do". In other words, meta-competencies (or -qualities/-abilities) are the characteristics underpinning the ability both to acquire experience and to learn from it, which is the key to development generally.

As the Brown and McCartney definition indicates, the notion of meta-competencies has been around for a good many years now. However, more recently, particular emphasis has been placed on the importance of learning to learn (see the quote from European Communities, 2007, earlier in this section) in the context of today's ever-changing (and doing so ever more rapidly) environment, particularly the working environment. Particular stress is laid upon the importance of continuous learning across the whole of one's life-span (also referred to as life-long learning; London, 2012).

ASSESSING THE SITUATION

Important though the person is, don't ignore situational factors – the design of the job itself, the organisation of the work more broadly, social/interpersonal relationships among co-workers, the quality of supervision and numerous others (Chapter 3, Box 3.9). These factors bear on the *opportunity* (Blumberg and Pringle, 1982) to perform. Job design features such as autonomy may have a facilitating effect (assuming requisite ability and motivation on the part of the performer). On the other hand, working conditions that are too hot, too cold, too noisy or over crowded are likely to impede performance. Even the weather can get in the way, as when rain stops play. Ideally, jobs (and the wider conditions of work) would be designed and organised so as to remove constraining factors and include ones that are enabling/facilitating.

When it comes to the backward-looking aspect of appraisal, regard should be paid to any impact that situational factors may have had. In particular, be aware of the risk of the fundamental attributional error that we referred to in Box 4.3 – that is, blaming the worker for poor performance without any acknowledgement or understanding of the situation. The impact of situational factors is a legitimate topic for discussion in the appraisal interview, though this may bring with it some risk of excuse-making on the part of the appraisee (Dobbins *et al.*, 1993). Against that, however, if there genuinely are constraining or inhibiting factors, then these need to be exposed so that, if possible, they can be remedied; or, if not, that there is a shared understanding about their impact. Adopting a diagnostic approach would seem to be particularly important in order to understand the causes of poor performance. What's the difference between what the performer is doing and what they should be doing? Does the performer know what is expected of them? Do they have the necessary skills, abilities, knowledge and motivation to carry out what's required? What factors in the workplace situation (or outside) are bearing on the performer and with what impact? These are examples of the sorts of questions that need to be asked in order to avoid making false attributions when assessing performance, to engender a sense of fairness and promote better performance.

IN SUMMARY

Given the complexity of performance as a concept, it is understandable that appraising performance is likewise complex. However, the complexity of assessment lies not in the methods – the choice is far from wide, fundamentally ratings and/or narratives. Rather, the complexity lies in deciding what to appraise. Outputs/goals? Behaviours – that is, process performance? Task performance and citizenship performance? How many dimensions? What about what the performer brings to the job – their competencies? And how are you going to take into account the impact of the situation?

DISCUSSION POINTS AND QUESTIONS

4.1 Adaptive performance or individual adaptability as a meta-competency: which is the more useful perspective in an appraisal context?

4.2 How do the different approaches to competencies help us in describing and assessing performance? What do they give us that assessing people against objectives does not?

4.4 What should organisations do to try to counter the effect of biases in appraisal?

4.5 What properties should an appraisal process have in order for it to be perceived as fair?

KEY REFERENCES

Pulakos, E. D., Mueller-Hanson, R. A., O'Leary, R. S. and Meyrowitz, M. M. (2012) *Building a High-Performance Culture: A Fresh Look at Performance Management.* Alexandria, VA: Society for Human Resource Management.

Staats, C., Capatosto, K., Wright, R. A. and Contractor, D. (2015) *State of the Science: Implicit Bias Review 2015.* Columbus, OH: Kirwan Institute.

Winterton, J., Delamare-LeDeist, F. and Stringfellow, E. (2006) *Typology of Knowledge, Skills and Competences: Clarification of the Concept and Prototype.* Luxembourg: Office for Official Publications of the European Communities.

REFERENCES

Blumberg, M. and Pringle, C. C. (1982) The missing opportunity in organizational research: Some implications for a theory of work performance. *Academy of Management Review*, **7**(4), 560–569.

Briscoe, J. P. and Hall, D. T. (1999) Grooming and picking leaders using competency frameworks: Do they work? An alternative approach and new guidelines for practice. *Organizational Dynamics*, **28**(2), 37–52.

Brown, R. B. and McCartney, S. (1995) Competence is not enough: Meta-competence and accounting education. *Accounting Education*, **4**(1), 43–53.

Burgoyne, J. and Stuart, R. (1976) The nature, use and acquisition of managerial skills and other attributes. *Personnel Review*, **5**(4), 19–29.

Butcher, D. and Harvey, P. (1998) Meta-ability development: A new concept for career management. *Career Development International*, **3**(2), 75–78.

Cavanaugh, C. and Zelin, A. (2012) *Learning Agility: A Hot Topics Paper Prepared by the SIOP Visibility Committee.* Bowling Green, OH: Society for Industrial and Organizational Psychology.

De Meuse, K. P., Dai, G. and Hallenbeck, G. S. (2010) Learning agility: A construct whose time has come. *Consulting Psychology Journal: Practice and Research*, **62**(2), 119–130.

Dobbins, G. H., Cardy, R. L., Facteau, J. D. and Miller, J. S. (1993) Implications of situational constraints on performance evaluation and performance management. *Human Resource Management Review*, **3**(2), 105–128.

European Communities (2007) *Key Competences for Lifelong Learning: European Reference Framework.* Luxembourg: Office for Official Publications of the European Communities.

Hall, D. T. and Kahn, W. A. (2002) Developmental relationships at work: A learning perspective. In C. L. Cooper and R. J. Burke (Eds) *The New World of Work: Challenges and Opportunities.* Oxford: Blackwell, pp. 49–74.

Heilman, M. E. (2012) Gender stereotypes and workplace bias. *Research in Organizational Behavior*, **32**, 113–135.

Heilman, M. E. and Eagly, A. H. (2008) Gender stereotypes are alive, well, and busy producing workplace discrimination. *Industrial and Organizational Psychology*, **1**(4), 393–398.

Heslin, P. A. and VandeWalle, D. (2008) Managers' implicit assumptions about personnel. *Current Directions in Psychological Science*, **17**(3), 219–223.

Klemp, G. O. Jr and McClelland, D. C. (1986) What characterizes intelligent functioning among senior managers? In R. J. Sternberg and R. K. Wagner (Eds) *Practical Intelligence.* Cambridge, UK: Cambridge University Press, pp. 31–50.

Lombardo, M. M. and Eichinger, R. W. (2000) High potentials as high learners. *Human Resource Management*, **39**(4), 321–330.

London, M. (2012) Lifelong learning. In S. W. J. Kozlowski (Ed.) *The Oxford Handbook of Organizational Psychology. Vol. 2.* New York: Oxford University Press, pp. 1199–1227.

Pedler, M., Burgoyne, J. and Boydell, T. (1986) *A Manager's Guide to Self-Development.* 2nd edn. Maidenhead, UK: McGraw-Hill.

Pulakos, E. D. (2007) Performance measurement. In D. L. Whetzel and G. R. Wheaton (Eds) *Applied Measurement: Industrial Psychology in Human Resources Management.* New York: Psychology Press, pp. 293–317.

Pulakos, E. D., Mueller-Hanson, R. A., O'Leary, R. S. and Meyrowitz, M. M. (2012) *Building a High-Performance Culture: A Fresh Look at Performance Management.* Alexandria, VA: Society for Human Resource Management.

Roberson, L. and Block, C. J. (2001) Racioethnicity and job performance: A review and critique of theoretical perspectives on the causes of group differences. *Research in Organizational Behavior*, **23**, 247–325.

Schippmann, J. R. (2010) Competencies, job analysis, and the next generation of modeling. In J. C. Scott and D. H. Reynolds (Eds) *Handbook of Workplace Assessment.* San Francisco: Jossey-Bass, pp. 197–232.

Spencer, L. M. and Spencer, S. M. (1993) *Competence at Work.* New York: Wiley.

Staats, C., Capatosto, K., Wright, R. A. and Contractor, D. (2015) *State of the Science: Implicit Bias Review 2015.* Columbus, OH: Kirwan Institute.

Williams, R. S. and Walker, J. (1985) Sex differences in performance rating: A research note. *Journal of Occupational Psychology*, **58**(4), 331–337.

Wilson, K. Y. (2010) An analysis of bias in supervisor narrative comments in performance appraisal. *Human Relations*, **63**(12), 1903–1933.

Winterton, J., Delamare-LeDeist, F. and Stringfellow, E. (2006) *Typology of Knowledge, Skills and Competences: Clarification of the Concept and Prototype.* Luxembourg: Office for Official Publications of the European Communities.

5 DESIGNING APPRAISAL SYSTEMS

If you are involved in the design of an appraisal process, there's a good chance that you won't be starting from scratch. In all likelihood there already will be something in operation and it's quite likely that it is seen as not working well. Assuming this to be the case, then the first question to be considered is what to do with what you already have. Well, much turns on what evidence you have about the existing arrangements. Have you done any systematic evaluation? If so, what does that tell you? In our experience, systematic evaluation tends not to happen all that often, so the chances are that all you will have to go on is of an anecdotal nature. There will be a feeling somewhere, probably at quite a senior level, that what's in place at the moment isn't cutting it. So, what to do?

It might be tempting to do a bit of tinkering or tweaking – basically keep most or all of what exists already and add on something that tackles what is seen as the problem. In our view, some of what we've seen over the past few years comes into this category – most particularly the application of forced ranking/distributions and so-called 'calibration' or 'moderation'. But it is difficult to see such practices doing much to motivate or develop performance – in our view, the primary purposes of appraisal. By sticking with some or all of what's in place already, it becomes all too easy to fall into the trap of simply adding more to what's there. For us, this points towards trying to start with as blank a slate as possible – a fresh look, in other words. This doesn't mean that some of the current approach cannot continue to be used – but we think it is preferable to begin by asking again the fundamental questions. Naturally, this includes the 'What's it for?' question; and our answer to this is 'to motivate and develop performance'. This then necessarily leads on to asking questions about what is meant by motivation, the nature of jobs and performance, and how jobs themselves are motivating. Many of the problems of appraisal systems can be identified as arising out of the design process. Get things wrong here and they are likely to stay wrong. Design needs careful thought and consideration of a number of issues, which we explore in this chapter.

AN INVOLVING AND CONSULTATIVE APPROACH TO DESIGN

If HR adopts a 'we know best' approach to designing appraisal, the odds will be stacked against coming up with something that comes near to fitting the bill. A consultative and involving design process that meaningfully involves those who will have to make appraisal work is needed. Such a design process was put forward many years ago by Mohrman *et al.* (1989) and is shown in Box 5.1.

Identify the critical players

Box 5.1 points to three main sets of critical players. It is hard to conceive of an approach to appraisal system design that doesn't involve some input from top management and the HR function. The HR department may be a source of relevant expertise and is likely to be involved in managing the design process; and top management commitment will be needed. But what is crucial is to ensure that the input of these two groups doesn't receive undue weight. The involvement of performers and their managers is paramount to help determine what the appraisal system should be for, what its constituent elements should be and how they should operate. Of course, it won't be possible for everyone (other than in smaller organisations) to take part in the design process, so what's important is that those who do get involved should be seen as broadly representative of the organisation as a whole – hierarchical level, function/department, type of job (clerical/administrative, managerial, production/operational, specialist/professional – e.g. scientists, engineers). There are various ways of achieving this: a multi-disciplinary design group/project team, focus groups, reference groups, surveys, for example. An illustration of a comprehensive consultation approach is given in Box 5.2.

Decide on a design process

Modifying an existing appraisal process or introducing a new one is a kind of organisational change. There's no one best way of bringing about change, but we advocate a participative approach on the grounds that this is likely to stand the greatest chance of coming up with arrangements that will fit a range of requirements. It helps to create the condition of readiness to change which is needed if the new process is to be put into practice successfully. And it increases the likelihood of ending up with a process that will be seen, at least on paper, as fair.

Assess the current organisational situation

It is inevitable that many aspects of the current situation will need to be analysed; and it is likely to be helpful to adopt some kind of framework for

BOX 5.1

Design process

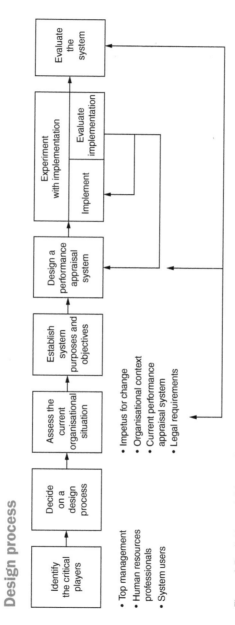

Identify the critical players
- Top management
- Human resources professionals
- System users

Decide on a design process

Assess the current organisational situation
- Impetus for change
- Organisational context
- Current performance appraisal system
- Legal requirements

Establish system purposes and objectives

Design a performance appraisal system

Experiment with implementation
Implement | Evaluate implementation

Evaluate the system

Figure 4 Realistic model for performance appraisal system design
Source: Mohrman *et al.* (1989)

BOX 5.2

AN EXAMPLE OF CONSULTATION AND PARTICIPATION IN APPRAISAL SYSTEM DESIGN

A motor manufacturer set up its own systems company, which decided to establish a new appraisal scheme to reflect its particular needs and circumstances. The principal consideration was to involve as many staff as possible in the design stage, not only to gain commitment, but to draw upon their extensive experience of appraisal in the past.

A series of discussion groups, each consisting of 12 employees representing a cross-section of staff from different divisions, organisational levels and occupational groups, was set up. Each group considered the need for an appraisal system and how present practices could be improved. Amongst the conclusions of these discussions were:

- Performance should be measured against agreed objectives.
- Elements of self-appraisal should be included.
- The overall performance rating should be dropped.
- The employee development element of the system should be kept separate from the appraisal of performance element.

The next stage was to draft an appraisal form and procedure that conformed to the groups' requirements. The personnel department, which had taken the lead in facilitating the consultation process, then presented the provisional scheme to senior management and staff unions as the basis for appraisal over a trial period. Despite some reservations, this was agreed. The four-month trial took place, and all appraised under the new system were asked for their views through questionnaires and interviews. The reactions were very favourable, though there were some suggestions for changes (in relation to details rather than the overall approach) that were incorporated in the final version of the scheme. This was accepted by senior management and staff unions and put into operation (Scott, 1983). It ran successfully for many years after that.

this analysis to help ensure that important factors do not get missed. One example is the list of questions suggested by Roch and Williams (2012), as shown in Box 5.3.

Though focused on appraisal, a diagnostic analysis inevitably will range over matters to do with the fit of appraisal with HR processes, organisational structure, the nature of the organisation's culture and the like. The structure

BOX 5.3

ILLUSTRATIVE QUESTIONS TO ASK DURING AN ORGANISATIONAL ANALYSIS

1. Who wants to change the performance appraisal system (or implement a new one)?
2. Does this organisation need a new performance appraisal system or is it possible that problems stem from other human resource practices such as selection or training?
3. Are performance ratings very political? That is, do raters use performance ratings to accomplish personal goals or gain advantages for their units?
4. How do employees perceive the performance appraisal system? Does it differ by organisational level?
5. For what purposes are performance ratings used in this organisation?
6. What are the goals of the performance appraisal system?
7. Is there an existing organisational competency model? If so, what is the role of this competency model in human resource practices (including performance appraisal)?
8. What aspects of the current performance appraisal system are successful?
9. What aspects of the current performance appraisal system are not successful?

Source: Abbreviated from Roch and Williams (2012)

and the culture of organisations are dynamically interrelated, and both need to be considered in drawing up plans for an appraisal scheme. Is the company a highly structured, bureaucratic one in which there is a great emphasis placed on formal observance of rules and procedures, and in which power is vested in individuals largely as a result of their position in the hierarchy? If so, then the appraisal scheme may need to be a rather formal process too, with clear guidelines, a fixed timetable, the appraiser firmly in control of the process and so on. But there is a potential tension here. Does appraisal simply reinforce the status quo, or can it be a tool for cultural change? Either could be true, depending on what's required. While it is unlikely that appraisal in itself will bring about change in an organisation's culture, it may have a part to play by reinforcing other changes that may be under way.

So, for example, with the numerous changes and pressures of recent times, many organisations have shifted to a style and structure that a few years ago would only have been found in advanced technology and computing companies. The de-layering process has removed levels of management; greater autonomy and profit/loss accountability have been given to individual operating units; the demand for speed in responding to market changes has increased (often necessitating changes in staffing and organisation, with more use of matrix management) and so on. Partly as a result of this, the power base of managers has changed and now often stems from their demonstrated expertise and competence as opposed to being legitimised simply by their rank in the hierarchy. Moreover, many of these changes have meant that managers now have much bigger spans of command, making traditional top-down appraisal much more difficult.

In circumstances such as these, a flexible and adaptable approach to appraisal is necessary, with a greater degree of local control over content and administration. This usually fits in well with appraisal that is primarily geared to motivation and development and has a high level of appraisee participation. But where assessment and comparison come into the picture as the focus for appraisal, difficulties arise. The use of standard report formats and rating scales, completed at fixed times by the nominated appraising manager to facilitate cross-company comparison, does not sit comfortably within the framework of organisations geared to flexibility and quick reaction.

Also, within a big organisation, it is quite likely that there can be marked variations in culture and attitude. An example of this will be found in quite a few local authorities, where the responses of the social services department and of the highways department to what is ostensibly the same appraisal scheme frequently differ in ways that reflect aspects of the staff groups involved. The former has a strong social work ethos, with considerable emphasis on interpersonal issues, so handling the appraisal interview process in an open but sensitive way becomes paramount. The latter department, whose staff are often professionally qualified engineers and the like, tends to have quite a different attitude. These staff are inclined to concentrate more on any quantitative elements in the scheme (which are usually to be found in the paperwork) and are usually stronger on directness than on subtlety in the communication process. Other departments that differ in terms of functions and staff make-up could just as easily exhibit these and other variations of response to appraisal. No doubt much the same is also true in some divisions of private-sector organisations.

How can these cultural differences be allowed for when devising the appraisal scheme? Again, the use of a core appraisal scheme with elements varied locally to meet specific needs and to increase its relevance is one option. Any good consultation process should bring to light what variations are needed. However, it is not always the case that the scheme itself has to be modified. In the example given above of the social work and highways departments, the problem is perhaps more one of orientating the training process and presentation of the scheme to address the likely differences in attitudes, reactions and skills.

It is important that appraisal and other HR practices fit with one another, and any review of appraisal inevitably means looking at other HR policies too. How widely this is done depends on what those other policies and practices are. There's also the question of how open to modification they are. Will they act as a constraint on any review of appraisal practice? Or do they need to change to fit with the new arrangements?

Establish system purposes and objectives

We've dealt with the 'What's it for?' question in some depth in Chapter 2. Rather than reiterate points that we've already made, we emphasise the importance of understanding appraisal from the perspectives of the most involved parties – performers and their line managers. What do they want from appraisal? As we showed in Chapter 2, they may have differing aims in mind. Though there is potential for conflict amongst these, it is likely to be more useful in practice to emphasise common interests – and all parties (the organisation included) share an interest in motivating and developing performance, albeit for varying reasons.

DESIGN AND TRIAL

At various points throughout this book we voice our doubts about the wisdom of a single, monolithic appraisal system being applied in a universal, inflexible way. There are common elements – the need to agree performance requirements, the need to give feedback – but these may mean somewhat different things in practice for different groups of staff. Which groups of staff to include is just one of the fundamental questions that needs to be answered during the design process. Here are some of the others. What do you mean by performance? Do you need ratings? What documentation do you need (whether paper or electronic)? Who will do what? How often? In this section we set out a range of questions that need to be answered during the design process.

Design questions

We'll start with what probably is the most difficult, the 'What do you mean by performance?' question. As we showed in Chapter 3, performance is a complex concept and that complexity has implications for appraisal. Do you want to express performance requirements in output terms? If so, you probably will incorporate goal-setting. But bear in mind that not all jobs have some kind of measurable output, so it would be a mistake to be slavish about adopting goal-setting. For some jobs there may still be a place for basing appraisal on a job description – after all, job descriptions do set out what the job is! But bear in mind their limitations – in particular, it is all too easy for them to get out of date, especially in a fast-changing environment. Bear in mind too that turbulent environments also may mean that goals may change more frequently than would be the case in a more stable setting. But is a job description too bare-bones? Perhaps the UK National Occupational Standards will fill in the gaps. Occupational standards specify

> the standard of performance an individual must achieve when carrying out a function in the workplace, together with the knowledge and understanding they need to meet that standard consistently. Each [standard] defines one key function in a job role. In their essential form [they] describe functions, standards of performance and knowledge/understanding.
>
> (Carroll and Boutall, 2011: 6)

Box 5.4 illustrates a single standard. Does this level of detail smack of overkill? Well, perhaps – after all, National Occupational Standards have been developed primarily for learning/training purposes and the need for a fuller specification is understandable in that context. That said, appraisal does, of course, have a forward-looking aspect and standards are a way of expressing performance requirements. They may have particular value when someone is new to a job.

The example does, though, serve to illustrate the point we've been making about the complexity of performance – we've illustrated just one standard, and any job will have several. This same issue potentially arises if you decide to use competencies. First, you need to decide which approach to competencies you wish to adopt – the 'dimensions of process performance' approach or the 'characteristics of the person' approach? If the former, will you focus just on task performance, just on citizenship performance or some combination of several aspects of performance? Will you want to try to have a common competency framework that applies to all jobs? This is tricky when it comes to task performance – after all, the dimensions of task performance differ across jobs. But a common framework ought to be more achievable when it comes to citizenship performance as these dimensions of performance are broadly similar across jobs in an organisation. And this is a good way of helping to ensure that these important behaviours don't get overlooked. Will you have a catalogue of process performance competencies from which managers and appraisees will be able to choose?

BOX 5.4

AN EXAMPLE OF A UK NATIONAL OCCUPATIONAL STANDARD

Identify potential victims of modern slavery

Overview	This standard is for workers who may be in contact with potential victims of modern slavery during the course of their daily duties. These duties may be carried out within an agency that is recognised as a formal referral point for modern slavery victims or it may be within other agencies that have contact with potential victims of modern slavery. It covers what you must do, know and understand in relation to the initial identification of potential victims of modern slavery. You will look for signs and indicators of modern slavery, and work with potential victims to address any immediate needs they may have. Potential victims of modern slavery may be adults, children or young people.
Performance criteria *You must be able to:*	1. maintain an up to date knowledge of signs and indicators of modern slavery 2. identify signs and indicators of modern slavery in line with current guidance 3. monitor those whom you come into contact with for indicators of potential modern slavery in line with organisational procedures 4. communicate at a pace and level suited to the potential victim using recommended communication techniques . . . 16. record all findings in line with organisational procedures 17. share information with relevant agencies where there is a statutory or other requirement to do so and in line with organisational procedures 18. comply with the rights and requirements of confidentiality when working with potential victims
Knowledge and understanding *You need to know and understand:*	1. Legislation, guidance and organisational procedures relevant to: 1.1 modern slavery 1.2 safeguarding and protection 1.3 health and safety . . . 16. how to access the range of support services available to potential victims of modern slavery 17. the importance of confidentiality and discretion 18. the importance of remaining open-minded when faced with situations involving potential victims of modern slavery 19. recording requirements of: 19.1 your organisation 19.2 national referral and reporting mechanisms

Source: Abbreviated from http://nos.ukces.org.uk/PublishedNos/SFJBMS01.pdf#search=social%20worker

What about the second perspective on competencies that we introduced – the idea that competencies are characteristics of the person? Will you want to try to include these? If so, will you want to include them as well as process competencies or instead of them? An example of a framework that includes both process competencies and person-characteristic competencies is provided by the US Competency Model Clearinghouse (www.careeronestop.org/ competencymodel/). This framework comprises several tiers of competencies, bringing together multiple perspectives. At the two lower levels, the focus is very much on who the person is/what the person has – 'Personal Effectiveness Competencies' (e.g. Integrity, Lifelong Learning) and 'Academic Competencies' (e.g. Reading, Critical and Analytical Thinking). The third tier comprises 'Workplace Competencies' (e.g. Planning and Organising, Teamwork). These three tiers are regarded as foundation competencies – generally required for jobs across the board. The fourth and fifth tiers are 'Industry-Wide Technical Competencies' (those required across an industry) and 'Industry-Sector Technical Competencies' (required within a particular sector of the broader industry segment). At the apex are 'Occupation-Specific Competencies' (as might be specified for a particular function, e.g. HRM) and 'Management Competencies' (e.g. Monitoring Work, Supporting Others).

Does such a framework seem all too complex? Well, it does illustrate what the implications really are if you want fully to embrace competencies. You need also to consider where you will get your competencies from. Some professional bodies have frameworks of one sort or another: will you use them? Will you buy in a framework from a consultancy? If you want to go down the route of using an established framework, then there may be cost- and time-saving benefits to be gained by doing so. But this doesn't necessarily mean that an already existing framework will fit your circumstances exactly. One of the main criticisms of the UK National Occupational Standards, for example, is that they ignore context – this is true of generic behavioural competency frameworks too. So, some tailoring is likely to be needed.

You may be thinking that going down the route of something that already exists is all very well, but tailor-making something from scratch would lead to a much better solution. We certainly don't want to rule this out. As Sparrow (1994) has pointed out, there are process benefits to be gained – for example, generating ownership of the behaviours/competencies that are identified. This is particularly the case because going your own way (if you are going to do it properly) necessarily means taking a participative approach to draw on the knowledge and expertise of job incumbents and others who are able to give an informed view. However, it is all too easy to cut corners. Cockerill *et al.* (1995), for example, are particularly critical of approaches that rely on invention; for example, when the senior team divines some list of competencies believed to be necessary for some imagined future dreamed up at an 'away day'. So, the do-it-yourself route is not for the faint-hearted. It is time-consuming. Do you have the expertise? If not, you could buy this in, but at a cost. For us, however, the main point is that if you are going to use a competency model, then it must be well-developed. Campion *et al.* (2011) set out best practice guidelines on competency modelling and Appendix A gives some introductory advice.

- *Do you need ratings?* Ratings have long been part of appraisal practice, and there have been decades of research exploring the merits (and psychometric properties) of different rating formats. But none of this research answers the question of whether ratings are needed. If you have opted to use performance-related pay, then that decision will push you in the direction of using ratings – at the very least, a single rating of overall performance. But be wary of overusing ratings: heed the warning that comes from users' perceptions of appraisal as a bureaucratic form-filling exercise. If you choose to concentrate on the motivational and developmental purposes of appraisal, then there may be less need for ratings, although they may have value when it comes to individuals assessing their own competencies against each other (as we discuss later in this chapter). But don't overdo it – limit ratings to the essential competencies. And be wary of the language used to describe the points on rating scales: there's nothing particularly motivating about 'average' or 'satisfactory'.
- *Who should be appraised?* On the basis that everyone in an organisation is a performer, then appraisal should apply to everyone. But this doesn't necessarily mean that all employee groups have the same perspective on what they want from appraisal. For example, a research scientist in a pharmaceutical company might have different desired outcomes in mind as compared to, say, a marketing manager or an operations manager involved in the manufacturing process. We return to the question of appraisal for professional groups in Chapter 8.

The extension of appraisal schemes to take in more categories and levels of employees does not have to mean that it is exactly the same scheme for all. There is some virtue in uniformity, but not a lot. An example of how the desire for bureaucratic convenience and similarity of assessment can be taken to extremes is provided by an appraisal report form used in many UK Government departments in the early 1970s. This form required all staff – from nuclear physicists to clerical officers, from first-level supervisors to senior managers – to be rated on the same set of dimensions. The notion that the same attributes were relevant to such a wide range of jobs is quite ludicrous. What we've said about the nature of performance and of competencies underscores this point.

The same *elements* of appraisal may be present in the appraisal scheme at different levels, in the sense that there may be some objective-setting and assessment thereof along with some consideration of behavioural aspects of performance, as well as feedback-giving and coaching; but the form, content and application of them should certainly vary to suit the circumstances. For instance, in jobs which allow for little personal discretion in determining work style and output, there may be limited scope for setting personal targets, in which case the results-orientated aspect of the appraisal would be diminished. For some unskilled and routine tasks, the purpose of the appraisal may be limited to simply acknowledging the part played by the individual and listening to any problems, views or ideas they want to raise. In the case of younger or less experienced staff, self-appraisal may be less helpful and appropriate as a method, as they may have difficulty in judging their own performance at this stage. The key here is flexible application with much discretion being at a local level – that is, in the hands of managers and those they are appraising.

So, performance appraisal has something to offer for all categories and levels of staff, but it is not the same in every case. The implication is that the organisation needs a very flexible framework for performance appraisal based on a small number of core principles/components, accompanied by sensible guidance on their application. It is important, though, to try to ensure that no staff group ends up feeling they are being treated as second-class citizens on the basis of different appraisal processes. A medium-sized UK county council found that when it had PRP for senior levels and not for the management grades immediately beneath, the latter felt that they were missing out in some way, and that they were earning their bosses' pay rises.

Who should do what?

The leading parties are appraisees and their line managers, but there may be supporting roles for others who can give an informed view of performance, as we illustrate below.

The immediate manager/supervisor

Although the practice of having appraisals done by the employees' immediate boss is still the norm, the case has become ever stronger for it not to remain so. The rationale advanced for the traditional, one-up appraisal is that the immediate boss is in the best position to assess and guide subordinates, because of the amount of contact and greater experience. However, the contact argument does not always hold good – probably less so these days than in earlier years. For example, one of the effects of de-layering has been to produce flatter management hierarchies. Some organisations have had this kind of structure for years anyway, and it does bring with it a problem for conventional appraisal systems. The norm has been for the individual's immediate boss to do the appraisal, with some input from the 'grandparent' – the boss two levels up. This becomes a less practicable arrangement when the structure of the management hierarchy means that each manager has many direct reports. The problem is further compounded in many instances by the geographical spread of the organisation. With fewer management levels, and greater internationalisation of businesses, the appraisee's immediate boss can increasingly be based in another part of the country, or in another country altogether. It thus becomes very difficult for a manager in this position to be in full command of the facts about his or her subordinates' performance and development needs. Nor does the 'greater experience' argument necessarily hold true: it is entirely possible that the manager won't actually have done the lower-level job, particularly in those organisations where there is a high degree of entry (beyond junior levels) from outside. Moreover, the concerns about the appraisers' objectivity and fairness in assessment have made this model problematic. All this strengthens the case for building up the performer's role.

Though some aspects of the manager's appraisal role may have become harder, managers continue to bear responsibilities for motivating their staff. They still have a part to play in agreeing the performer's job responsibilities and agreeing required competencies so that both performer and manager are clear about what the job is; they still have to check on progress and how well the job is being done, and they still have to give feedback – expressing appreciation and giving praise for work well done and providing coaching (for performance improvement if that's needed or to help develop new skills).

Self-management/self-appraisal

Since the mid-1970s, there has been a pervasive increase in the degree to which appraisal systems have been structured to allow and encourage participation by the performer. Much of this participation has been in the backward-looking aspects of appraisal, and we will come on to this in a moment. But there is no less of a case – indeed, quite possibly a stronger case – for the job performer's active involvement in shaping what the job is and how it should be done. This is especially important in a context of employee engagement.

Carrying out an analysis of appraisal goals through the eyes of the key stakeholders might lead you to an employee-centred definition of appraisal along the lines that we showed in Chapter 2 (page 32) in the quote from Buchner (2007: 66). Buchner (2007) also suggests a range of questions for employees to ask: to illustrate the potential for active appraisee involvement in the forward-looking aspect of appraisal, we show in Box 5.5 questions that focus on the goal-setting process. Clearly, these questions point to a much wider and more active role in appraisal for the employee than traditionally has been the case, even though the appraisee's involvement has broadened somewhat over the years. Initially, it was limited to giving the individual a form to assist in preparing for the appraisal, listing headings that formed an agenda for the appraisal interview and inviting the person to think about them beforehand. This moved on to including sections on the report form for the appraisee to add their own comments on the appraisal, and to register any disagreement if necessary. Eventually, some organisations adopted an appraisal process that involved both appraiser and appraisee completing nearly identical appraisal forms, discussing them in an interview, and filing a single agreed report on the basis of this. In addition, self-assessment is usually an integral element in 360° feedback.

There are numerous advantages to incorporating self-review into the appraisal process. It is said to engender more commitment on the part of the person appraised, because of its participative nature. It reduces defensiveness by encouraging the appraisees to take the lead in reviewing their own

BOX 5.5

ILLUSTRATIVE PERFORMANCE APPRAISAL QUESTIONS FROM THE EMPLOYEE'S PERSPECTIVE

Goal setting

- What information do I have or need to make informed decisions about my job priorities?
- What are the current goals or standards that govern my work, and what do I think of them?
- Which goals are most important and relevant to me, my work unit, my organisation, and why?
- Given my strengths and the organisation's priorities, where should the most challenging and difficult goals be placed?
- Do I know how to write a specific goal? Are my goals sufficiently specific?
- What is my personal tendency when setting goals?
- Once I have set a goal, what is my commitment level?
- What can I do to strengthen my commitment to a difficult goal?
- What do I need to put in place to monitor my progress?

Source: Buchner (2007: 67)

performance, rather than having an assessment imposed on them. It
encourages appraisees to think about their own performance and development
needs in a focused way. It promotes fairness by giving appraisees a voice and
increases acceptance of the appraisal process (Roberts, 2003). And by giving
the perspective of two people – the appraiser and the appraisee – it should lead
to more balanced assessment than if it rested on either one alone.

But there are some potential problems that inhibit its use. Possibly the greatest
of these is the danger of inflated or excessively lenient self-assessments (Jones
and Fletcher, 2002). This can certainly happen, sometimes through a
fundamental lack of objectivity on the part of the appraisee, sometimes
because the situation is not one that motivates the individual to be accurate,
and sometimes because the nature of the exercise does not facilitate accurate
self-assessment. Research (Mabe and West, 1982) suggests that while there are
individual differences in self-assessment objectivity, on average people have
the capacity to be reasonably accurate in reporting on their own behaviour.
Whether they will deploy that capacity, however, is another matter. If the
motivational context of the situation is such that immediate decisions on
rewards depend on it, then it is likely to strain anyone's objectivity and honesty,
and people will be more inclined to be lenient in their self-assessments.
Finally, if the invitation to self-assess is not framed appropriately, then it can
promote inaccuracy (Jones and Fletcher, 2004). The latter is likely to arise
when people are asked to compare themselves with others, especially if the
others concerned are not all that familiar to them. It is often the case that
people simply don't have the information to gauge their effectiveness against
that of colleagues and peers, and asking someone to make this kind of
comparison is giving them a task they are likely not to be able to do very well.

All this serves to suggest that self-appraisal will do best where:

• the immediate boss does not see enough of the appraisee to be left as the
  only source of the appraisal data;
• there are no reward decisions based solely on the outcome of the appraisal
  process;
• the nature of the self-assessment is such that appraisees compare
  themselves against their own personal standards, and not against other
  people's.

This last point needs some elucidation. One of the most effective ways of using
self-appraisal is to ask the person appraised to assess their performance against
what they see as their own 'norm'. Thus, they might be invited to say what
they feel they have done best and least well over the last year, or – in a more
specific form – on which of various listed attributes or competencies they feel

themselves to be strongest and weakest. For example, an individual may rate him- or herself high on information collection and handling but low on delegating to subordinates, but the high rating does not imply that this person is better than average in the department, nor does the low rating imply being worse than average – they both reflect variations against that appraisee's notional individual standard. Used in this way, self-appraisal has been found to be more discriminating and less subject to the 'halo effect' than appraisal done by others (Williams, 1989).

Self-appraisal probably has the greatest potential in an appraisal system geared primarily to motivation and development. Nonetheless, it is likely to be important in any type of appraisal system, since the individual's self-assessment will be on the agenda implicitly, if not explicitly, and it is better that it is overtly brought into play in some fashion as part of the formal process. Self-appraisal, like most things, can probably be taken too far, though. There is no more value in basing appraisal exclusively on appraisees' views than there is on appraisers', so it is unlikely that schemes that seek to do this will be very effective.

Appraisal by peers

The formal involvement of peers in the appraisal process is something that has only recently become popular, largely in the context of 360° feedback systems, of which more in the next sub-section. It has a longer history, and greater appeal, in academic and teaching institutions, where there is often a dislike of formal hierarchical management structures. In universities, it is commonly an important input to promotion decisions, external assessors being asked to comment on the candidates' work and its impact on the field. In theory, appraisal by peers should have a lot to offer, because peers may be in a position to give a unique insight into an individual's team contribution – no small concern when the pressure on people to achieve might sometimes lead them to put their own concerns ahead of the team effort. In fact, though, peer rating in general is not all that accurate or unbiased, judging from some of the research evidence (Antonioni and Park, 2001). However, because it takes place largely within the context of multi-source, multi-level feedback systems, it will be dealt with in Chapter 7; it will also be mentioned in connection with the appraisal of professional groups (Chapter 8).

Multi-level, multi-source appraisal

This consists of assessments made on an individual (the 'focal manager') by subordinates, peers and bosses, plus, in some cases, clients. Usually it also requires the person appraised to do a self-rating. Because this has become a major approach to appraisal and development in the last few years (under the banner of 360° feedback), it is examined separately and in depth in Chapter 7.

Appraisal by superiors

This heading refers not to the traditional one-up appraisal process, but to the situation in which several bosses may contribute to the appraisal. It is, like peer appraisal, multi-source, but it is not necessarily multi-level appraisal. Where an individual works on a series of different projects over a year, serially or simultaneously, each with different project leaders, it becomes very difficult to identify any one person who should be the formal appraiser. The two approaches that most often find favour here are either to have a series of separate, project-specific appraisals; or to have one appraisal at the end of the review period to which all those who have managed the individual contribute. The former has some merit, but it does suffer from the lack of an overall view; it is quite likely that an individual will vary in performance (or, more accurately, be seen to) from one project to another, not least because of the different team make-up and the relationships that result. The alternative method has more to recommend it: a manager is nominated to collect the appraisal information from all the individual's team/project leaders throughout the year, and to base the appraisal on that. If there are reward implications, then again it is easier to deal with them on an overview basis. There is, of course, nothing to prevent there being informal review sessions with individual managers at the end of each project as well – indeed, this practice probably should be encouraged.

Appraisal by subordinates

Finally, and on a rather different note, there is the possibility of subordinates appraising their bosses – upward appraisal. This is not so much a question of 'Who should appraise?' as 'Who should appraise whom?'. Appraisal by subordinates is most often encountered in multi-level/source appraisal schemes, dealt with in Chapter 7, though there it is slightly diluted by being just one of several sources of feedback. While it is possible to have upward appraisal without having a 360° feedback scheme, the issues and problems are much the same in each case, and so will be left to Chapter 7.

What documentation do you need?

It is hard to see how there could be none at all – that implies there are no appraisal arrangements. But there are dangers of overload, so the one golden rule is to keep it to a minimum. The success of appraisal lies not in the paperwork, but in the aims and attitudes of the participants. There is a need for adequate background documentation to explain the scheme when it is launched, and there may be a need for some reference material (but be wary of overdoing this). For example, advice on goal-setting (perhaps with examples) is likely to be helpful (and may be part of the training materials). If you have gone down the route of using competencies, these will need to be specified, and it is possible that you will need a competency catalogue or directory depending on the competency framework (or frameworks) that you are using. These days there is a strong likelihood that much, perhaps all, of the documentation is going to be held electronically.

Be clear about what needs to be written down (or exist in electronic form) and retained. This applies whether you have an electronic form or a paper one. So far as the forward-looking aspect of appraisal is concerned, there needs to be agreement over performance expectations – objectives (both performance and learning/developmental), required behaviours – and it would be reasonable for these to be recorded. But bear in mind that at least some of this may exist already in some printed or electronic form, in which case it is important that it is accessible. Bear in mind, too, that what's recorded as the performance contract at the beginning of the review period may need to be periodically revised during the review period, particularly for jobs in turbulent environments. Who should do the recording? Well, it doesn't have to be the manager. Indeed, in an employee-centred approach to appraisal, there is a strong case for the performer to be in the lead when it comes to writing things down.

The same is true of the backward-looking aspects too. At the very least, there ought to be something to help the performer prepare for the annual appraisal interview – this is an event that is unlikely to go away. The record of the discussion should note the main points of evidence that support the assessment made. What it does not have to do is to try to give a blow-by-blow account of the discussion, or to go into much detail. This kind of appraisal record usually generates more trouble than it is worth, and often reduces the appraisal to a kind of tortuous drafting session, with more emphasis on the formal record than on the substance of the discussion.

It is important to have regard for useability – or risk engendering or reinforcing a view of appraisal as bureaucratic form-filling. Given the desirability of brevity – nobody wants to see six-page blockbusters landing on the desk (or page after page of an electronic form) waiting to be completed on each appraisee – it is probably worth getting some professional help in the actual layout and presentation of the form (whether paper-based or electronic). This should facilitate the development of appraisal paperwork that is professional in appearance (i.e. visually pleasing without being distracting), economical in its use of space, and effective in generating the information required.

Do the completed appraisal forms need to be kept? Well, this depends on purpose. If appraisal is intended to be about motivation and development, then there may not be a need to keep the forms for any great length of time – keep them only for as long as they are useful for that motivational/developmental purpose. And this probably means that it is just the job holder and their manager who need to keep the forms, though it may be useful for there to be some notification to HR that the event has taken place. The HR department may need to be sent a copy of the forms if the appraisal information is to be part of the process of determining pay or some talent management purpose.

In the UK there's no statutory requirement to keep performance appraisal records; but if an employer does so, then bear in mind the likely need to comply with the requirements of the Data Protection Act (1998). So, for example, you need to specify (and tell the employee) why you are keeping the information and you should keep the data for no longer than is necessary to satisfy that purpose. The Advisory, Conciliation and Arbitration Service (ACAS) and the Information Commissioner's Office (ICO) in the UK both provide useful guidance on personnel record-keeping.

Frequency/timing

When appraisals should take place is not always easy to decide. The preferred pattern seems to be for them all to be done within a limited period, partly for administrative reasons – all the forms can be sent out together, all the information sought by HR can be collected at once; and partly because of organisational inertia – this is the way it always has been done! Of course, there may be a genuine need to fit with other aspects of performance management. If the objectives set in appraisal are to link with the wider team and organisational objectives, if they are to relate to the business plan as a whole, then inevitably the appraisal process has to occur at a time that coordinates with these. The implication is that objective-setting will take place fairly soon after the business plan for the year has been laid down (but bear in mind the risk of the cascading process taking longer than you might hope – Chapter 1, Box 1.5). Where PRP is a feature of the situation, the review of people's progress against objectives and the reward decisions arising out of it are made at a point when the results for the previous year are known (because the reward decisions generally rest on the amount of funds available for distribution in this form). If the organisation holds a separate appraisal session to focus on development needs, this can be timed with rather more flexibility.

The disadvantage of this 'set period' approach is that the load on appraisers is concentrated over just a few weeks, leaving them little time for anything else and probably feeling a bit jaded by the end of the process, too. This risks reinforcing any negative views of appraisal that may already be held (or encouraging them if they haven't yet set in) and risks interfering with getting on with the day job. It also does not necessarily match well with varying individual circumstances; an appraisee may have started the job only a few weeks before, or it may be that the appraiser is new to the position. For these reasons, some organisations have chosen to ask for appraisals to be done on the anniversary of the appointment to the current post, or have staggered them through the year on some other basis. Ideally, timing should be determined by the requirements of the job, not an arbitrary timescale imposed by HR.

The same point applies to frequency, perhaps with even greater force. In particular, with the predominance of results-orientated appraisal, what was formerly the most usual practice – holding appraisals annually – makes less sense. The problem is that objectives are susceptible to changing circumstances, and for a great many jobs, progress against them needs to be reviewed more frequently than just once a year. Consequently, many organisations have a formal review and objective-setting session annually, but encourage the appraisers to hold interim reviews either quarterly or half-yearly. Apart from checking that objectives are still relevant, these also provide the opportunity to take remedial action if the performer is having difficulties. No additional paperwork need be involved in interim reviews, though any changes may have to be added to the original statement of agreed objectives.

The periodicity of appraisals may vary for other reasons, too. For *some* older staff nearing retirement, it may be that appraisals – or some elements of them – are less meaningful. They might be given the choice of opting out for a year, though not for more than that. On the other hand, with younger staff who are new to the job or to the organisation, there is arguably a need for an appraisal session within the next six months and two in the first year, especially if there is a probationary period. Here, of course, we are talking about some kind of reasonably formal review session. Informal feedback and review should happen as performance (or the performer) requires – to coincide with completion of an objective or as a problem arises, for example.

Experiment with implementation: trialling/piloting

It is easy to underestimate the scale of introducing appraisal, whether something substantially new or a more modest refresh. It ought to be more obvious, of course – here is something that potentially will affect everyone in the workplace and some people will be affected in two ways, given that they will be on both the giving and receiving end of appraisal.

It is risky to assume that appraisal will be implemented as intended, as we discussed in Chapter 1. So, some piloting is appropriate. It gives the opportunity to test out the documentation and support materials, develop and trial the training, etc. – are the forms useable, are the competencies clear, do the different parties understand what they are expected to do, is what they are expected to do actually doable? If problems are revealed, then they can be tackled and resolved before full implementation. Bear in mind that in a large organisation, introducing appraisal is a substantial task, especially if new or substantially different from what has gone before. To avoid the dangers of overload, a progressive implementation process has much to recommend it.

Evaluate the system

We suspect that this too often is *ad hoc* and unsystematic. We return to this theme in Chapter 10.

USING INFORMATION TECHNOLOGY IN APPRAISAL

There are two principal aspects to the use of information technology (IT) in appraisal. The first concerns using IT to support and facilitate the administrative aspects of appraisal; for example, an electronic record taking the place of paper forms, online competency dictionaries and the like. For such benefits to be realised, it would seem likely that the system needs to be user-friendly: managers and appraisees will need to fully understand the system and be comfortable with it. As Farr *et al.* (2013: 84) note, "no matter how high-tech a system is, it cannot run well if people are not willing to use it appropriately". And bear in mind the risk of IT reinforcing the worst of the bureaucratic excesses sometimes associated with appraisal! Hirsh (2006) confirms this concern, finding that managers saw a disadvantage of computerisation in that it simply encouraged HR to ask for yet more information on skill profiles, etc. That said, an example of an unusually thorough and carefully constructed online performance management system is given in Box 5.6.

Second, there is electronic monitoring of performance, which affords the ability to record a huge amount of data on multiple dimensions of work performance (Stanton, 2000). This facilitates a more continuous and detailed collection of performance data in some jobs – e.g. call centres – and has the capacity to do so in a non-obvious, even covert manner. However, bear in mind that such monitoring may give at best a partial picture of performance. Call-centre jobs are a good example. It is very easy to measure a whole range of objective performance indicators, such as call volume or call duration. But these measures tend to be silent when it comes to matters such as call complexity and outcomes – a particular call may take longer than the norm because it is complex, but if it is resolved in a way that engenders customer

BOX 5.6

AN EXAMPLE OF IT USED TO FACILITATE PERFORMANCE MANAGEMENT

FinServe is a large, global financial services group. Having undergone years of rapid growth, including mergers and acquisitions, there was a perceived need to ensure that its PM systems were applicable to the new shape of the organisation and that they delivered value. This led to the development of a new online PM system which combined corporate and local ownership. Three core competencies (Client Orientation, Teamwork and Professional Behaviour) were identified, along with a number of supplementary, flexible competencies; all parts of the business included the core competencies, but they were free to choose from among the latter those that were most valuable and relevant to them. Each competency is defined in terms of four levels of performance, and each level is described by a set of observable behaviours. Business leaders, HR and managers can create and define the role profiles they see as critical and determine the competency expectations for each of these – a degree of flexibility and sophistication that would be difficult to achieve in anything but an IT-based system.

When it comes to making an assessment of an individual's performance, the system collates multiple raters' assessments and generates a performance 'skyline' to highlight strengths and weaknesses. The line manager assigns his or her own ratings in light of this information and their own view of the person's performance. The system allows the appraiser to see how the level of competence being shown matches the level required by the role. It also generates a recommended overall rating by calibrating managers' ratings against required competency levels.

The system allows for continuous access to update and adjust objectives and for appraisers to enter notes and observations on performance or goal achievement at any point in the year, and for the person appraised to obtain that ongoing feedback. It also facilitates HR giving feedback to line managers about the distribution of their ratings and how these compare to other, more widely based distributions of ratings. The HR department is also able to take data off the system to identify 'blind spots', which are skill gaps for teams or departments, and to assist in developing action plans to deal with them.

The flexibility allowed by the system is considerable, and there are many more aspects of it than can be outlined in this brief description. The organisation found the new approach to be superior in terms of providing a more accurate picture of employee development needs, and results have been reassuring in terms of its acceptability to users.

satisfaction, then the time may be seen as well spent. This reinforces the importance of taking into account the impact of situational factors, not least because doing so may promote appraisee confidence in the system and may foster satisfaction and a sense of fairness (Cardy and Miller, 2005).

Note that such electronic monitoring may fall within the scope of the UK's Data Protection Act (1998): the Employment Practices Data Protection Code published by the Information Commissioner's Office gives further guidance on this. Quite apart from any issues of legality, from a performer's perspective, some forms of electronic monitoring may be experienced as unduly intrusive:

> One of the characteristics of my worst managers is micro-managing. One manager used to comment about the time on which I log in to the instant messenger as an indication for when I started working. The other manager (for whom I worked remotely) was frustrated that he does not know where I am in any given time and asked me to install a webcam on my desk so he could see me all day.
>
> (Nurick, 2012: 41)

A related use of IT is in the feedback process; many software packages are available to record and aggregate performance ratings and written observations, and to make the information available online. The use of IT in these ways potentially helps in making the appraisal process more manageable, especially where multiple rating sources are involved. However, it also raises many questions about appraisees' reactions and possible effects on PA outcomes. How do people feel about being monitored in this way – are there shades of 'Big Brother' about it? Do they perceive the feedback so delivered to be credible? Do they attend to it, or switch off? Does it have the same impact as face-to-face feedback? At present, only limited research and experience are available to try to answer such questions (Fletcher, 2001), and in some cases the evidence is rather indirect. Nonetheless, it is worth looking at what we know so far, if only because commercial organisations promoting software-based solutions will become more rather than less prevalent, making it important for HR practitioners to understand some of the issues.

Do people welcome feedback from electronic sources? Is computer-based appraisal too 'impersonal'?

The findings here are broadly positive. There is some reason to believe that feedback is *more* likely to be sought through electronic mail than through face-to-face meeting. A possible reason for this is that there may be less apprehension about the assessment and less emotion in getting feedback from a computer, and perhaps with good reason if a computer-based system helps focus the appraiser's attention on job-relevant behaviours and reduces the influence of potentially biasing interpersonal factors (Fletcher and Perry, 2001). Supporting this, one study (Weisband and Atwater, 1999) found that the potentially biasing effects of the appraiser's personal liking for the appraisee on their ratings were less where the ratings were made electronically. These findings perhaps illustrate that the more impersonal nature of entering and communicating assessments via a computer might lead to greater objectivity – which is clearly desirable in appraisal. Maybe as a consequence of this, individuals seem to trust feedback that they obtain on the computer more than feedback provided directly by their supervisor, which is important for actually taking it on board; of course, there is a certain irony in this if the feedback comes from the same source (the supervisor) in the first place. There is also evidence that feedback provided by computer results in better work performance and learning than when the same feedback is provided by a human (Fletcher and Perry, 2001). But, on the downside – is the cost of this impersonal approach also a loss of sensitivity? Will it lead to less tact in handling the feedback situation – because apart from anything else, there is no chance to directly observe the reactions of those on the receiving end? So, although performance feedback conveyed online may reduce face-to-face confrontation and be less emotionally laden, it may still lead to disagreement and resentment if individuals tend to be less polite and show less concern for others when communicating it.

Will more and quicker feedback be better feedback?

One of the benefits of computer monitoring of performance is that it has the potential to make more information available and do it faster, without the need to wait for a scheduled appraisal review to receive it. A basic psychological principle is that quicker feedback is more effective, so rapid feedback mediated by IT should enhance learning and be beneficial. The question of the value of *more* feedback is less clear-cut. There is the possibility of habituation effects – people getting so much feedback that they cease to give it much attention. Is there a risk of the performer becoming overwhelmed by the volume of data that electronic performance monitoring can generate? What may be important here is the extent to which the appraisee is able to exert some degree of control over an electronic feedback-giving process. Where such monitoring is used to exercise control over the performer, it might be expected that the performer reaction will be less favourable than in circumstances where the performance monitoring enables control by the performer and where the monitoring is used for developmental purposes (Johnson and Gueutal, 2011). Cardy and Miller (2005: 143) suggest: "It may be that computer-generated feedback that performers access and interpret on their own is less threatening than situations in which the person is a powerless and passive recipient of feedback from a supervisor."

At the present time, the verdict has to remain open on the impact that ongoing feedback from monitoring will have on appraisal. One potential consequence, though, stems from the fact that many of the jobs most susceptible to this kind of performance monitoring are often not covered by formal PA schemes at present; it may be that the availability of such quantitative performance measures begins to bring the staff in these roles within formal organisational PA arrangements. Also, it seems possible that computer-based systems may enable the investigation of bias, not least by collecting the data that allow HR to identify any systematic group differences that emerge. If computers are to be brought into the PA process, they should perhaps facilitate or supplement rather than replace face-to-face feedback – it seems likely that there will continue to be a need for the latter (and for training in how to handle it), probably in much the same form as appraisal takes now. Quite a lot depends on the broader organisational and work context; computer-based performance feedback systems may be most effective when employees frequently use and have access to computer technology, in which case getting feedback this way will come more naturally.

One more caveat

With personal (including performance) data stored on a PC, there is a danger to confidentiality: those appraised may reasonably seek reassurance as to who will have access to their appraisal data held on an IT system, and what security is in place to protect it. This is an understandable risk. And it shouldn't be assumed that unauthorised access is just an internal organisational problem. For example, in June 2015, the Office of Personnel Management in the United States announced a large-scale data breach involving the theft of wide-ranging personal data about millions of federal employees.

Though the potential for further applications of IT in the appraisal field may be considerable, the impact to date is unclear, particularly when it comes to appraisal effectiveness (Farr *et al.*, 2013). There seem to be potential advantages, particularly in enabling efficiency benefits, but there are also risks – a potential 'dark side':

> [T]echnologically aided appraisal can result in workers concluding that the performance management system is there to trip them up. Far from being a partnership focused on maximizing performance, technology can help divide managers from workers and instill an adversarial climate.
>
> (Cardy and Miller, 2005: 162)

Two things we can be sure of – the first, that some people will herald IT applications as the answer to all previous problems; the second, that they most definitely are not. We will probably learn about their best use the hard way, as usual. Some companies will rush into applying them, and we can all stand back and watch and learn from the results. It is always tempting to think that a system or a new piece of technology can get us off the hook when it comes to the messy business of handling relationships at work and managing performance, but while it can help, it will never do more than that.

IN SUMMARY

The changes that organisations have gone through in recent years, and their continuing evolution, make it even more essential that appraisal practices are developed that offer a degree of tailoring to the context and circumstances of the different parts of an organisation. Consultation with the main stakeholders in formulating the appraisal scheme is crucial to the success of this. The shift in organisational structures – and in particular the move to 'flatter' hierarchies – has implications for who contributes to the appraisal of an individual. The range and level of staff covered by appraisal arrangements have increased, and this also requires a more flexible approach to ensure that the process is relevant to their varying needs. The administration of appraisal schemes is still often too cumbersome, with an excessive emphasis on forms. While the growing role of IT in delivering the appraisal process can lead to swifter and more efficient operation of the scheme, the more ambitious use of computers in appraisal – for example, in delivering feedback on a more regular basis – raises many issues to which we do not at present have answers.

DISCUSSION POINTS AND QUESTIONS

5.1 How do we get 'buy-in' to appraisal during the design stage?

5.2 Who should contribute to the appraisal of an individual employee? Is there a role for self-assessment – if so, how much reliance should we place on it?

5.3 What can information technology contribute to performance appraisal? Will it make the process more objective? Will it help in making feedback more acceptable? What are the 'dark side' aspects?

KEY REFERENCES

Campion, M. A., Fink, A. A., Ruggeberg, B. J., Carr, L., Phillips, G. M. and Odman, R. B. (2011) Doing competencies well: Best practices in competency modeling. *Personnel Psychology*, **64**(1), 225–262.

Farr, J. L., Fairchild, J. and Cassidy, S. E. (2013) Technology and performance appraisal. In M. D. Coovert and L. F. Thompson (Eds) *The Psychology of Workplace Technology*. New York: Routledge, pp. 77–98.

Roberts, G. E. (2003) Employee performance appraisal system participation: A technique that works. *Public Personnel Management,* **32**(1), 89–98.

REFERENCES

Antonioni, D. and Park, H. (2001) The relationship between rater affect and three sources of 360 degree feedback ratings. *Journal of Management,* **27**(4), 479–495.

Buchner, T. W. (2007) Performance management theory: A look from the performer's perspective with implications for HRD. *Human Resource Development International,* **10**(1), 59–73.

Campion, M. A., Fink, A. A., Ruggeberg, B. J., Carr, L., Phillips, G. M. and Odman, R. B. (2011) Doing competencies well: Best practices in competency modeling. *Personnel Psychology,* **64**(1), 225–262.

Cardy, R. L. and Miller, J. S. (2005) eHR and performance management: A consideration of positive potential and the dark side. In H. G. Gueutal and D. L. Stone (Eds) *The Brave New World of eHR: Human Resources Management in the Digital Age.* San Francisco: Jossey-Bass, pp. 138–165.

Carroll, G. and Boutall, T. (2011) *Guide to Developing National Occupational Standards.* www.gov.uk/government/uploads/system/uploads/attachment_data/file/304239/nos-guide-for-_developers-2011.pdf (accessed 17 January 2016).

Cockerill, T., Hunt, J. and Schroder, H. (1995) Managerial competencies: fact or fiction? *Business Strategy Review,* **6**(3), 1–12.

Farr, J. L., Fairchild, J. and Cassidy, S. E. (2013) Technology and performance appraisal. In M. D. Coovert and L. F. Thompson (Eds) *The Psychology of Workplace Technology.* New York: Routledge, pp. 77–98.

Fletcher, C. (2001) Performance appraisal and performance management: The developing research agenda. *Journal of Occupational and Organizational Psychology,* **74**(4), 473–487.

Fletcher, C. and Perry, E. (2001) Performance appraisal and feedback: A consideration of national culture and a review of contemporary trends. In N. Anderson, D. Ones, H. Sinangil and C. Viswesvaran (Eds) *International Handbook of Industrial, Work and Organizational Psychology.* Thousand Oaks, CA: Sage, pp. 127–144.

Hirsh, W. (2006) *Improving Performance through Appraisal Dialogues.* London: Corporate Research Forum.

Johnson, R. D. and Gueutal, H. G. (2011) *Transforming HR through Technology: The Use of E-HR and HRIS in Organizations.* Alexandria, VA: Society for Human Resource Management.

Jones, L. and Fletcher, C. (2002) Self-assessment in a selection situation: An evaluation of different measurement approaches. *Journal of Occupational and Organizational Psychology,* **75**(2), 145–161.

Jones, L. and Fletcher, C. (2004) The impact of measurement conditions on the validity of self-assessment in a selection setting. *European Journal of Work and Organizational Psychology,* **13**, 101–111.

Mabe, P. A. and West, S. G. (1982) Validity of self-evaluation of ability: A review and meta-analysis. *Journal of Applied Psychology*, **67**(3), 280–296.

Mohrman, A. M., Resnick-West, S. M. and Lawler, E. E. (1989) *Designing Performance Appraisal Systems: Aligning Appraisals and Organizational Realities*. San Francisco: Jossey-Bass.

Nurick, A. J. (2012) *The Good Enough Manager: The Making of a GEM*. New York: Routledge.

Roberts, G. E. (2003) Employee performance appraisal system participation: A technique that works. *Public Personnel Management*, **32**(1), 89–98.

Roch, S. G. and Williams, K. J. (2012) Building effective performance appraisals from an analysis of work. In M. A. Wilson, W. Bennett Jr, S. G. Gibson and G. M. Alliger (Eds) *The Handbook of Work Analysis: Methods, Systems, Applications and Science of Work Measurement in Organizations*. New York: Routledge, pp. 419–436.

Scott, S. B. (1983) Evolution of an appraisal programme. *Personnel Management*, August, 28–30.

Sparrow, P. R. (1994) Organizational competencies: Creating a strategic behavioural framework for selection and assessment. In N. Anderson and P. Herriot (Eds) *Assessment and Selection in Organizations. First Update and Supplement*. Chichester, UK: Wiley, pp. 1–26.

Stanton, J. M. (2000) Reactions to employee performance monitoring: Framework, review and research directions. *Human Performance*, **13**(1), 85–113.

Weisband, S. and Atwater, L. (1999) Evaluating self and others in electronic and face-to-face groups. *Journal of Applied Psychology*, **84**(4), 632–639.

Williams, R. (1989) Alternative raters and methods. In P. Herriot (Ed.) *Assessment and Selection in Organisations*. Chichester, UK: Wiley, pp. 725–736.

6   APPRAISING, IDENTIFYING AND DEVELOPING POTENTIAL

Most of the content of the previous chapters has focused on the appraisal of performance, albeit with an eye to motivating and developing individuals over the review period. Traditionally, however, appraisal has a longer-term perspective in contributing to the assessment and development of potential. In recent years, with the so-called 'war for talent' (Michaels *et al.*, 2001), this has been given greater attention and prominence, and that is reflected in the more lengthy treatment of the subject here than might traditionally be associated with a book on appraisal.

In times of economic uncertainty – which is just about all times now – development and career planning are often seen as less important aspects of appraisal. This is perhaps not surprising, as it is harder to project ahead and to envisage growth with confidence; many organisations have de-layered and downsized and consequently have fewer promotion opportunities on offer. The pattern of career progression is thus less stable for many people, and less likely to be continued within the same organisation. However, these circumstances – far from suggesting that promotability and potential should be taken off the appraisal agenda – indicate that the career progression of the individual needs to be addressed with much greater care. If there are fewer promotions to be had, then it is even more essential that the process of deciding who will get them is seen to be fair and effective. If career development opportunities increasingly lie outside the organisation, then the latter cannot rely quite so much on the loyalty and company commitment of individual employees as a motivating force. The 'old deal' whereby organisations offered 'cradle to grave' employment in return for loyalty and motivation is no longer sustainable in many companies (Sparrow and Cooper, 2003). Moreover, the nature of career development, either inside or outside the organisation, is changing. With flatter organisations and fewer senior positions, for many people, development is going to involve sideways moves or job enlargement rather than a straight promotion. In effect, a new contract has to be instituted whereby the organisation undertakes to assess individuals' potential and to help them develop – ultimately, if necessary, outside the organisation. As part of this, self-development needs to be encouraged; if organisations are less able to guarantee future opportunities, then individuals can be provided with the experiences and skills to become more autonomous in facilitating their own career progression (for a wider discussion of this, see e.g. Conway and Briner, 2005; or Sturges *et al.*, 2005). This is the so-called 'new deal' – development in return for commitment while employed. There has to be some balance between organisational and individual needs in appraisal, and only by retaining the assessment and development of potential as part of the appraisal process (in the widest sense) can this be achieved.

Deciding the best methods for assessing and developing potential is not at all straightforward, however. One obvious basis to work from is present performance, as reflected in appraisal and other data. But the reason for having an assessment of potential is precisely because present performance is by no means a completely reliable indicator of future performance, particularly at higher organisational levels. While Silzer and Church (2009a) point out that an individual's adaptability, learning orientation and other attributes may be stifled by their current work context, it is true in most cases that if an individual is not performing well at their existing level, they are very unlikely to do better at more senior levels, and will probably do even worse. The relationship between performance and potential is nicely illustrated by the grid used in the UK National Health Service Leadership Academy Talent Management Conversation Tool (NHS, 2014: 9); see Box 6.1.

The question is, which of the majority of staff who are performing satisfactorily in their current jobs have the latent ability and aptitude to be promotable to the next level, or progress even further? How are those latent abilities and aptitudes to be assessed? The main methods for doing this are described and evaluated below. Before looking at them, though, there is a broader issue to consider: what is it, from the organisation's viewpoint, that people are being assessed and developed *for*?

Although there is a huge amount written on the subject of talent development, the actual concept of 'potential' remains highly variable in the way it is interpreted and operationalised. Indeed, a thorough treatment of this subject would take a book in itself (for a fuller treatment, the reader is referred to Silzer and Church, 2009a). For many organisations, identifying and developing talent are about finding individuals who have the potential to be effective in different, wider and more senior future roles. This may imply a track to a specific post in some cases, but often it is more open-ended, and is about being able to operate successfully in a range of possible higher-level positions. To

NHS Talent Grid Conversation Tool

BOX 6.1

	Professional talent	Developing talent, ready soon	Ready now
Readiness to move	Shows promise to continue to advance in their professional field or into a wider leadership role within 3–5 years if they have the capacity and ambition to do so, but equally valuable where they are.	Demonstrates the potential, ambition and motivation to develop at their current level and potentially progress in their career within 1–3 years into new and wider challenges.	Demonstrates the potential, ambition, motivation and experience to perform at the next level now or within the next 12 months into new and wider challenges.
Performance and behaviours			
Exceeds expectations Outstanding performance against objectives, achieves more than what is expected of them, and demonstrates role modelling of behaviours required beyond their role.	**Professional in field** (High potential) • High performance in own field. • Role models behaviours of organisation/role. • Consistent results and brings added value to tasks given. • Possibly reached, expert, stage in their career, likely to move on in the medium future, outside of own specialism. • Emergent wider skills.	**Key generalist** (Pivotal and flexible) • High performance with consistency of results across a variety of assignments and brings added value to tasks given. • Acts wider than professional background. • Role models behaviours of organisation/role. • Low-moderate potential ambition to move on, possibly happy to stay in current position. • Secondary pool to fill critical positions; perhaps move one level; likely to shift to key or high professional roles over time.	**Role model** (High potential to go further) • A role model with the highest levels of performance, potential and ambition to move on. • High performer, bringing added value to assignments with lots of potential and capacity for immediate advancement. • Role models behaviours of organisation/role. • Demonstrates mastery of current assignment. • True organisation asset – role model. • First call to fill critical positions.
Meets expectations Meets the expectations for performance against objectives and behaviours required at the level for their role.	**Future professional in field** (Needs stretching) • Good reliable performance. • Behaves professionally in line with role. • Showing upward potential but less ambitious to move outside of field.	**Solid generalist** (Solid/adaptable) • Good rounded performance. • Behaves professionally in line with role. • Meets expectations. • Works wider than professional background. • Some potential to do more in long term if ambition and development allow.	**Future emergent potential** (Capacity for key roles) • Individual with high potential. • Good rounded performance. • Behaves professionally in line with role. • Has the capacity to be a consistent talent, or with stretch move to higher levels.
Partially met expectations Below 'met expectations' against performance objectives and behaviours required at the level for their role.	**Developing professional** (Needs stretching) • Current low demonstration of performance and behaviours required of role. • Being supported to reach their potential. • May be in the wrong role.	**Developing generalist** (Needs stretching) • Low performance but showing moderate potential over time outside of professional role. • Being supported, needs pushing and stretching to reach full potential. • May be bored, under-used or in the wrong role.	**Transition employee** (New to role, needs support) • New to post or assignment. • Have yet to demonstrate results, or high potential in a new position/development assignment. • Future performance will allow assessment of where they align to the grid longer term.

Source: NHS (2014)

facilitate the latter, organisations increasingly institute ways of assessing individuals with such potential, and then put them on fast-track development programmes (Silzer and Church, 2009b). But while this kind of activity is now commonplace, the notion of potential is found to vary, as was shown by Karaevli and Hall (2003), who surveyed 13 major organisations and found that none of them had the same definition of this construct. Silzer and Church (2009a) report the most common descriptions of potential they found across 20 large organisations to rest on having the ability to move into senior management positions (35 per cent of their sample), having the ability to be effective in a job two levels above the current one (25 per cent), having the capability to take on wider leadership roles (25 per cent) and showing a consistent track record of exceptional performance.

Although more career development than before will lead to movement between organisations rather than simply within them, it remains important for organisations to try to identify what their needs are likely to be. If they do not, then there is a good chance that they will end up with the wrong mix of abilities and competencies for the situation they find themselves in a few years down the line. Techniques for analysing their requirements are largely those discussed in relation to competency-based appraisal in Chapter 4 (especially that based on meta-competencies described on pages 74–7) and in competency modelling, outlined in Appendix A. However, they will also be mentioned again below in relation to some of the methods of appraising potential, specifically those that are focused on longer-term potential rather than short-term competence to tackle a job the next level up.

THE CONVENTIONAL APPRAISAL PROCESS AS A MEANS OF ASSESSING SHORT- AND LONG-TERM POTENTIAL

For a long time, the appraisal of performance and promotability and/or long-term potential were both parts of the same exercise and recorded on the same form – and indeed still are in some organisations. The problems of linking the discussion of current performance with rewards, which include promotion, led to many appraisal schemes separating the two functions out. As a result, it has become common for the appraisal of potential to be carried out at a different time of the year and to be written on different report forms from the appraisal of ongoing performance.

The main role for appraisal in the context of career development is as an opportunity to discuss short-term training and development needs, and for the appraisee to talk over career aspirations with the appraiser. But the conventional appraisal process has been found severely wanting as a means of assessing long-term potential, though it does have a more worthwhile contribution to make to immediate promotion decisions. The problems of using performance appraisal in this context of potential are numerous:

- As a means of assessing current performance – which is the basis of the promotion/potential judgement – its accuracy leaves a lot to be desired, as has been noted several times in this book in discussing the problems and biases that all too often seem to afflict appraisal ratings.
- The direct linking of promotion or other rewards to the performance discussion may have detrimental effects on the latter (as noted in Chapters 1 and 2).
- Managers are sometimes reluctant to lose their best people, and it is not unknown for this to affect their written assessments of potential.
- The manager's own style may inhibit the opportunity for a subordinate to demonstrate potential.
- Where judgements about long-term potential for senior management levels are needed, line managers are not necessarily the best people to comment, as they may not have reached that level themselves and therefore do not possess first-hand experience of what is required.
- The limited breadth of perspective of individual managers can mean that they are unaware of the performance standards required for promotion and of the range of opportunities available – which may give rise to the creation of false (unduly high or low) expectations in the appraisee.

Several of these problems (and particularly the last one) are accentuated in appraisal schemes that are highly devolved and line-owned, which suggests that in such circumstances it is especially unwise to let the assessment of potential rest solely on the appraisal process. However, even in centrally driven appraisal schemes, given all the other demands and burdens placed on the annual appraisal, it does not seem very sensible to add this one. Perhaps the best contribution that the annual appraisal can make is as a short-listing mechanism: if appraisees are consistently performing at a high level (and perhaps have demonstrated this with more than one boss), then they are worth considering for promotion by whatever other review or assessment method is used. This way, the line manager still has a direct influence on promotion decisions, but not the deciding one. An example of how appraisal can be used in combination with other inputs and methods is reported by Catano *et al.* (2007) and summarised in Box 6.2.

CAREER REVIEW PANELS

One of the most common methods of making assessments about potential and feeding them into career planning is through the use of career review panels

BOX 6.2

AN EXAMPLE OF AN APPRAISAL-BASED PROMOTION SYSTEM

The Royal Canadian Mounted Police carefully developed a new appraisal system with a view to using it in making promotion decisions. Officers were appraised on a set of eight core competencies, which themselves had been arrived at through an extensive and systematic process of development. Each competency was described in different behavioural terms according to differing rank/responsibility levels. Candidates completed a Performance Report for Promotion (PRP), giving two examples that illustrated their performance level on each competency (i.e. 16 in all). An independent referee was approached to verify the examples given by the officer. The PRP also contained a set of BARS (see Chapter 4) for each competency. Again, these had been developed through a careful and systematic process. The officer's immediate boss completed these ratings, and could add further comments if he/she wished to. The officer had the opportunity to see the ratings and to record agreement or disagreement on the form; if there was a disagreement that could not be reconciled, the officer could record what he or she thought the rating(s) should be.

The next step was for the PRP to be viewed by a Promotion Review Board consisting of three senior officers. Their purpose was to resolve any disagreements over ratings and also to act as a check on over- or underrating by individual line managers; they thus exercised a moderating function and could enhance consistency of standards. The Board's final set of ratings were summed and fed directly into the promotion decision, which rested on a combination of the rating score, and the score from a job simulation exercise (JSE) – the latter presented the candidate with a set of 48 scenarios that might be encountered at the next level up (the level being promoted to) and asked which of a set of alternative responses would be the most effective and appropriate in dealing with them – see the section on 'Behaviourally based interview methods' later in this chapter. Again, this JSE was the result of careful, empirical development and offered objective scoring. So, in effect the promotion process offered an assessment of past performance and competence (the ratings), including a self-assessment, and a future-orientated measure of how an individual might perform at a higher rank (the JSE), with each of the two components being given equal weight in the final decision.

Considerable emphasis was given to providing training to all participants in the promotion process, and the promotion process was subject to thorough evaluation. For a full and excellent account of this work, see Catano *et al.* (2007).

(CRPs) (also known by a variety of other, similar names). These CRPs usually consist of a panel of senior managers, convened by the HR department, who periodically review either all managers at a specific level, or on a selective basis. Their task is to make some assessment of the promotability of individuals and to draw up a career plan for them. In doing this, they will have access to appraisal forms and possibly to additional reports made by appraisers specifically for this purpose. They may also interview staff if they feel this would be helpful. Throughout their deliberations, they have input from HR, which should help inform them of the range of opportunities available, the people who might fill them, and talent management generally in the short and medium term.

The advantages of this approach are that it is flexible, it provides a wider perspective than can be achieved by any one appraiser, it still involves line management, it has credibility because of the senior level of the people on the panel and it does not interfere with the normal appraisal process. The limitation of CRPs is that they remain largely dependent on the input from the performance appraisal to assess potential (though that input might relate to a broader time span and the appraisee's performance under more than one appraiser). Thus, they are still in the position of trying to judge potential on the basis of present performance. Also, some or all members of the panel may have little or no direct contact with the people whose potential they are trying to assess. Looking at the pros and cons of CRPs overall, while they are helpful in making decisions on short-term promotions, the method seems to have most to offer where it is used as a career-planning mechanism based on assessments of potential done by other means.

THE INTERVIEW IN ASSESSING SHORT- AND LONG-TERM POTENTIAL

The interview still seems to be the most popular way of deciding suitability for promotion to a specific post. The form of the interview may vary, from a one-to-one interview with the manager who has a vacancy to fill to a panel interview where HR and other departments are represented. How candidates are chosen to attend for the interview can be based on personal applications to the manager concerned, on appraisal data and on psychometric test results. Leaving the last-mentioned of these aside for the moment (it will be dealt with in depth below), the use of the interview usually takes a fairly conventional form. Typically, questions focus on:

- the individual's career so far, and the reasons for the decisions they have taken;
- the attraction of the position they are applying for and how they would tackle it;

- the way they perceive the fit between their experience and abilities and the position they are applying for;
- future career aspirations and direction;
- various hypothetical questions of the 'What would you do if. . .?' and 'How would you do such and such?' variety.

The advantages of interviews are that they are fairly easy to arrange, and that they are usually considered to be an essential part of the promotion process, if only so that the manager with the vacancy to fill can have a say in who is appointed, and the candidates can meet the person they would be working with. Alas, all that might be said of interviews in general applies to them in this context too. The typical, unstructured interview by the untrained interviewer remains an abysmal selection tool, for the many reasons that the research spanning three-quarters of a century has demonstrated. The outcome is as likely to be determined by the biases of the interviewers, and what they have failed to find out, as by anything more positive. Happily, this does not mean that the interview is devoid of value in contributing to the assessment of potential, as more recent developments in interview techniques show.

Behaviourally based interview methods

It has long been known that more structured approaches to interviewing increase its effectiveness. There are now a number of structured, behaviourally based interviewing techniques that are applicable in assessing promotability and potential and have been shown to be valid – in other words, they predict performance with some success; according to Anderson *et al.* (2008), their validity ranges from .44 to .56. There are two basic types, one which focuses on past performance, and is sometimes called the past-behaviour interview (PBI), though probably more often it is simply referred to as a competency-based interview; and one which focuses on future behaviour, which is called the situational interview.

Competency-based interviews

If the competencies or dimensions relevant to effective performance in the post are known, then it is possible to develop a structured interview around them. Thus, if it is known that organisation and planning are key elements in the job, then a series of questions on this theme can be drawn up to assess the extent to which the candidate has demonstrated a capacity for planning and organisation.

Examples might be:

- 'Tell us about how you establish the priorities in your present job.'
- 'Can you outline an example of how you have achieved a difficult goal through careful planning?'

- 'Describe how you go about planning and organising your own work and time.'
- 'What was the most difficult planning task you have had? Tell us about it.'

Questions of this kind yield useful information and are targeted on the important aspects of the job, and they do deal with actual rather than anticipated behaviour. But they all relate to what the individual has done in the past, at a lower level, with the limitations that implies. Nonetheless, there is considerable evidence in support of their validity (Taylor and Small, 2002).

Normally, a 45-minute interview of this kind will cover three to five competencies; trying to deal with more leads either to very superficial coverage or very long interviews. As has been implied above, you are dealing with a kind of 'scripted' interview here, drawing on a pool of maybe six or seven questions per competency. It would not be the intention to ask all the questions under each heading, but simply to ask enough to get a measure of the individual's capability. Although the initial question list is set, the interviewers do of course ask probing follow-up questions for clarification. The reasons for having a pool of questions are (a) that some questions are not relevant to the experience of some candidates, or they have little to offer in answer to them; and (b) that the questions may otherwise become too predictable and well known within the organisation. At the end of the interview, the assessors make ratings of the individual on each competency, based on the evidence of the behaviour the person has described (and *not* on his or her behaviour in the interview). It is best to have two interviewers if possible, so that one can be concentrating on making notes on the answers while the other asks the questions; they can swop round on this responsibility from competency to competency or from interview to interview.

Competency-based interviews yield useful information and do deal with actual rather than anticipated behaviour. A potential criticism of the method is, however, that it reflects individuals' work approach at present or in the past – and possibly when they were operating at a lower organisational level – rather than what might be demanded of them in the future. Several other concerns have been raised too. First, there is sometimes a degree of initial resistance from those doing the assessment to the idea of having their freedom limited by the straitjacket of preset questions. This does not seem to last long, though; they quickly become quite comfortable with it and like not having to think up questions for themselves. They also appreciate the thoroughness and fairness of the method. But there is another perspective here: the candidates. What do they think? Research suggests a mixed reaction; many of those assessed this way feel that competency-based interviews are fairer. They also see them as more obviously job-related than alternative approaches – which they are.

On the downside, though, candidates who have encountered competency-based interviews on more than one occasion complain that the interviews were 'boring' and easily fakeable. If the style and content of interviews become too predictable, it does not take very much intelligence to 'manufacture' convincing episodes showing how one demonstrated achievement orientation, interpersonal sensitivity, etc.; the danger of synthetic behavioural evidence seems very real. The only way round this is to spend more time on each question, probing the answers in such detail as to make faking very difficult to sustain.

Situational interviews

The situational interview involves quite a sophisticated technique and one that takes some time to develop – it is described in Box 6.3. One of the strengths of the situational interview is that it seeks to project candidates forward into their anticipated behaviour in the role they are being assessed for. It is true that because people say they will act in a particular way when faced with a situation, it is not necessarily the case that they do so in reality. However, the evidence for the validity of the situational interview is some reassurance here (Day and Carroll, 2003). Apart from anything else, at least the situational interview tells you whether the candidates *know* what the right answer is, irrespective of whether they will really act that way.

There is some evidence that different types of behaviourally based interview may predict different outcomes in a selection situation. Specifically, competency-based interviews give better indicators of an individual's cognitive ability, task performance and managerially relevant personality attributes, while situational interviews are better at predicting the fit between the individual and the organisation in terms of work styles and values (Krajewski *et al.*, 2006). Perhaps the best advice is to use a combination of both. Whatever the relative merits of the various approaches to behaviourally based interviewing, all such structured interviews are likely to be better at yielding accurate assessments than unstructured interviews (Anderson *et al.*, 2008). Panel interviews also seem to be superior to one-to-one interviews in this respect (Weisner and Cronshaw, 1988). Without the use of behaviourally based methods, the interview as a means of assessing potential is likely to be little more than an exercise in impression management.

USING PSYCHOMETRIC TESTS IN ASSESSING POTENTIAL

Psychometric testing is a complex topic, the full scope of which is beyond this book – readers are referred to Coaley (2014) for a fuller treatment of the subject. Any organisation willing to invest the money in either buying in

BOX 6.3

THE SITUATIONAL INTERVIEW

This novel approach to interviewing requires the organisation first to carry out, or have access to, a critical incidents job analysis (see Appendix A p. 248) of the position to be filled. The incidents identified will describe various situations and problems that typically arise in the job. The steps in constructing the situational interview are then as follows:

1. A group of managers familiar with the job and level at which the vacancy or vacancies exist selects a number of incidents that they agree on as being characteristic of the job and as sampling the main attributes necessary to perform effectively in it. So, for example, they may choose a reported incident where a manager had a problem with a subordinate because of a complaint about sexual harassment from another member of staff. The manager concerned passed it on to personnel to handle rather than dealing with it personally.

2. These incidents are turned into questions. In the case of the example given, it might be: 'One of your subordinates comes to you with a complaint about sexual harassment from another of your subordinates. You suspect it is true, though you have no other evidence to go on. What would you do in this situation?'

3. The group of managers would then be asked to say, independently and on the basis of their knowledge of staff of varying standards at this level, how good, mediocre and poor performers would deal with the situation outlined. When they have done this, they discuss their answers to check that there is a good level of agreement in each case. In the example used here, they might come up with a set of benchmark answers like this:

   - *Good performer:* tries to deal with the situation themselves, but gathers further information from the parties involved before coming to a judgement about what action is appropriate.
   - *Mediocre performer:* passes the matter on immediately to personnel without any attempt to gain further information or taking any responsibility for it.
   - *Poor performer:* calls in the party alleged to be doing the harassing and issues a stern warning without seeking further information and without giving them an opportunity to answer the allegation.

Answers reflecting these three strategies might be scored 1, 3 and 5 respectively. A complete set of questions and graded answers is arrived at through the same process, in such a way that all the key dimensions of the job are covered. The example used here might reflect both judgement and supervisory ability.

4. The interview takes place and candidates are posed the questions. Their answers are taken down by one of the interviewers (the method requires a panel of at least two).

5. Candidates' answers are scored, preferably independently by two or more raters, in terms of how they relate to the benchmark answers. The raters then discuss their marks and come to an agreed assessment.

This approach to interviewing sounds just like presenting a set of hypothetical questions, and it is – but with some crucial differences. It is based on real work situations and job analysis. The questions are chosen to cover the important performance dimensions, and the answers are quantitatively rated on how they compare with good and poor performers in the actual job. It is certainly a more demanding form of interview in terms of time and managers' involvement, but it has been shown to have good validity if used appropriately (Latham and Sue-Chan, 1999) – so at least it is time well spent. Also, it probably sounds more daunting to construct than it actually is.

It may strike the reader that this sounds rather like an orally administered questionnaire, and so it will be no surprise to learn that it can indeed be delivered and scored in pencil and paper form or using a computer-administered format – sometimes called a Situational Judgement Test or a Job Simulation Exercise (see Box 6.2).

external consultants or in getting their own staff trained in testing can make use of the methods described below. Companies producing tests offer good (but fairly costly) training, and it inevitably tends to focus on their own particular products. It is therefore advisable first to get some independent advice as to what, *if any*, are the most appropriate kinds of tests for the situation, and whether it is going to be more cost-effective to get company staff trained or to have it done by an external agency.

How can tests assess potential?

The huge growth in the use of psychometric tests (Wolf and Jenkins, 2006), both here in the UK and elsewhere in Europe, has included an increase in their use to assess promotability and potential. What is the basis for thinking that psychometric tests can contribute to the assessment of potential? There are two broad categories of tests that need to be looked at here: one covers cognitive (intellectual) abilities; and the other deals with personality attributes – though, strictly speaking, the latter are not 'tests' as they do not involve right or wrong answers. The argument that cognitive tests have something to say about potential is the strongest, or at least the most straightforward. It goes something like this:

- In many administrative, managerial and professional roles, a good level of intellectual ability is needed to perform effectively.
- The higher individuals go within these roles (up to a point), the greater the demands made on them, and the greater their ability needs to be to cope.
- We therefore need to know that any candidates for higher responsibility levels have the intellectual potential – or learning capacity – to perform effectively: we saw in Chapter 4 (pages 74–7) that certain 'meta-competencies' are associated with the ability to learn from experience and to reach higher organisational levels. One of the ways to assess this is to compare an individual's cognitive/learning abilities against those of people already successfully performing at such levels.
- Because they can show whether an individual matches up to the intellectual level associated with people already at higher levels, tests can also give some indication as to whether individuals who are performing well in their present job are actually at their ceiling or whether they have the intellectual resources to progress further.

The question might be asked as to whether educational qualifications might not serve the same purpose. They can, but not nearly so well. The advantage of tests is that they often show up intellectual potential that is not evident in academic achievements. There are all sorts of reasons for this, but essentially it comes down to the fact that educational qualifications reflect a great deal else besides intellectual ability – home background and opportunity, parental attitudes, motivation, adolescent problems and rate of maturity, quality of teaching and so on. Not surprisingly, then, psychometric tests given to adults are very often found to be more predictive of job success than are educational qualifications. Moreover, with grade drift and a tendency for more people to get high exam grades at all levels, academic results become less useful as a means of discriminating between different levels of ability. The evidence, both in the UK and the USA, shows a strong relationship between cognitive test scores and measures of both training and job performance, especially in more complex jobs (Bertua *et al.*, 2005).

It is a little more difficult to specify the role of personality measures in assessing potential. In terms of promotability to a particular job, the case is fairly straightforward. Here, the demands of the job and the person specification for it will suggest some personality attributes that are likely to be essential for effective performance and some that are likely to be counterproductive. A personality questionnaire may thus be useful in providing some data on these qualities. However, when the issue is one of longer-term potential to perform effectively some years in the future at a higher level and across a range of jobs, the requirement is much less clear-cut. It is less certain what personality attributes will be needed. There are two main alternatives to follow. One is to give personality measures to existing high performers at this level and see if any particular pattern emerges. The problem here is that any profile that emerges tells you about how things are now, not necessarily about how things should be or will be in the future – see Box 6.4.

BOX 6.4

AN EXAMPLE OF BOARD-LEVEL ASSESSMENT

A medium-sized company had got into some difficulties and as a result had been acquired by a much larger engineering and electronics firm. The management of the latter decided that they wanted to know more about the capabilities and capacities of the existing board of directors of the company they had acquired, so they decided that the entire board of directors should be put through a battery of personality and cognitive ability tests by an occupational (work) psychologist. The test profile that emerged showed a remarkably consistent pattern: most of the directors were intellectually highly able, but operated in a style that seldom exploited their potential in this direction. They were all strongly task-orientated, extremely high in drive and energy, quick to react, disinclined to think strategically, individualistic and uncooperative. The one exception to this was the MD, who was intellectually less capable than his colleagues but was the only one of them who had some capacity for teamwork and was probably the only one who could get them to move in the same direction. It was not difficult to see how the nature of the work in that company and the tendency for people to be attracted to (and promote) individuals like themselves had brought about this group of directorial clones. The recipe had worked for some time, and the company had grown rapidly to become very successful. Unfortunately, when the market changed and competition increased, they did not seem to have the resources within the board to respond to it; they all continued to charge ahead in the same way, without thinking through a new strategy. The point of this example is that if one took the personality pattern of the high performers in this organisation as the model for assessing the potential of more junior managers, the result would be pretty disastrous in a few years' time. It does not mean that there is no value in taking account of the personality pattern of senior managers (quite apart from anything else, it may say a lot about the organisation and how it is likely to function), but to be guided entirely by that would be a mistake. An analysis of future directions and needs has to be built into the picture.

The other alternative for guiding the use of personality measures in assessing long-term potential is reasonable deduction (or informed guesswork). It is probably going to be the case that some characteristics are *not* going to be helpful. People who are emotionally unstable, extremely low in drive, excessively aggressive and so on are much less likely to make progress to the top. People who are flexible, dynamic, outgoing, emotionally stable, etc. are more likely to be effective and to perform at higher levels. However, there are obvious limitations to this kind of approach, and it will only be helpful with some of the more extreme cases.

A competency analysis of the work conducted at this level will help, and also give some pointers as to what will or will not facilitate performance. But trying to relate personality questionnaire data – and, indeed, other psychological test scores – directly to competency descriptions raises some problems. The root cause of the difficulty is that competency frameworks and psychological test dimensions usually describe behaviour at different levels. An individual competency description typically focuses on a broad pattern of surface behaviour relating to some aspect of work performance. To take the example used earlier, a competency labelled 'organisation and planning' will be described in terms of such positive and negative behaviours as 'can link own plans with wider strategic objectives', 'prioritises demands made on his/her time', 'carefully monitors progress', 'initiates action without thinking it through' (all these are taken from actual examples of descriptors for such a competency). When the psychologist looks at this range of behaviour, several different psychological constructs are likely to seem relevant: thoughtfulness, analytical thinking, caution, impulsiveness and so on. In other words, the psychological dimensions are often much narrower in nature, and several different ones may be relevant to any one competency. Even with very work-focused personality measures this remains true.

So it becomes quite complicated to line up the psychological test dimensions with the competencies. In a few cases, there are actually no very clear or close relationships between the two; competencies that revolve around the notion of business sense or business awareness often come into this category. More usually, though, a number of psychological constructs seem to be relevant to each competency. A common problem that then arises is that no single psychometric test can be found to fit the bill: no one of them will offer measures of all the psychological dimensions that the analysis of the competency framework throws up. This being the case, the choice is either to use a lot of different tests – not attractive in terms of time or cost – or to decide to prioritise and perhaps use just one or two that cover as many of the key competencies as possible; the latter is normally the course adopted.

Another perhaps more fundamental and difficult issue that arises is when the psychological analysis of what is involved in the competencies suggests that the competencies do not make psychological sense. Either the psychological qualities required for different behaviours described under a single competency conflict with each other, or the same thing is true across two (or more) different competencies – implying that it is unlikely that an individual could be high on both. By way of illustration, take a competency called 'achievement orientation': the behavioural descriptions frequently include such things as 'sets targets beyond those required', and 'wants to be the best'. The psychological profile for individuals with very strong achievement motivation is not always one that fits very comfortably with the teamwork and interpersonal competencies, which often emphasise the capacity to put personal credit to one side in favour of the team, or imply giving higher priority to team cohesion and individual well-being than to personal goals.

Yet another issue that can arise stems from almost the opposite phenomenon; namely, the same psychological factors contributing to different competencies. A common example would be a trait like 'emotional control' contributing to the assessment of such competencies as customer relations, resilience, interpersonal sensitivity and so on. Having the same psychological factors relating to different competencies can cause problems in being able to discriminate between the latter and assess them independently. Sometimes the problem lies in the quality of the original work done in identifying the competencies. But in other cases it goes deeper, and reflects an unrealistic expectation of what people can achieve. The underlying assumption of some frameworks is that the competencies are all compatible and that it is possible to be strong in all of them. Psychologically, there are grounds for challenging this assumption. More pragmatically, though, the advice might be to leave plenty of time to think through the use of personality questionnaires and other psychometric tests in this context, and to realise that they seldom map neatly onto competencies. Other assessment methods will be needed. If they are used sensibly, though, personality questionnaires can contribute to the prediction of competency (Dulewicz and Herbert, 1996; Salgado et al., 2001; Barrick and Mount, 2012).

The ways in which tests are used

There are a variety of ways in which tests are applied in assessing potential and promotability:

- They may be given to external candidates as part of a selection procedure, not only to assess suitability for the job vacancy, but also to get some idea of the individual's potential beyond that.

- Internal candidates for a promotion vacancy may be given a battery of tests to assess their suitability for the promotion in question.
- Individuals may go through a testing session as part of a career assessment process that is not related to a specific promotion or job vacancy, but which has the assessment of potential as one of its aims (see Box 6.5).
- Tests are often included as an element of the assessment centre process, which will be described shortly.

Quite often the testing of candidates is done within the organisation by those appropriately trained. But at middle and senior levels, it is common practice to send the individuals to an outside consultant – usually a registered occupational psychologist (also known in European countries as work psychologists, and in North America as industrial and organisational [I/O] psychologists) – to conduct what is known as an Individual Psychological Assessment (Fletcher, 2011a, 2011b); see Box 6.4 for an example of this approach being adopted.

Apart from the higher level of expertise offered by taking this (possibly expensive) route, the main reason for it is political. Middle and senior management candidates are less happy to be put through such a searching assessment process by someone who may be junior to them in the organisation. The form of these assessments typically includes a battery of cognitive ability tests – numerical, verbal, logical reasoning and (perhaps) creative thinking – and one or two personality measures, as well as an in-depth interview with the consultant. The result is a report to the company which covers various aspects of work performance, and (where appropriate) an assessment of the candidate's suitability for a particular promotion vacancy, based on a job description and person specification. If the aim of the assessment has been more general, the report will include an assessment of overall career potential and will review career alternatives against the background of the individual's strengths and weaknesses. There is almost invariably some kind of feedback session with the candidate, where the assessor goes over the findings and discusses them with the individual, who may also receive a copy of the report. There is evidence that this kind of approach can show a good level of predictive validity (Silzer and Jeanneret, 2011; Weldon *et al.*, 2014).

It is never suggested that tests are sufficient by themselves to assess potential. They should always be employed as an additional input to other sources of information, such as existing performance, career progress to date, and possibly an interview. Their results and implications have to be interpreted in the light of all this information. An example of combining them with assessment centres is given in Box 6.5.

BOX 6.5

USING PERSONALITY QUESTIONNAIRE INPUT AT AN ASSESSMENT CENTRE FOR PROMOTION

A large international accountancy and consulting firm used the process outlined here for assessing director-level staff for making the next step up to partnership. The individuals had to be 'sponsored' by the partner they worked for in order to go through the assessment process. The first stage was to complete a well-known general personality questionnaire (the NEO), which was then followed up with a profiling interview conducted by an occupational psychologist. This would cover the candidate's background and work history, and elicit behavioural examples of situations and challenges they had dealt with. The psychologist would probe any particular areas of concern that had been flagged up by the individual's personality profile.

Within the next week or two, the candidate would attend a demanding two-day assessment centre (AC), where they would be assessed on six competencies. On the third day, the assessors reviewed the evidence under each competency for each candidate, coming to an agreed rating in each case, indicating whether the candidate had performed at partnership level or still needed development. The psychologist attended this assessment session, their function being to outline the strengths and weaknesses observed from the profiling interview on each competence. However, the aim of this was in part to present the candidate in a wider perspective than just their performance in the AC – to reflect a more enduring picture of how the individual had performed in their career so far, and to put their performance in the previous two days into a broader context. As part of this, the psychologist used the personality and interview data to help explain, if explanation was necessary, how and why the candidate might have behaved as they did – for example, showing inconsistency across different types of exercise or between their normal in-the-job performance and how they fared in the AC. This would inform the assessors' discussions and in some cases shade their final competency assessment in one direction or another – especially where there were implications for whether shortfalls in observed AC performance were likely to be easily remediable or not. Thus, although there was not a direct feed-in of personality 'scores' to the assessments made, they nonetheless had an indirect influence in many instances.

ASSESSMENT CENTRES

The term 'assessment centre' (AC) is used to describe the process whereby a team of assessors uses an integrated series of assessment techniques to assess a group of candidates. Those techniques typically include psychometric tests, interviews, peer ratings and simulation exercises. It is the last mentioned of these that constitute the core of the AC. They are meant to simulate or sample the kinds of work that an individual has to do at the level they are being selected for. These can include group problem-solving tasks, individual decision-making exercises (e.g. in-tray exercises), business games and interview role plays. Again, as with psychometric testing, this is a topic worthy of a book in itself, and the reader can be directed to an excellent one by Povah and Thornton (2011). The discussion of ACs offered here will be limited to a general outline of their use in assessing and developing potential, examination of some of the main issues associated with this method, and an evaluation of its worth.

Setting up and running ACs

As with so many aspects of appraisal, the first stage is to identify the key attributes for effective performance at the target level – the level in the organisation at which you are trying to assess the potential to perform successfully. This usually involves some kind of competency analysis (see Appendix A). Once the necessary competencies or behavioural dimensions have been decided, it becomes possible to judge what kinds of exercise might be used to assess them. The usual practice is to aim to have at least two, and preferably more, AC assessment techniques contributing to the assessment of each dimension. This ensures that the behaviour in question is sampled on separate occasions on different kinds of task, and possibly by different assessors – so providing a basis for making reliable judgements. A matrix is usually drawn up, with assessment exercises across the top and the competencies assessed down the side.

The simulation exercises should represent the work at the target level as accurately as possible, and to this end, managers already at that level should be involved in providing material for the exercises. It is possible to buy AC exercises off the shelf from various consultancies and test producers, but most organisations rightly want the content and nature of the exercises to reflect their own work and culture as closely as possible – which means constructing them from scratch, probably with some help from a consultant experienced in this field. Once the dimensions, exercises and other assessment methods are devised and decided on, a timetable for the AC event and administrative matters, such as where it is to be run, can be settled. Two other vital issues have to be confronted while all this is going on. Who are to be the assessors and how are they to be trained? And how are the candidates to be nominated for the AC?

The assessors should largely be managers in the organisation who are working at the target level, so at least they know the work and demands associated with it at the present time. Their involvement has two other benefits: it ensures input and part-ownership of the AC process by the line, and it gives the AC a degree of credibility with senior line management as a result. Getting this line input is far from easy, as it requires a considerable time commitment from the managers concerned. They need to be trained, and then to be able to act as assessors on enough AC events (assuming that there is a series of them) to maintain a consistent standard. The importance of the training cannot be overstated; the value of the whole AC rests on it. The assessors should have the background and rationale of the method explained, gain some experience of doing some or all of the exercises themselves, and be given instruction in behavioural assessment. In particular, they need to become thoroughly familiar with the competencies or dimensions they are assessing, and what kind of behaviour is covered by each of them, so that they can correctly classify the candidates' behaviour when they see it. Ideally, the performance of the assessors themselves should be monitored, as they certainly differ in effectiveness (Stillman and Jackson, 2005).

Apart from the line-manager assessors, there will usually be some HR representatives and possibly also one or more outside consultants. Including the latter is very desirable, for two reasons. First, where occupational psychologists are concerned (and they often feature in this role because of their expertise in devising ACs), reviews of the research evidence suggest that their success in predicting performance from ACs is greater than that achieved by line managers (Arthur *et al.*, 2003). Second, even with all the sophistication of the AC method, there is still a danger of the assessors selecting people they see as being similar to themselves. In other words, the AC becomes a glorified cloning process. The presence of external assessors reduces the chance of that happening.

How the candidates for the AC are to be identified is never altogether straightforward. The basic options are:

- self-nomination
- nomination by the boss
- qualification through passing exams, etc.

Nomination by the boss has the advantage of being based on current performance, but given the inadequacies of appraisal as an assessment mechanism, relying solely on this source may mean that some good candidates are missed. Self-nomination is the best in terms of scanning all possible candidates who might have potential and who could have been overlooked. However, this can also lead to some very unsuitable candidates putting themselves forward, with two unfortunate consequences: they waste the organisation's resources by taking places on ACs which are costly to run, and they may set themselves up for experiences of failure that could be very discouraging or even damaging to them. There is some virtue in the argument that says that where self-nomination is allowed, there should be a first-stage screening process involving psychometric tests. There are a few organisations where certain objective criteria, typically passing professional exams to some level, are used to determine who should attend ACs. Where there are such criteria and they are relevant to the assessment of potential, then nomination is much more clear-cut.

The typical ratio of candidates to assessors is 2:1 or 3:1, and the number of candidates attending any one AC is normally within the range of five to fifteen. The duration of the AC depends on the number of assessment techniques it contains, but is usually 1–3 days. The last day or part of it is devoted to the assessors' conference, where each candidate's performance is reviewed in turn; all the information is scrutinised, candidate by candidate, and final ratings on each dimension agreed. The candidate will be given an Overall Assessment Rating (OAR), which generally boils down to a judgement that the individual (a) has high potential, (b) possibly has high potential, or (c) does not appear to have high potential at the moment. The first two of these lead to fast-track development status.

In due course, the outcome of the AC and observations on the candidates' performance in it will be conveyed to them in an individual feedback session. This is usually given by one of the assessors and/or a personnel representative, and the candidate's line manager may also be present – which is important if the latter is to assist the candidate in implementing any development plans. The implications of the AC for career progression will be thoroughly discussed and whatever action is needed put in hand.

Issues in the use of ACs

Some of the practical problems in using ACs have already been mentioned. There are, however, a number of other issues that HR practitioners need to be aware of:

- *Self-fulfilling prophecies*. There is some danger of letting ACs create crown princes and princesses. Once individuals have been identified as having potential, special attention and resources are lavished on them, so it may not be surprising if they do well. The expectation that they will be high performers can also influence perceptions of their actual performance. It is important, then, that such individuals are subject to particularly careful assessment to see that they are living up to their promise. Equally, the judgement in an AC that an individual does not have high potential must not be allowed to become the kiss of death, with no further interest or resources being directed to their career progression. This leads on to the next issue.

- *The feedback process.* The feedback given after ACs leaves a lot to be desired and tends to be one of the weakest features of their operation. The primary problem is that it comes too long after the event to capitalise on it. If the feedback is to be meaningful, it has to be given while the experience is still fresh in the participants' minds; a week or more after the event is far too long. Also, it has to be especially sensitively handled with individuals who have not done well in the AC. It has been found that failure in an AC (one aimed at identifying managerial potential) reduced psychological well-being and some aspects of motivation at least six months after the event (Fletcher, 2011c). There is sometimes a need for counselling on a longer-term basis, so that individuals do not feel that their career is somehow over and that they are no longer valued; not everyone can be a high-flyer.

- *Cost-effectiveness.* There is no doubt that ACs are the most expensive assessment process to run. It is impossible to give a precise cost per candidate, since the content and duration of ACs vary so much, as does the number of candidates put through them (obviously, the set-up costs as a proportion of total costs diminish with increasing numbers put through the AC). Utility analysis shows that the financial benefits of better selection using ACs far outweigh the expense of the method; see Woodruffe (2007). This does not mean, though, that it is impossible to achieve nearly as good results through using cheaper methods. The main alternative to ACs is using psychometric tests, which are certainly cheaper and almost as predictive of future performance as are ACs, though perhaps not quite (Krause *et al.*, 2006). The debate about the relative cost-effectiveness of the two methods will go on and on, but in a sense there can never be an answer. The reason is that there is no way of financially evaluating either the superiority of the AC as a development tool or its face validity (the extent to which it *looks* as though it is measuring what it claims to) for both candidates and assessors. However, the experience of being trained as an assessor on an AC seems to improve a manager's assessment skills in other situations, such as performance appraisal (Macan *et al.*, 2011) – another valuable consequence of the method.

- *Preparing the candidates.* Because of its unique and demanding nature, the AC has the potential to throw some people a little off balance. It is important to give candidates an idea of what to expect. It is also desirable to break them in gently, by having less demanding exercises, or 'unfreezing' exercises, first. Anxiety generated by the AC itself which is not generally characteristic of the candidate can adversely affect and distort performance at ACs (Fletcher *et al.*, 1997; Fletcher, 2011c), and assessors need to be aware of this. Having said that, even ACs are not immune from candidate impression-management tactics (McFarland *et al.*, 2005).

- *The use of competencies/dimensions.* There is much academic debate about these, and whether ACs really measure them in the way they claim to – the emerging evidence is generally positive (Kudisch *et al.*, 1997; Lievens, 2001). One thing is clear, however – that the assessment dimensions used in ACs should not be too numerous. It has been shown that more dimensions do not mean more refined judgement – quite the opposite. It is probably better to focus on a smaller number of essential competencies and to train assessors to rate them effectively than to go for long lists of 15 or more dimensions (Arthur *et al.*, 2003).

An evaluation of ACs

A lot of the faith in ACs is due to their high face validity – and also because of the scientific evidence in their favour, which is overwhelmingly positive in terms of their ability to predict career potential and success (Povah and Thornton, 2011). However, neither of these means that an AC is actually doing a good job. It is just as easy to set up and run a bad AC as it is to carry out a poor interview. So, one cannot generalise with ACs – because some are good, it does not mean they all are. If, however, they are set up and run in a careful and professional manner, and if they are subject to evaluation and monitoring, they are the best and most thorough method available.

The use of ACs is quite flexible – they can be employed for assessing the potential of:

- junior and middle managers for more senior levels;
- first-line supervisors for junior/middle management;
- scientific, professional and technical staff for general management or for management within their own specialism.

What they are not usually acceptable for is the more senior levels. While there are exceptions, many senior managers are reluctant to engage in AC-type assessment procedures. The politics and status of operating at this level do create difficulties in running and assessing such things as group exercises. Senior managers are therefore more likely to be put through an external, psychometrically based, individual assessment procedure when being considered for promotion.

Development centres and other approaches to assessing promotion and potential

Some of the issues associated with ACs that were outlined above have led to an increased use of a rather different version of the method, known as the development centre (DC). Essentially, this is similar in format to the AC, but the focus is much more on the training and development needs of the individual than on coming out with an overall rating of potential – indeed, no OAR is provided at all. The idea is to capitalise on the learning potential of the AC exercises and to use the information they generate to build a development plan for each participant; see Povah and Thornton (2011) for a full consideration of DCs. This largely removes the problem of some people being branded as failures or, come to that, as crown princes/princesses. The assessors may include more HR, management development and training staff, though senior line managers will often still be involved. It is difficult to formally evaluate DCs in the way one can ACs, because their output is individually tailored and there is no clear-cut criterion against which to measure their success. However, such evidence as there is suggests that results are variable, and not quite as good as they perhaps should be given the cost of setting up and running DCs (Halman and Fletcher, 2000; Povah and Thornton, 2011).

There are many hybrid approaches to assessing potential, especially where the aim is to identify high-flyers from an already senior and highly selected group. An example is given in Box 6.6.

BOX 6.6

AN EXAMPLE OF ASSESSING FOR HIGH POTENTIAL

Individuals who reach Senior Civil Service status within the UK Civil Service have already progressed a long way and in most cases will have been through several demanding assessment stages. However, it was decided to seek to identify within this cadre a group of individuals who had the potential for accelerated development that would equip them for top management in a relatively short space of time. The appraisal of their capacity to deliver dynamic leadership went through several stages:

1. Individuals could put themselves forward or be nominated within their own department, which would assess them in ways that varied somewhat from department to department, but which resulted in a very limited number of candidates being put forward for the central assessment process run by the Cabinet Office.

2. Each candidate who went forward presented a portfolio of evidence. This included:

- a quantitative (ratings-based) and a qualitative (free-written) self-assessment against the competencies being assessed
- copies of the last three performance appraisal reports
- an assessment and ranking from their own department
- a brief CV.

3. The candidates completed, online, two psychometric measures, both focused on leadership.
4. All this evidence was placed before a panel of three interviewers, consisting of a permanent secretary (in effect, the chief executive of a Government department), a non-executive director of a Government department (who came from a background career outside the Civil Service) and a consultant occupational psychologist – again, none of these were civil servants.
5. After reviewing the evidence, the panel conducted a competency-based interview of each candidate lasting 45–60 minutes, made an assessment against the competencies and a recommendation as to whether the individual should be placed on the new High Potential scheme.

Just over a hundred candidates attended the central assessment process in the first year the scheme operated, and around 50 per cent were selected for accelerated development. Those who were chosen subsequently attended a development centre to help tailor a development plan specifically for them, which was followed by a comprehensive series of activities and strong central support to widen and enhance their leadership capacities.

This scheme is an example of using multiple assessment methods and stages in appraising potential, and is notable for the mix of high-level internal and external assessors used (Fletcher, 2006).

IN SUMMARY

There is still a place for the annual appraisal in assessing promotability, but where the appraisal is of the traditional kind, its role is a limited one. The way in which so many organisations have taken to using psychometric tests and assessment centres in recent years suggests that this point has been widely recognised. As a trend, it looks set to continue and strengthen for some time yet. One of the advantages of this kind of strategy is that it allows appraisal of performance to be very much line-led, but puts the assessment of potential into a wider perspective that cannot usually be provided by line management alone.

It also offers a superior level of objectivity and predictive power in assessment. If handled sensibly, tests and ACs can still leave line managers with a substantial role in implementing career development plans and decisions for their staff. Where it is felt that tests and ACs are not the most appropriate techniques, the development of behavioural interviewing has a lot to offer.

Whichever approach to assessing potential is used, it remains essential that there is an attempt to identify the needs of the organisation in the years ahead (see Appendix A on competency modelling in this context). The competencies or skill dimensions arrived at through such a process can be built into the appraisal of performance *and* potential, and a clearer picture will emerge of the likely career opportunities and pathways. With this information, both the organisation and its employees can take decisions and make plans. If the latter know what the options are, and have also been put through assessment methods that give them feedback about their skills and strengths, they are in a much stronger position to direct their own careers. Various techniques such as career planning workshops and workbooks and development centres can help them further in this respect.

DISCUSSION POINTS AND QUESTIONS

6.1 What useful contribution can performance appraisal make to promotion decisions – and what are its limitations in this respect? How can we use other methods to compensate for those limitations?

6.2 What is 'potential'? Why, and how, should we measure it?

6.3 Analyse the strengths and weaknesses of assessment centres compared to using psychometric tests in assessing potential?

6.4 Critically evaluate the systems for making promotion decisions and for identifying high potential amongst existing staff in either your own organisation or one you are familiar with. What changes would you make to improve them?

KEY REFERENCES

Catano, V. M., Darr, W. and Campbell, C. A. (2007) Performance appraisal of behavior-based competencies: A reliable and valid procedure. *Personnel Psychology*, **60**(1), 201–230.
Coaley, K. (2014) *An Introduction to Psychological Assessment and Psychometrics.* 2nd edn. London: Sage.

Povah, N. and Thornton, G. C. III (2011) *Assessment Centres and Global Talent Management*. London: Gower.

Silzer, R. and Church, A. H. (2009a) The pearls and perils of identifying potential. *Industrial and Organizational Psychology*, **2**(4), 377–412.

REFERENCES

Anderson, N., Salgado, J., Schinkel, S. and Cunningham-Snell, N. (2008). Staffing the organization: An introduction to personnel selection and assessment. In N. Chmiel (Ed.) *An Introduction to Work and Organizational Psychology: A European Perspective*. Oxford: Blackwell, pp. 257–280.

Arthur, W., Day, E. A., McNelly, T. L. and Edens, P. S. (2003) A meta-analysis of the criterion-related validity of assessment center dimensions. *Personnel Psychology*, **56**(1), 125–154.

Barrick, M. R. and Mount, M. K. (2012) Nature and use of personality in selection. In N. Schmitt (Ed.) *The Oxford Handbook of Personnel Selection and Assessment*. Oxford: Oxford University Press, pp. 225–251.

Bertua, C., Anderson, N. and Salgado, J. F. (2005) The predictive validity of cognitive ability tests: A UK meta-analysis. *Journal of Occupational and Organizational Psychology*, **78**(3), 387–410.

Catano, M. V., Darr, W. and Campbell, C. A. (2007) Performance appraisal of behavior-based competencies: A reliable and valid procedure. *Personnel Psychology*, **60**(1), 201–230.

Coaley, K. (2014) *An Introduction to Psychological Assessment and Psychometrics*. 2nd edn. London: Sage.

Conway, N. and Briner, R. B. (2005) *Understanding Psychological Contracts at Work: A Critical Evaluation of Theory and Research*. Oxford: Oxford University Press.

Day, A. L. and Carroll, S. A. (2003) Situational and patterned behavior description interviews: A comparison of their validity, correlates and perceived fairness. *Human Performance*, **16**(1), 25–47.

Dulewicz, S. V. and Herbert, P. (1996) General management competences and personality: A 7-year follow-up. *Henley Management College Working Paper Series*, HWP 96/21.

Fletcher, C. (2006) Where the assessment centre may not reach: Assessing candidates for the top levels in a UK Government context. Paper presented at the 33rd International Congress on the Assessment Centre Method, London, September.

Fletcher, C. (2011a) Individual psychological assessments in organisations: Big in practice, short on evidence? *Assessment and Development Matters*, **3**(2), 23–26.

Fletcher, C. (2011b) Assessment for top management selection. *Assessment and Development Matters*, **3**(4), 11–14.

Fletcher, C. (2011c) The impact of ACs and DCs on candidates. In N. Povah and G. C. Thornton, III (Eds) *Assessment Centres and Global Talent Management*. London: Gower, pp. 115–130.

Fletcher, C., Lovatt, C. and Baldry, C. (1997) A study of state, trait and test anxiety and their relationship to assessment centre performance. *Journal of Social Behavior and Personality*, **12**(5), 205–214.

Halman, F. and Fletcher, C. (2000) The impact of development centre participation and the role of individual differences in changing self-assessments. *Journal of Occupational and Organizational Psychology*, **73**(4), 423–442.

Karaevli, A. and Hall, D. T. (2003) Growing leaders for turbulent times: Is succession planning up to the challenge? *Organizational Dynamics*, **32**(1), 62–79.

Krajewski, H. T., Goffin, R. D., McCarthy, J. M., Rothstein, M. G. and Johnston, N. (2006) Comparing the validity of structured interviews for managerial level employees: Should we look to the past or focus on the future? *Journal of Occupational and Organizational Psychology*, **79**(3), 411–432.

Krause, D. E., Kersting, M., Heggestad, E. D. and Thornton, G. C. III (2006) Incremental validity of assessment center ratings over cognitive ability tests: A study at executive management level. *International Journal of Selection and Assessment*, **14**(4), 360–371.

Kudisch, J. D., Ladd, R. T. and Dobbins, G. H. (1997) New evidence on the construct validity of diagnostic assessment centers: The findings may not be so troubling after all. *Journal of Social Behavior and Personality*, **12** (special issue on assessment centres), 129–144.

Latham, G. P. and Sue-Chan, C. (1999) A legally defensible interview for selecting the best. In R. S. Barrett (Ed.) *Fair Employment Strategies in Human Resource Management*. Westport, CT: Quorum Books/Greenwood Publishing, pp. 56–67.

Lievens, F. (2001) Assessors and the use of assessment center dimensions: A fresh look at a troubling issue. *Journal of Organizational Behavior*, **22**(3), 203–221.

Macan, T., Mehner K., Havill, L., Merial, J. P., Roberts L. and Heft L. (2011) Two for the price of one: Assessment center training to focus on behaviors can transfer to performance appraisals. *Human Performance*, **24**, 443–457.

McFarland, L. A., Yun, G., Harold, C. M., Viera, L. and Moore, L. G. (2005) An examination of impression management use and effectiveness across assessment center exercises: The role of competency demands. *Personnel Psychology*, **58**, 949–980.

Michaels, E., Handfield-Jones, H. and Axelrod, B. (2001) *The War for Talent*. Boston, MA: Harvard Business School Publishing.

NHS (2014) *Talent Management Conversation Tool: A Guide for Managers and Employees*. NHS Leadership Academy. www.leadershipacademy.nhs.uk/wp-content/uploads/2014/10/PH6023-Leadership-Academy-Talent-management-guide1.pdf (accessed 30 December 2015).

Povah, N. and Thornton, G. C. III (2011) *Assessment Centres and Global Talent Management*. London: Gower.

Salgado, J. F., Viswesvaran, C. and Ones, D. S. (2001) Predictors in personnel selection: An overview of constructs, methods and techniques. In N. Anderson, D. Ones, H. Sinangil and C. Viswesvaran (Eds) *International Handbook of Industrial, Work and Organizational Psychology. Vol. 1*. London: Sage, pp. 165–199.

Silzer, R. and Church, A. H. (2009a) The pearls and perils of identifying potential. *Industrial and Organizational Psychology*, **2**(4), 377–412.

Silzer, R. and Church, A. H. (2009b) Identifying and assessing high potential talent: Current organizational practices. In R. F. Silzer and B. E. Dowell (Eds) *Strategy Driven Talent Management: A Leadership Imperative*. San Francisco: Jossey-Bass, pp. 213–280.

Silzer, R. and Jeanneret, R. (2011) Individual psychological assessment: A practice and science in search of a common ground. *Industrial and Organizational Psychology*, **4**(3), 270–296.

Sparrow, P. and Cooper, C. L. (2003) *The Employment Relationship: Key Challenges for HR*. London: Elsevier.

Stillman, J. A. and Jackson, D. J. R. (2005) A detection theory approach to the evaluation of assessors in assessment centres. *Journal of Occupational and Organizational Psychology*, **78**(4), 581–594.

Sturges, J., Conway, N., Guest, D. and Liefooghe, A. (2005) Managing the career deal: The psychological contract as a framework for understanding career management, organizational commitment and work behaviour. *Journal of Organizational Behavior*, **26**(7), 821–838.

Taylor, P. J. and Small, B. (2002) Asking applicants what they *would do* versus what they *did do:* A meta-analytic comparison of situational versus past behaviour employment interview questions. *Journal of Occupational and Organizational Psychology*, **75**(3), 277–294.

Weisner, W. H. and Cronshaw, S. F. (1988) A meta-analytic investigation of the impact of interview format and degree of structure on the validity of the employment interview. *Journal of Occupational Psychology*, **84**, 275–290.

Weldon, P., Fletcher, C. and MacIver, R. (2014) Individual psychological assessments: A predictive validity study. *Proceedings of British Psychological Society Annual Occupational Psychology Conference*, Brighton, UK, January. [Online publication only.]

Wolf, A. and Jenkins, A. (2006) Explaining greater test use for selection: The role of HR professionals in a world of expanding regulation. *Human Resource Management Journal*, **16**(2), 193–213.

Woodruffe, C. (2007) *Development and Assessment Centres: Identifying and Developing Competence*. London: Human Assets Ltd.

MULTI-LEVEL, MULTI-SOURCE FEEDBACK FOR APPRAISAL AND DEVELOPMENT

7

Chapter 5 looked at the issue of who should appraise, and touched on the subject of multi-level, multi-source appraisal, also known as 360° feedback. This generally means an individual being rated by subordinates, peers, superiors and – sometimes – clients or customers, as well as doing a self-assessment. Since the middle of the 1990s, this kind of feedback system has spread with tremendous speed across both public and private sectors and is now in widespread use. The actual percentage of companies applying it is hard to gauge, as findings tend to conflict. Carruthers (2003) reports that 90 per cent of Fortune 1000 companies in the USA use 360° feedback, and 85 per cent of top Australian corporations do also. On the other hand, an international survey of over 1,000 organisations by Mercer (2013) reported that only 22 per cent used formal 360° feedback systems. However, the balance of evidence suggests that the higher figures are closer to the mark. Another international study (Brutus *et al.*, 2006) suggested not only a continuing increase in use, but also a more diverse range of applications.

THE TYPICAL 360° FEEDBACK SYSTEM

Although there are many minor variations, most systems of this kind are rather similar. The main elements, and how they are handled, are as follows.

The questionnaire

This generally presents a series of statements about the 'focal' manager's behaviour and effectiveness; the managers receiving feedback used to be referred to as the 'target' managers, but this made it sound like they were being shot at! Often – but not always – the behaviours are linked to the key competencies identified as being associated with high performance in that organisation. Each competency will be described by a set of indicators of the sort we saw in Chapter 3, Box 3.3, and each of those will be rated either in terms of the effectiveness of the individual in relation to that behaviour, or the frequency with which it is displayed (see Box 7.1 for examples of the kind of rating scale typically used).

BOX 7.1

TYPICAL RATING FORMATS USED IN 360° FEEDBACK QUESTIONNAIRES

Rating Scale – example 1

The individual is simply rated on their level of effectiveness in terms of each specified behaviour:

Extremely effective
Very effective
Effective
Mostly effective
Partially effective
Not effective

Rating Scale – example 2

This focuses on the frequency with which a behaviour is demonstrated, rather than the level:

Always displays this behaviour
Nearly always displays this behaviour
More often than not displays this behaviour
Sometimes displays this behaviour
Seldom displays this behaviour
Never displays this behaviour

So, if there are eight competencies thought relevant to a particular role, there might be something like five to seven questions asked in relation to each one, giving a rating form of around 40 to 50 questions. Some companies mix all the questions up together; some group them under their relevant competency heading. The better examples of such systems offer the respondents the alternatives of saying, in relation to any particular question, either that they think this is not relevant to the job or that they have not had the opportunity to assess it, so allowing them to skip that rating. Other variations on the rating task include such practices as asking raters to rate the relevant attribute in terms of actual level displayed, and then in terms of desirable level for the job in question. Most forms also provide a free-written section in which other observations may be made. These are sometimes helpfully structured by asking such questions as, 'What should he (or she) do more of?' or 'What should he (or she) do less of?'.

The raters

The focal manager completes a self-rating and is independently rated by colleagues. Many organisations allow the focal manager to choose who contributes to the rating process, based on whom the individual feels is in the best position to comment on their performance. The number of raters ranges from three to as many as twenty, depending on circumstances. One view frequently taken is that there should be a minimum of five people giving ratings, so that a degree of anonymity can be maintained. Usually, the raters will be peers, subordinates and the immediate boss; sometimes, other superiors in a position to comment on performance may also be included, which is especially helpful when the focal manager has been working in several project teams. Clients or customers, generally but not necessarily external to the organisation, figure in some systems. The focal manager's self-ratings are not entered into the aggregate of the ratings of others, but put alongside them to point up any differences.

The feedback process

There are three main elements to this. The first is the person who collects the feedback; the second is the feedback report and how the data are represented within it; and the third is the manner in which this information is conveyed to the focal manager. The completed ratings are now most often entered on a computer and fed into a software program which aggregates them for each feedback source (peers, subordinates, etc.). They will normally go either to a designated source in HR or to an external consultant; less often, they go to a senior manager. If the 360° system is manual rather than software-based, then whoever collects the ratings has the task of collating them in a form that will be helpful to the recipient. Whichever way it is done, the output will usually present an average 'score' on each competency, broken down by rating group, perhaps putting the self-rating alongside it. Providing the numbers in each group are sufficient, this preserves anonymity for the respondents. In some cases, where the number of colleagues contributing feedback is small and breaking them down into groups would make them individually identifiable, their ratings are simply put together and presented as overall figures. This is understandable, but has the disadvantage of failing to identify any differences in perspective between subordinates, peers and others involved, which may have considerable significance in terms of development implications. The other problem with averaging ratings, either within or across rater groups, is that information about the range of assessment is lost. It is quite possible for someone to come out as rather middling on an attribute because one group of, say, subordinates assessed him or her as high and another group as low on that behaviour; such a difference can stem from favouritism or from different role relationships, for example. It thus seems desirable to represent the ratings of different groups separately. This should not compromise anonymity, providing there are enough raters in each category. Quite reasonably, there is usually less concern over the immediate boss's ratings being identifiable.

Free-written comments can be listed verbatim, though it is more useful for a summary of the themes emerging to be included in the report. This can help illuminate the ratings, and give some leads in terms of development needs. It is not uncommon for 360° feedback systems to specify a criterion level of performance, defined by ratings above a certain value, and to highlight ratings that fall short of this or that significantly exceed it. Various profile charts, graphs, etc. are frequently used to present the information in a more striking manner, when the system is IT-based. In some 360° systems, the focal manager's ratings may be viewed against a normative base reflecting such ratings received from a larger sample. The latter may be based on the organisation as a whole, or across several different organisations, or on particular management levels or professional groups. However, the broader the sample is, potentially the less relevant it is to the specific focal manager and his or her context.

Just how the assessment is communicated to the manager does to some extent reflect the background and purpose of the feedback process. In organisations where there is still considerable sensitivity about this kind of feedback, the report may simply be sent to the focal managers and the initiative left with them as to whether they show it to, or discuss it with, anyone else, and whether they choose to take any action on it. Often, though, the report is discussed with a coach, the individual's line manager or someone from HR, with a view to producing a development plan based on the feedback. A few – perhaps rather brave – organisations operate a process whereby the content of the feedback is actually discussed by the focal manager face to face with some or all of the feedback givers, the event being facilitated by an HR manager. In these cases, the concern over preserving anonymity is obviously rather less! This is not a common practice and does require skilled handling to ensure that the focal manager does not become too defensive and that the feedback given is expressed in a constructive manner. Open discussion of the content of the feedback does have the major advantage of allowing clarification. Ratings alone can often be a little ambiguous. By way of example, one manager said,

"I was accused of not giving enough credit to my subordinates, but I still don't know whether this was because I did not thank them enough for work done well or if it really was down to the fact that I did not recommend two of them for promotion last year." Note his use of the word 'accused'!

An interesting and well-presented case study of the introduction of a multi-source feedback system is provided by Clifford and Bennett (1997). They describe how initial work on management standards in the UK Automobile Association (AA) was used as a basis for implementing a 360° system to bring about a culture change. A 50-item management standards questionnaire, with the response to each question given on a clearly described six-point effectiveness scale, was used to gather feedback. Each participant sent the questionnaire to their boss and to their first- and second-level reports; respondents were encouraged to explore what they valued most, or least, about the participant. Feedback was handled by internal HR staff and line managers specially trained for the purpose. The aim was for each participant to emerge with a prioritised development plan. Clifford and Bennett's account gives a picture of a carefully handled process systematically monitored in terms of its operation and impact. Box 7.2 presents a further illustration of such a scheme, this time operated within the context of a specific management development programme.

BOX 7.2

AN EXAMPLE OF 360° FEEDBACK USED IN THE CONTEXT OF MANAGEMENT DEVELOPMENT

This was an application of 360° as part of a career-review workshop run for middle managers in a public-sector organisation that deals with financial strategy and regulation. A key element of the workshop was the input to participants provided by psychometric test data and colleague feedback, and how this could help inform their thinking about future career development. The 360° questionnaire covered seven competencies and consisted of 41 items rated from (6) extremely effective to (1) very ineffective. The participants were given the questionnaires to distribute to their respondents 3–4 weeks before the event, and when completed they were returned directly to external consultants who compiled a report for each manager. On the afternoon of the first day of the workshop, a consultant led the group through a session on psychometric tests (their pros and cons, and how they should be interpreted), before distributing to each participant confidential details of their scores on the personality and cognitive tests taken pre-workshop. After they had looked at these and had a chance to raise general questions, the session moved on to look at 360° feedback, and how it should be interpreted. The participants were then given their feedback reports and dispersed to read through them individually. The final session of the day was given to talking through general issues and questions arising from the feedback, and how it might relate to the psychometric data.

Before the second stage of the workshop process, which was a week later, each participant – having had some time to consider the test data and the feedback – had an individual session with a consultant to discuss the implications and possible development steps. After this, they attended the final group elements of the workshop.

One feature of this organisation's use of 360° feedback was the care they were willing to go to in checking that the questionnaire used did what it was supposed to; in other words, they carried out an analysis to see:

- whether raters were using the full range of the rating scale;
- whether different rater groups showed any specific biases;
- whether the items related to each competency were correlated with each other rather than with items relating to other competencies;
- whether there were any items to which respondents found difficulty in replying.

In light of this, they were able to do some fine-tuning of the questionnaire. Particular strengths of the approach taken to using 360° here were the way it was integrated with psychometric data to give a broader picture, and the extent to which support and assistance were provided to participants in helping them understand the information and its implications, and in formulating development plans accordingly.

Why has 360° feedback caught on?

Having briefly described and illustrated the kind of process involved, it is worth asking why it has become so widely adopted, and why diverse organisations have seen it as a worthwhile activity. The reasons they usually offer revolve around:

- *Empowerment.* Feedback gives subordinates a 'voice' in how they are managed, peers a voice in how this person relates to them as a member of the team and customers a voice in how they are dealt with. As such, 360° feedback is an empowering mechanism that gives people an input and a degree of control they might not otherwise have.

- *More rounded assessment.* Traditional approaches to appraisal and assessment are top-down and inevitably limited in perspective. The use of multi-source feedback is inherently fairer and gives a more rounded and balanced perspective on the individual. This does *not* necessarily mean a more objective one, though, as we shall see.
- *Enhances awareness of competencies.* Many organisations have spent a fortune on developing competency frameworks, but the problem then is getting people to understand what they mean and to use them as the performance language of the company. Basing the 360° questionnaire on the competencies and their descriptors can help raise awareness of them and make staff more familiar with the wording and concepts used.
- *Powerful learning potential.* This really is at the heart of most applications of feedback – the impact it can have and the potential for using this to generate behavioural change. Feedback is hard to get on a day-to-day basis, and the higher in an organisation one goes, the more this is true. So 360° assessment may represent the first real feedback an individual has received in a long while, and coming from all his or her colleagues, it is hard to ignore.
- *Improved self-awareness – and performance.* One of the explicitly stated aims of 360° feedback is to increase levels of self-awareness, on the grounds that holding a view of oneself that is sharply different from the way other people see you is likely to be detrimental to performance. So, the notion is that 360° feedback provides a chance to compare self-assessment against the perceptions of others, and to gauge the 'gap'. Over successive feedback episodes, the notion is that people become more realistic in their self-perceptions, and hence the gap between their assessments and the assessments made of them by others becomes smaller. As will be seen below, the research evidence supports the notion that greater self-awareness *is* associated with better performance.

THE BURNING ISSUE – APPRAISAL OR DEVELOPMENT?

While initially most applications of 360° feedback were set in a developmental context, later there was a marked shift towards using it as a direct or indirect input to appraisal. Appraisal and development are not mutually exclusive, of course, but which of these purposes gets the greater emphasis in a multi-source feedback scheme has a bearing on a number of important decisions as to how it is operated:

- *Is it to be mandatory or optional?* If it is an aspect of the appraisal process, it is more likely to be mandatory: you can hardly have a number of people opting out of part of the appraisal. Actually, both practices can be found in the same organisation; e.g. a large company in the telecommunications field had it as mandatory for top management layers and optional for middle management (where they reported around 60 per cent take-up).

- *Is it to be done annually?* If it is part of appraisal, then presumably it will be an annual event, with the implications this has for the resources needed to administer it. But as a development event, it could reasonably be done on a more intermittent basis, or even as a one-off.
- *Who decides who is to contribute to the assessment process?* As we have noted, the focal manager often chooses his or her own assessors – in developmental schemes. But is this acceptable in an appraisal context? There may be some dangers here. Allowing people to choose who makes an input to their appraisal process can offer an opportunity for the more Machiavellian-inclined to bias the process by arranging a reciprocal process of back-slapping. Whether this actually happens, at least in any significant proportion of cases, is not known.
- *Who is responsible for follow-up action?* In development, the focal manager often works with an HR manager or consultant to develop an action plan, or is left to work it out by him/herself. But in the context of appraisal, the individual's boss is more likely to be involved.
- *If it is to be part of an appraisal process, is it to be linked to rewards?* In a minority of UK organisations, this link has existed for some while (Handy *et al.*, 1996). It has also been related to pay in some US companies (e.g. FedEx) and their UK operations for some years.

360° feedback and appraisal: the pros and cons

Some HR practitioners and management writers have expressed concern about having 360° feedback as an input to appraisal, with the attendant possibility of a link with pay, so it may be worth running through the arguments for and against. Before doing that, though, it may also be worth reminding ourselves of some of the reasons why top-down appraisal schemes have failed so often in the past:

- They are perceived to be unfair by appraisees, in part because they reflect the limited perspective of one person (the boss).
- They have been found to be poor assessment devices: appraisal ratings predict little and are subject to many distortions (Murphy, 2008).
- Appraisals seem too often to result in demotivation and defensiveness, with the result that they are avoided by both parties (Latham *et al.*, 2005; Iqbal *et al.*, 2014).

On the face of it, 360° feedback seems to offer a way round some of these problems. So let us look first at the case for making it part of the appraisal process. The arguments go like this:

- Team work and managing staff are vital aspects of most managerial and professional jobs. If this is the case, then should managers/professionals not be assessed by those people who are in the best position to comment – namely, peers and subordinates–and should that assessment not be part of the appraisal of performance?
- Much is said (see previous section) about 'empowering' employees. By putting subordinates' feedback into the appraisal process, one is indeed empowering them: they are able to exert some influence over how they are managed and treated.
- Making 360° feedback part of appraisal overcomes the problem of potential bias in an appraisal that rests on one person's assessment. In theory, multiple levels and sources of appraisal data should lead to a more objective, well-rounded picture of the individual's contribution, strengths and development needs. It should consequently promote higher levels of trust in the fairness of the process. Thus, assessments from a wide range of colleagues and the decisions made on the basis of them may be legally – and possibly ethically – more defensible.
- Finally, if 360° feedback is all it claims to be, why should it not be included in appraisal? Doing so is a useful way of sending a message to people that this process, and what it reflects, is something that the organisation takes seriously.

Well, this all sounds quite convincing, but what about the other side of the argument? Here are the reasons offered for keeping 360° feedback as purely a development tool:

- Once you put it into the appraisal system, it will undermine the trust of those giving the ratings, which is necessary for the whole thing to work. The result will be poorer quality of information from subordinates in particular, and probably peers too. There is some research evidence to back this up: peer ratings given as an input to appraisal tend to be less reliable, less valid and more lenient than when they are given for developmental purposes (Pollack and Pollack, 1996); and subordinate ratings have been found to be of lower quality when used for appraisal purposes (Greguras et al., 2003). There are some methodological limitations on the studies in this area which makes it hard to draw firm conclusions (Jhun et al., 2012), but there does seem to be an overall trend for 360° feedback to be perceived as leading to more constructive behaviour change when it is being used for developmental rather than administrative purposes (Smither *et al.*, 2005).

- Associated with this, focal managers will become more defensive and less ready to accept the feedback because of the potentially damaging consequences for them; its potential to generate constructive development activity will be reduced.
- It could lead to political game-playing. You might get subordinates asking for rises, changes in duties, etc. just prior to the time they and their manager know that they are going to be asked to contribute their assessments. Managers might be tempted to court popularity.
- To run the system on an annual basis is time-consuming and costly – not least because everyone is involved. So, if you are a line manager, you may complete feedback questionnaires on four subordinates, on three peers and (as upward feedback) to two bosses, not to mention your own self-assessment – a total of ten questionnaires, and it could easily be more! Imagine more or less everyone in the organisation doing this simultaneously; no wonder some people might suffer 'rating fatigue'.
- Are the accuracy and quality of the assessment ratings provided in 360° feedback *really* better than what tends to come out of a traditional appraisal system? Or are we just swapping one set of biased perceptions for a whole raft of them, which – far from arriving at some objective truth – simply obscure the picture? For example, we know that the extent to which appraisers personally like appraisees influences their assessment of them (Lefkowitz, 2000) – is the same true for peers and subordinates giving ratings in a 360° exercise? Unfortunately, the answer seems to be yes (Antonioni and Park, 2001; van Hooft *et al.*, 2006). Indeed, Bailey and Fletcher (2002a) found that there was even an effect in the opposite direction – the quality of focal managers' relationships with feedback givers influences the former's perceptions of the credibility of the feedback being offered. There is also evidence that 360° assessments are no more immune to ethnic bias than are other forms of appraisal (Alimo-Metcalfe and Alban-Metcalfe, 2003).

Now the whole question looks a bit less straightforward, doesn't it?

In a way, the arguments matter little, because the fact is that many organisations do incorporate 360° feedback in appraisal, and more probably will do so. Perhaps the most important thing is at least to consider the issues flagged above and to monitor how the system operates in the appraisal context. As will be seen below, there is certainly cause for concern about the accuracy and quality of the ratings provided, although fortunately this does seem to be open to remedial action. It is the link with rewards, though, that should give rise to the greatest hesitation.

The debate here is really no different from that in relation to appraisal in general. Since the mid-1960s at least, the research literature has been pretty consistent in suggesting that direct pay links do little for the quality and effectiveness of appraisal; reward issues get in the way of constructive discussion of development needs. There is no reason to believe that this will not happen to some extent if there is a pay link to 360° feedback. Some organisations say that this does not happen in their experience – but you need to look rather carefully at how thorough the 360° systems they operate actually are, and precisely what the pay link is. Obviously, if the relationship with pay is very indirect, it may exert little influence. Quite apart from the reactions of staff to links with pay, though, is the justification for linking with pay. This rests on the assumption that 360° ratings are accurate and psychometrically sound, which, as we shall now see, may not always be justified.

THE QUALITY OF 360° FEEDBACK

Concerns about the quality of conventional appraisal ratings can be found at various points in this book and in the research literature (e.g. Kluger and DeNisi, 1996). Unfortunately, many of the same problems seem to arise with 360° feedback, as is exemplified by a study in a multinational oil company (Fletcher *et al.*, 1998). In this case, the company (Shell) had wisely introduced its scheme (which was designed for them by an external consultant) on a pilot basis in just one division, and then asked independent academics (occupational psychologists) to evaluate it. The scheme looked like a lot of others, with 80 performance descriptors rated by peers, subordinates and clients nominated by the focal manager, as well as by the immediate boss and the individual concerned. The performance descriptors were meant to relate to three broad competencies that the company used. When the ratings from this system and other data were analysed, it was found that:

- the behavioural descriptors did not correspond to the competencies they were meant to correspond to;
- they were so intercorrelated that, in effect, most of them were redundant and all that was being measured was an overall dimension of 'good – bad';
- the ratings did not show a relationship with any other criterion measure of performance used in the company;
- there seemed to be systematic biases that affected specific groups of raters.

The inescapable conclusion from this analysis of the pilot scheme was that any development plan arising out of the feedback process could be seriously misguided. If such ratings had been fed into an appraisal process, and possibly been linked to reward decisions, the basis for the assessment and the equity of those reward decisions would have been called into question. All is not doom and gloom, however. On the basis of the analysis, the independent academic consultants were able to redesign the scheme, which, among other things, involved cutting the rating form to half its original length and rewording a number of items. When the revised scheme was piloted and evaluated, it showed vastly superior psychometric qualities compared with the original; the behavioural descriptors lined up with the competencies as they were supposed to and the ratings correlated with the external criterion measure of performance. The company's careful approach to 360° feedback was thus justified. Instead of launching a system across the company on the basis of blind faith and a superficial appearance of relevance, they had taken it one stage at a time and looked critically at what they were doing. They ended up with something that was less time-consuming and much more effective than what they started out with; indeed, what they started out with was not effective at all.

What this example suggests is that 360° feedback systems are rather like psychometric tests. Their value is difficult to assess on the basis of appearance alone; 'face validity' is not a guarantee that they are actually doing what they claim to be doing. Also, like tests, they may have a powerful impact on the recipient of the feedback, and could lead to important job and career consequences for those assessed. If we take this analogy further, then it seems reasonable to advocate that 360° feedback systems should be subject to the same kind of design process and monitoring that one would associate with properly developed psychometric instruments. They should be able to demonstrate that the assessments they offer are acceptable in terms of their psychometric properties; that they do reflect the dimensions or competencies they claim to; that they can show some relationship with other measures of performance and so on. At present, our suspicion is that very few UK 360° feedback systems meet such a specification, or at least they are unable to produce any evidence to that effect. In the longer term, if they become part of the appraisal process without following this path, it seems quite possible that they will face the same kinds of legal challenges that tests have encountered – and deservedly so.

EFFECTIVENESS: WHAT THE RESEARCH SAYS

If we want to evaluate this kind of feedback process, what criteria might we use? The first issue is one we have already touched on above – does the questionnaire measure what it claims to, or to put it another way, is it valid? The way to check this is to see how ratings given as part of 360° feedback correlate with other, independent, measures of performance. There is certainly some supporting evidence here. Conway *et al.* (2001) report a meta-analysis showing that peer and subordinate ratings account for significant and unique variance in objective performance measures (profit, productivity, etc.). Erikson and Allen (2003) found that store managers' multi-source ratings correlated with store revenues, sales and profit margins. There are some less positive findings in terms of correlating with simulation exercises or tests (van Hooft *et al.*, 2006), but these are in a sense less relevant criteria. Various studies (Beehr *et al.*, 2001; Ostroff *et al.*, 2004; Smither and Walker, 2004) have found relationships between feedback ratings and performance appraisal ratings. There have also been studies that did *not* find correlations with appraisal ratings (e.g. Brett and Atwater, 2001), though they are in a clear minority. But appraisal ratings are perhaps less convincing as 'proof' of the validity of 360° feedback, as there is always the possibility of some contamination (that is, the feedback may have influenced the appraisal assessment). Also, there would seem to be little point in having 360° feedback if what came out of it correlated highly with appraisal ratings – the whole point is to capture the viewpoints of different groups on the expectation that they *will* differ in some respects.

So, there is plenty of support for the potential validity of 360° feedback ratings if the questionnaire is constructed properly in the first place. But quite apart from whether these systems are accurate, in the sense of measuring what they say they do, what do they actually *achieve* – do they lead to an improvement in performance? Are they effective in *developing* focal managers? Certainly, many managers receiving this kind of feedback feel that it is potent, and they seem to have a broadly positive attitude to it (Fletcher and Baldry, 1999), but does that mean they respond constructively and modify their behaviour and style? In the UK, Tyson and Ward (2004) found that senior managers significantly improved on competency ratings after such feedback. Dai *et al.* (2010) in an unusually thorough and well-controlled study demonstrated that such feedback led to significant improvement in targeted competencies. Perhaps slightly less direct evidence comes from a study by Atwater and Brett (2006), who found that after managers had been through a 360° process, their staff showed more positive attitudes and a higher level of engagement. Pulling together the evidence available at that time, Smither *et al.* (2005) did a meta-analysis of 24 studies that had examined changes in 360° feedback episodes over successive applications. This was a large sample, consisting of up to 7,000 managers, and some of the studies covered incorporated control groups in their design. Overall, they found that focal managers' ratings from all feedback-giver groups tend to improve over successive feedback episodes, though not by a huge amount, and there is also quite a lot of variability in how much change is observed. Interestingly (as noted earlier), they also found that where feedback was used for development, it resulted in greater behavioural change than when it was used as an input to appraisal. While this may support those who feel that 360° feedback should not be part of the appraisal process, it could also be interpreted in quite another way – perhaps those giving feedback for appraisal were more conservative and realistic in assessing the extent to which the focal managers' performance had improved.

One other more indirect point should be made on the research. It was noted earlier that an aim of feedback is to make the recipient more self-aware, with the underlying assumption that having a wide disparity between one's self-perceptions and how others see you is probably unhelpful in performance terms. The research supports this: there are a number of studies showing that people who are self-aware (i.e. their self-assessment is broadly in line with how others see them) are also assessed more highly on independent measures of performance (Fletcher, 1997; Atwater *et al.*, 2005).

Asking a more complicated question

In terms of evidence, it looks promising, if somewhat mixed (Fletcher, 2015). The extent to which people change their behaviour following feedback is, as noted above, neither always great nor completely consistent. Instead of asking the very broad question as to whether 360° feedback is effective, we should probably be asking a rather more complex and refined question – more like, what kind of feedback, delivered in what manner, from what source, given to what kind of managers will bring about what specified improvements? There seem to be a number of factors that impact on the effectiveness of the process; here are just some of them:

1. *What people do with the feedback.* London and Smither (1995) followed up 252 managers over a five-year period and found that those who discussed the feedback with those who had provided it showed significantly more improvement in ratings than those who did not. Somewhat similarly, managers who work with a coach to review feedback and set development goals show more improvement than those who do not (Smither *et al.*, 2003). Tyson and Ward (2004) confirm the importance of building in coaching follow-up to feedback.

2. *Initial level of performance of the focal manager.* Some studies (e.g. Walker and Smither, 1999) have found that managers who initially received less favourable ratings put more effort into subsequent

development activity than those whose ratings were higher – presumably because there was more need for them to do so. Bailey and Fletcher (2002b) found that, over time, feedback led to a perception of increased competence and lowered development needs. Of course, much depends on the nature of the organisation and what is made available for following up the development implications of the feedback – there is no point generating development recommendations if there are no resources and time provided to act on them.

3. *The credibility of the feedback source.* If we look at the feedback literature in general (Kluger and DeNisi, 1996; London and Mone, 2015), we find that over and over again, the credibility of the source – the degree to which those receiving the feedback have trust in that source – comes through as being a very important factor in acceptance of the feedback. Is that true for 360° systems too? In which case, do some sources of feedback have more impact than others? Bailey and Fletcher (2002a) conducted a study in public- and private-sector organisations, and found that the most accurate feedback was perceived as coming from people who report directly to the manager, and that the extent to which it was seen as accurate (or credible) was influenced by the amount of contact those people had with the focal manager and the quality of relationship between the two of them. However, feedback from the boss was seen as the most important, even if it was not accurate! Perhaps there is good reason for this – if, in your eyes, your boss has the wrong idea about your performance (and this is not likely to be a case of you worrying that he or she thinks you are too good), then it is all the more important to know so that you can do something about it. Rather ironically, then, despite 360° feedback being used to give a more rounded and fairer assessment than the boss alone can provide, the boss still remains the most important input to it – power counts for more than accuracy or credibility! A few organisations, concerned that feedback from the boss might 'swamp' the feedback messages from other raters, have decided to leave the boss out of the 360° process altogether (which technically makes it 270° feedback!).

4. *The gender and cultural background of the focal manager.* There is some reason to believe that gender differences will be found in the operation of multi-source, multi-level feedback systems. Typically, the self-ratings of female managers are found to be closer to the ratings made of them by their colleagues than is the case for male managers; the latter tend consistently to overrate themselves compared with how they are seen by others (Fletcher, 1999). This needs to be taken account of in the interpretation of the feedback ratings; it should not be assumed that this lower level of agreement in the case of male managers implies less

accuracy or validity of the ratings made of them. The more realistic interpretation is that quite a few male managers are not quite as self-critical as they should be!

The cultural background of those giving and receiving feedback is likely to be significant. There are well-recognised differences among cultures in attitudes to communication; some cultural groups may be much more reticent about giving frank feedback, especially to superiors; and the attitude to receiving it is also likely to reflect this – this will be dealt with in more detail in Chapter 9, pages 187–9. There are many other factors that could be listed here – including a whole host of individual differences – such as personality (e.g. Bernardin *et al.*, 2009; Randall and Sharples, 2012), self-efficacy (Bailey and Austin, 2006) or other aspects of self-evaluation (Bono and Colbert, 2005) which are perhaps of more academic than practical interest. Keeping that emphasis on the practical, the next part of this chapter is devoted to outlining what we can now recognise as 'best practice' in the field.

BEST PRACTICE IN DEVELOPING AND IMPLEMENTING 360° FEEDBACK

Some years ago, the first author (Fletcher) wrote an article on 360° feedback in an HR jourrnal, only for a consultant to write in to the letters page a couple of weeks later saying it was "not rocket science" and line managers could be trusted to be given the tool and allowed to run with it themselves. He was, of course, quite right – it is not rocket science. However, as we saw above, it is all too easy to design a 360° questionnaire that does not measure what it claims to. And it is also quite possible to do a degree of damage to individuals by not handling feedback carefully. Indeed, some people working in this field use the acronym SARAH to describe the pattern of reaction some focal managers go through on receiving their feedback:

Shock
Anger
Rejection
Acceptance
Help!

The aim is to get the feedback recipient to the point of Acceptance, because some never get past the first two or three stages, and can suffer accordingly. Those who get angry and reject the feedback are storing up trouble for themselves and others, and need some help to move on. And the research (e.g. Brett and Atwater, 2001) is clear in telling us that less positive feedback does not magically become more acceptable when it comes from sources other than the boss. So managing the feedback at the individual level is not so straightforward either. Fortunately, there is now sufficient experience with and research on 360° feedback to provide organisations with guidelines to follow in this domain. What follows, then, is a summary of the wisdom on best practice.

Planning to introduce a 360° programme

The culture of an organisation and the timing have to be right for the introduction of these feedback processes. The adoption of a full 360° approach should ideally stem from a steady evolution in appraisal and development practices. It is unlikely that a 360° scheme would be accepted where there has been little or no history of appraisal of any kind: it would represent too radical a step. Even where there is an ample history of appraisal, one of the main problems is that many potential participants who are new to such feedback feel very apprehensive about it in advance. The managers being assessed frequently voice concerns that they feel their position may be undermined, and that subordinates and even peers can use the opportunity to exercise any grudges they hold. Subordinates, on the other hand, may fear some retaliatory punitive action by the managers if they are critical of them.

If high levels of mutual trust exist, such problems may not arise, but it seems that mutual trust is more the exception than the rule. Thus, as we have seen, most feedback schemes promise anonymity for the raters. But at least as important as this is the need to consult participants in the scheme (feedback contributors as well as focal managers) about it in advance – in terms of how the scheme will be structured and operated, aspects of its content, who will have access to the feedback reports and so on. Only by following that kind of approach are fears likely to be allayed and enough trust built up to let the scheme flourish.

Developing the questionnaire

The main points to follow here are:

- *Focus as far as possible on rating relevant (see the earlier discussion of the different ways of describing performance in Chapter 3)* **observable** *behaviours*. It is no use asking subordinates to comment on the strategic thinking capacity of their boss – first, it is mainly cognitive in nature and little of it may be visible in terms of overt behaviour; second, such of it as may be expressed behaviourally may not be manifested to more junior staff anyway. Make sure that respondent groups are asked to comment on what they are likely to be able to offer a judgement on; namely, behavioural outputs they are in a position to observe and are capable of assessing.

- *Do not ask those giving feedback to rate too many competencies – concentrate on the key competencies for the feedback purpose.* Some feedback questionnaires are insufferably long. It might be OK to ask 100+ questions on a one-off basis, but if you are going to ask people to complete such questionnaires for a number of colleagues, and maybe more than once for each of them, then 'ratings fatigue' will set in fast! It is usually best to focus on just a few key competencies, and these are probably mostly going to be in the interpersonal domain, because that is what 360° feedback is especially good at accessing. It is probably best to aim for a maximum of around 40 questions: so, at 5–7 questions per competency, that means no more than 6–7 competencies.
- *Check that the questions do indeed relate to the competencies.* This goes back to the issues highlighted in relation to the oil company example mentioned earlier in this chapter (page 148). At its most basic, it means checking to see if there is more correlation between the answers to the questions within a single competency than there is between them and questions relating to other competencies. For further details, see Fletcher *et al.* (1998). If this kind of analysis is beyond the expertise of anyone in your organisation, an external consultant should be able to carry it out, or (more cheaply) a student on an MSc course in Occupational/ Organisational Psychology might do it for their MSc dissertation research.
- *Ensure that the rating scale allows for sufficient range of response.* The first author (Fletcher) recalls seeing a financial services company 360° system that was great in most respects, except that its output failed to identify anyone as having any development needs! The reason for this was the wording of the rating scale for each item – it basically left the feedback giver the choice of saying that this person was either really good in terms of the specific behaviour, or poor. Most people when responding to these questionnaires do not want to sound too critical or undermining in their comments, and for the focal managers, it is easier to take feedback that says they are generally doing OK, but there are some things to work on. The rating scale, then, has to be worded to make it possible for some weaknesses to be conveyed in such a way that it is acceptable to both parties. This may mean having a positively skewed rating scale; that is, one that offers more positive rating points than negative ones. This has been found to encourage raters to spread their ratings (Jones and Fletcher, 2002, 2004). As indicated earlier (page 139), one form of wording frequently adopted presents the questions in terms of how often the focal manager has demonstrated the behaviour or how typical it is of them (Not at all/To a small extent/To some extent/To an adequate extent/To a large

extent/To a very large extent). An alternative is to frame the rating in terms of levels of effectiveness, and to add the development implications (e.g. Reasonably Effective: Some development need indicated). Apart from the wording of the rating scale, it is also important to allow respondents the opportunity to say either that they have not had the chance to observe the behaviour or that they feel it is not relevant to the role.

• *Include scope for qualitative comments as well as ratings.* There are some feedback systems that consist *only* of free-written comments, and some (more) that have only quantitative ratings. Most, however, are based on ratings with some provision for additional written comments at the end, perhaps in relation to each competency covered by the questionnaire. As noted earlier, the inclusion of this qualitative feedback can flesh out the ratings and help explain some of them more fully. There is a risk, though – allowing written comments is opening Pandora's box – you do not know what you will get. The danger is that people can use the opportunity to say things that are irrelevant, tactless or hurtful, or just not constructive. This seldom happens, but it is a possibility. In the context of performance appraisal reports, rather than 360° output, Wilson (2010: 1925) found that appraisers made "overwhelmingly positive comments" and that there was a lack of consistency between narrative comments and the actual ratings made – which suggests that the leniency effects one sees with the performance markings recorded on appraisal forms may be replicated in the form of written comments also. While there is some limited evidence of narrative comments adding nothing positive to post-feedback development in a medical setting (Vivekanandra-Schmidt *et al.*, 2013), the broad view of the research (Atwater and Brett, 2006) suggests that combining rating-based and textual feedback is the most effective approach.

Implementation

The first thing to say is – do not try to roll it out across the organisation in one go. 'Right first time' is not something that works terribly well with 360° feedback. If at all possible, like the oil company case described in this chapter on page 148, do a pilot run in one division first, and monitor that carefully. If all goes well, much of what needs to be done is reasonably straightforward. Those giving feedback need to be told what the timescales are; just sending out questionnaires and asking for them to be returned soon is a recipe for non-completion. Usually, respondents should be asked to return them within a week. Who these people are, how many of them to include, and how they are to be approached are things to be decided. Sample size (the number of raters) is an issue on two counts. First, the assessment has to be based on a big enough sample to ensure that it is valid; if it is small, there is a danger that one individual rater's experiences or bias will have a major impact on the average rating. Second, the sample of raters has to be big enough that individual sources cannot be identified; a minimum of four or five subordinates is usually suggested from this point of view. The implications for the time and administrative effort involved are clear.

The number and identity of the raters may have been agreed at the consultation stage. Often, the focal manager decides whom to ask for feedback, but where the exercise is linked to appraisal, the choice of respondents is generally determined by the focal manager and their boss together. Whoever is responsible, it is likely that they will appreciate or need guidance from HR on how many people to approach and in which categories (i.e. how many peers, subordinates, etc.). All those completing questionnaires have to be told how to return them (if this is not automatically done on a software-based system). Although, on the face of it, all this is simple enough, there will inevitably be queries and problems that arise, including those that stem from actually trying to complete the questionnaire, and in some organisations it has been found useful to establish a helpline when the exercise is started.

Report and follow-up action

Some 360° feedback reports, especially those generated by software packages, produce reams of paper – endless charts, tables and text, to the extent that the recipient may feel rather overwhelmed by the sheer volume. It is important for the report of the feedback received to be sufficient to give a clear picture, but not in such detail that the focal manager will have difficulty seeing the wood for the trees. Most such reports include the following information:

1. bar charts showing the average rating given on each competency by each group of raters (peers, boss, etc.) as well as the self-rating;
2. where the questionnaire is reasonably short, a similar analysis to that above, but this time in relation to the individual behavioural items which make up each competency. And arising from this, identification of specific behaviours that have been rated as less effective and/or requiring development action;
3. a highlighting of the highest-rated competencies, and the lowest-rated;
4. if this is not the first feedback episode, a comparison of ratings this time with the previous occasion and any marked changes that emerge;
5. a listing of free-written comments relating to each competency (should the system have allowed for these);
6. analysis of behaviours that feedback givers have felt they could not make a rating of for one reason or another.

The extent to which the second of these is important varies – if it is a long questionnaire, it can lead to a lot of graphs. But the individual items that attract low ratings do need to be flagged up. The use of average ratings is understandable and useful, but it is unfortunately not enough on its own. This is because one can have an average subordinate rating of 5 on a scale that goes from 1 (low) to 7 (high) – which sounds fine in itself – but it can be arrived at by having three subordinates rating you as 3 and another three rating you as 7, which is rather less fine. This is not uncommon – it may arise from bias (see Chapter 4, Box 4.3), with a manager treating subordinates differently, having an 'out' group and an 'in' group, or it can arise from different subordinates seeing different aspects and samples of their boss's behaviour. Whatever the reason, it is important to know the range and spread of the ratings given, not just the averages.

Feedback reports vary also in the extent to which they provide any interpretation or commentary on the ratings. Some will provide a 'gap' analysis, focusing on the degree of match, or mismatch, between self-ratings and ratings from others. This is a crude but useful measure of self-awareness. Where a report is being sent directly to the focal manager – especially if it is to be left to the individual to decide whether to share the content with anyone else – it is essential that some help is given in understanding the feedback and putting it in a context. Without this, the focal manager might have some difficulty in assessing the meaning of what is being conveyed – is it the results of an opinion survey, is it like a psychological test, is it common for subordinates to see you differently from the way your peers do, and if they do, what does that mean? These and many other questions can come to mind when reading the output from 360° feedback, and focal managers need guidance to use it.

The most important advice, though, is to encourage the recipients of the feedback to share it with someone else, and if at all possible, build this into the system from the outset. The evidence is clear and consistent (Fletcher, 2015) that sharing and discussing feedback lead to more positive outcomes. The discussion might be with a consultant, someone from HR or even with a peer. The purpose of discussion is not just to clarify and understand what has been said, but also to decide what action is appropriate. Again, most focal managers (and their bosses, come to that) need some help in thinking through the kinds of development activities that might be appropriate and available, and then putting them together in the form of a development plan. Some software-based systems automatically raise a list of potential development steps in relation to each competency that the 360° questionnaire has covered. It follows on from this that for any 360° system to be useful, the resources have to be in place to facilitate the development action that arises out of it. Tyson and Ward (2004) confirm the value of coaching being integrated into the feedback process. The actual approach taken to using 360° feedback in coaching is beyond the scope of this book and is a topic that itself needs more attention, but the reader is referred to McDowall and Kurtz (2008) and Nowack (2009) as useful sources.

Although there is much written on it (see London and Mone, 2015), one issue that is seldom if ever addressed in a practical context is the extent to which the feedback given is positive or negative in overall tone, and the extent to which it deviates from the individual's own self-view; that is, the extent of the 'gap' in the gap analysis mentioned above. It has long been known that most people have a limited tolerance for criticism in a conventional top-down appraisal, and as was pointed out at the beginning of this chapter, the same is probably true in relation to 360° feedback. If a feedback report shows that an individual's self-view is substantially more positive than the feedback given, then it would be wise to have some mechanism for identifying this at an early stage – preferably before the individual has been given the feedback – so that some kind of support strategy can be put in place. This might either be in the form of arranging for a facilitator to be present when the report is given, or in terms of the text provided around the feedback.

Using norms

Where the sample of focal managers and feedback givers is large enough, it is possible to develop norms – in other words, to show the average rating achieved on any competency (broken down by feedback group if desired) and, in some cases, some measure of the distribution of ratings; for example, in terms of standard deviation. This kind of normative data can be useful to the individual, to see how their ratings compared with colleagues or with equivalent groups within the organisation. It can also be valuable for an organisation if a consultancy company providing the 360° system can show the distribution of ratings on some or all of the questionnaire items that has been accumulated from applications in other, similar organisations – this can afford a degree of benchmarking, so that a company can see how their focal managers as a group fare against similar groups elsewhere. Here the dividing line between psychometrics and 360° feedback can become a little blurred.

As indicated, normative data can be very informative. But to obtain them, the organisation may have to trade off the desirability of having a set of questionnaire items that are tailored to its culture and needs against the need to have some fairly generic set of items that have been used across a range of different companies. The other caveat is that many aspects of organisational context – including the background reasons for deploying 360° feedback and the way it was introduced – may vary from one company to another, and these could well impact on the pattern of feedback ratings that emerge in any one place. In which case, the whole point of using normative data to make comparisons is undermined.

Evaluation

A lot of time and effort can go into setting up and running a multi-source feedback system, and given the strong feelings and reactions it can generate amongst participants, it is wise to make evaluation a rather more urgent priority than it might be with some other HR processes. Some of the research evidence on the validity and effectiveness of 360° feedback has already been presented (pages 149–51), but in what follows, the focus is more on the *practical* guidance on what to look for and how to go about it. The criteria against which to evaluate 360° feedback break down into short-, medium- and long-term outcomes.

Short-term evaluation

Perhaps the most pressing thing is to get some quick feedback on the feedback, so to speak. It is vital to identify anything going wrong as early as possible. The kinds of information that need to be sought in the short term are as follows.

Is the system acceptable to the users?

In other words, how did those giving the feedback and those receiving it feel about the process, how it worked, what came out of it and so on? Getting initial reactions (e.g. from staff associations or focus groups via informal soundings or a short questionnaire) to these basic questions is worthwhile, because it may allow remedial action to be taken early, before the system has rolled out to other groups.

Does the system identify development needs?

The main purpose is to get feedback to encourage improvement where it is necessary – so are any potential areas for improvement identified for most people? There will obviously be some for whom little improvement is possible or necessary, but these should be very few. Do the majority of focal managers report that they got useful development directions from the exercise? Do the feedback ratings show sufficient range to indicate some areas needing development?

Has the feedback questionnaire functioned effectively and measured what it set out to measure?

This is a bit trickier, because it involves the kind of statistical analysis that was mentioned previously in this chapter in relation to the oil company example. See page 155 for suggestions on this.

Medium-term evaluation

This level of evaluation is unlikely to take place if 360° feedback is used as a one-off development exercise, but if it is applied more than once, it becomes very relevant. There are two aspects to it.

Do focal managers show an increase in self-awareness?

Given that increasing self-awareness is an oft-declared purpose of 360° feedback, this is something we might be very interested in. If the data from each application of 360° are kept, it is possible to see if the level of agreement between focal managers' self-ratings and the ratings of others has increased; that is, if they have become more 'realistic' in their perceptions of their competencies. While there are several quite sophisticated ways of computing this self–other rating gap measure (see Fletcher and Bailey, 2003), the simple subtraction of the self-rating from the ratings of each other group on each competency should be enough to show if there has been a shift. It will obviously also be of interest to see if the ratings of the focal manager have increased in favourability over time, as this might indicate perceived improvement.

Has there been development activity taken as a result of the feedback?

It is one thing to check, in short-term evaluation, if development needs have been identified, but quite another to see if they have been acted upon. After a reasonable amount of time has elapsed following the feedback, it should be possible to either ask the focal managers (or their bosses) what action was taken and/or to see what record of development activity relating to the feedback exists in the HR department.

Long-term evaluation

Few, if any, organisations do long-term evaluation, though fortunately there is some research into this, as described earlier (see Smither *et al.*, 2005; Dai *et al.*, 2010). The kind of outcomes that are longer-term in nature are as follows.

Do ratings of managers by others show a pattern of improvement over time, with successive feedback episodes, in relation to the areas that needed such improvement?

Are there any hard measures of performance that show improvement? These are notoriously difficult to come by, and even when they are available, so many other factors impact on performance that it may not be realistic to expect 360° feedback to show a direct effect on it.

Are there any signs of a culture change?

This is even more difficult, but since 360° feedback is a culture-change instrument, it is reasonable to ask whether after some applications of it there are signs of people becoming more comfortable with seeking, giving and accepting feedback. For example, do the focal managers show a greater likelihood of talking to the feedback givers directly about their views?

A recap on best practice

Best practice in multi-source feedback demands that attention be given to careful preparation of the ground for all parties before it is introduced, expertise in designing the questionnaire, staged implementation, and the provision of an appropriate report and follow-up support mechanisms for those receiving the feedback. There are other aspects of good practice that are not dealt with here – for example, in relation to using software in this field (Atchley *et al.*, 2001). It is to be hoped that the discussion above will be enough to demonstrate that such feedback processes are certainly not straightforward, and although there are potential benefits from applying multi-source assessment and feedback, failure to think it through carefully at the outset can lead to no positive outcomes being achieved, or worse still, some actual damage being done. In view of this, putting evaluation strategies in place is essential, and these may focus on the short-, medium- and long-term impact of feedback.

SOME TRENDS AND ISSUES IN MULTI-SOURCE FEEDBACK USE

Over time, and with greater familiarity, there have been some changes in the way multi-source feedback has been deployed. The main one – the shift to using it in appraisal – has already been mentioned. However, there are others. For example, there has been a shift towards applying it in a more focused way to particular groups or for more specific purposes. An example of this is the use of feedback as a diagnostic tool in team development, or as a team-building aid in itself. Also, it may be called for in relation to the development of an individual senior manager, whose coach may personally approach and interview a whole range of people who work with this manager. This usually provides very 'rich' information, though of course it usually does not present anything in normative form. The coach typically analyses the themes emerging and records verbatim (but usually anonymously) the comments made under each one.

There was almost too much demand for 360° feedback interventions in some organisations – HR was being bombarded with requests for bespoke questionnaires for specific teams, individuals, bits of the company and so on. Apart from the danger of multi-source feedback being seen as a panacea and applied rather blindly, this can place quite a strain on resources. Moreover, this enthusiastic embrace of the method can very occasionally lead to improper use – for example, a Health Authority accessing feedback information which had been collected under a 'development only' guise, and then using it in a disciplinary process against the individual concerned. Clearly, this is unethical.

Finally, there is the question of cultural differences between focal managers and feedback givers and the possible impact such diversity might have. However, that will be discussed in detail in Chapter 9.

IN SUMMARY

Over recent years, we have seen a shift in emphasis from 360° feedback as a development device to its use in appraisal. It can be used for both purposes, though if it is to be part of appraisal, it should be treated as just one input to the process, rather than taking centre stage. The enthusiasm and the speed with which such feedback was embraced is remarkable. Fortunately, as outlined above, there is a growing body of evidence suggesting that, if it is well designed and implemented, this kind of process can lead to changes in behaviour, increased competency levels and other desirable performance outcomes. However, the level of success achieved will depend on a wide range of variables that need to be taken account of. The concept of multi-source, multi-level feedback seems to suit the move towards the less hierarchical, more flexibly structured, and knowledge-based organisations of the future. But the parallels with psychometric testing are striking. Tests are often presented as easy to use, but actually they are only easy to use badly. And the merits of any one test are difficult to judge on superficial characteristics alone. The rush to use tests in the 1980s is similar to the wholesale adoption of 360° systems since the mid-1990s. In the case of tests, it led all too often to poor practice, the presentation of deficient instruments to the market, and – ultimately – to increasing legal challenges. There is every chance that 360° feedback systems will follow the same route if they are not introduced more carefully and examined more critically than is usually the case at present.

DISCUSSION POINTS AND QUESTIONS

7.1 Should we use 360° feedback as an input to appraisal, or employ it only as a development tool? What are the arguments and evidence you would use to argue either way?

7.2 How does the use of 360° feedback in your organisation match up to best practice – what are the strengths and weaknesses?

7.3 What factors are likely to determine whether 360° feedback will have a positive effect with any particular individual focal manager?

7.4 How would you evaluate 360° feedback – what do you feel are the most important things to look for, and how would you go about it?

KEY REFERENCES

Dai, G., De Meuse, K. and Peterson C. (2010) Impact of multi-source feedback on leadership competency development: A longitudinal field study. *Journal of Managerial Issues*, **22**(2), 197–219.

Fletcher, C. (1997) Self-awareness – a neglected attribute in selection and assessment. *International Journal of Selection and Assessment*, **5**(3), 183–187.

Fletcher, C. (2015) Using 360 degree feedback as a development tool. In K. Kraiger, J. Passmore, N. R. dos Santos and S. Malvezzi (Eds) *The Wiley Blackwell Handbook of the Psychology of Training, Development and Performance Improvement*. Chichester, UK: Wiley–Blackwell, pp. 486–502.

London, M. and Mone, E. M. (2015) Designing feedback to achieve performance improvement. In K. Kraiger, J. Passmore, N. R. dos Santos and S. Malvezzi (Eds) *The Wiley Blackwell Handbook of the Psychology of Training, Development and Performance Improvement*. Chichester, UK: Wiley–Blackwell, pp. 462–485.

Ostroff, C., Atwater, L. E. and Feinberg, B. J. (2004) Understanding self–other agreement: A look at rater and ratee characteristics, context and outcomes. *Personnel Psychology*, **57**(2), 333–376.

Smither, J. W., London, M. and Reilly, R. R. (2005) Does performance improve following multi-source feedback? A theoretical model, meta-analysis, and review of empirical findings. *Personnel Psychology*, **58**(1), 33–66.

Tyson, S. and Ward, P. (2004) The use of 360 degree feedback technique in the evaluation of management learning. *Management Learning*, **35**(2), 205–223

REFERENCES

Alimo-Metcalfe, B. and Alban-Metcalfe, J. (2003) It don't matter if you're Black or White: Not according to 360-feedback. *Proceedings of the British Psychological Society Annual Occupational Psychology Conference, Brighton, 8–10 January*. Leicester, UK: British Psychological Society, pp. 63–66.

Antonioni, D. and Park, H. (2001) The relationship between rater affect and three sources of 360 degree feedback ratings. *Journal of Management*, **27**(4), 479–495

Atchley, S., Coomber, J. and Goodge, P. (2001) Guidelines for using 360 degree software. *Selection and Development Review*, **17**, 7–9.

Atwater, L. and Brett, J. (2006) Feedback format: Does it influence managers' reactions to feedback? *Journal of Occupational and Organizational Psychology*, **79**(4), 517–532.

Atwater, L., Ostroff, C., Waldman, D., Robie, C. and Johnson, K. M. (2005) Self–other agreement: Comparing its relationship with performance in the US and Europe. *International Journal of Selection and Assessment*, **13**(1), 25–40.

Bailey, C. and Austin, M. (2006) 360 degree feedback and development outcomes: The role of feedback characteristics, self-efficacy, and importance of feedback dimensions to focal managers' current role. *International Journal of Selection and Assessment*, **14**(1), 51–66.

Bailey, C. and Fletcher, C. (2002a) When do other people's opinions matter? The credibility of feedback from co-workers. *Proceedings of the British Psychological Society Occupational Psychology Conference, Blackpool, January*. Leicester, UK: British Psychological Society, pp. 109–113.

Bailey, C. and Fletcher, C. (2002b) The impact of multiple source feedback on management development: Findings from a longitudinal study. *Journal of Organizational Behavior*, **23**(7), 853–867.

Beehr, T. A., Ivanitskaya, A. L., Hansen, C. P., Erofeev, D. and Gudanowski, D. M. (2001) Evaluation of 360 degree feedback ratings: Relationships with each other and with performance and selection predictors. *Journal of Organizational Behavior*, **22**, 775–788.

Bernardin, H., Tyler, C. and Villanova, P. (2009) Rating level and accuracy as a function of rater personality. *International Journal of Selection and Assessment*, **17**, 300–310.

Bono, J. E. and Colbert, A. E. (2005) Understanding responses to multi-source feedback: The role of core self-evaluations. *Personnel Psychology*, 58(1), 171–203.

Brett, J. F. and Atwater, L. E. (2001) 360 degree feedback: Accuracy, reactions and perception of usefulness. *Journal of Applied Psychology*, **86**(5), 930–942.

Brutus, S., Derayeh, M., Fletcher, C., Bailey, C., Velazquez, P., Shi, K., Simon, C. and Labath V. (2006) Multisource feedback systems: A six-country comparative analysis. *International Journal of Human Resource Management*, **17**, 1888–1906.

Carruthers, F. (2003) Nothing but the truth. *Australian Financial Review*, November 14, p. 78.

Clifford, C. L. and Bennett, H. (1997) Best practice in 360-degree feedback. *Selection and Development Review*, **13**(2), 6–9.

Conway, J. M., Lombardo, K. and Sanders, K. C. (2001) A meta-analysis of incremental validity and nomological networks for subordinate and peer ratings. *Human Performance*, **14**(4), 267–303.

Dai, G., De Meuse, K. and Peterson, C. (2010) Impact of multi-source feedback on leadership competency development: A longitudinal field study. *Journal of Managerial Issues*, **22**(2), 197–219.

Erikson, A. and Allen, T. (2003) Linking 360 degree feedback to business outcome measures. Paper presented at the 18ᵗʰ Society for Industrial and Organizational Psychology Conference, Orlando, Florida.

Fletcher, C. (1997) Self-awareness – a neglected attribute in selection and assessment. *International Journal of Selection and Assessment*, **5**(3), 183–187.

Fletcher, C. (1999) The implications of research on gender differences in self assessments and 360 degree appraisal. *Human Resource Management Journal*, **9**(1), 39–46.

Fletcher, C. (2015) Using 360 degree feedback as a development tool. In K. Kraiger, J. Passmore, N. R. dos Santos and S. Malvezzi (Eds) *The Wiley Blackwell Handbook of the Psychology of Training, Development and Performance Improvement*. Chichester, UK: Wiley–Blackwell, pp. 486–502.

Fletcher, C. and Bailey, C. (2003) Assessing self awareness: Some issues and methods. *Journal of Managerial Psychology*, **18**(5), 395–404.

Fletcher, C. and Baldry, C. (1999) Multi-source feedback systems: A research perspective. In C. L. Cooper and I. T. Robertson (Eds) *International Review of Industrial and Organizational Psychology. Vol. 14*. New York and London: Wiley, pp. 149–194.

Fletcher, C., Baldry, C. and Cunningham-Snell, N. (1998) The psychometric properties of 360 degree feedback: An empirical study and a cautionary tale. *International Journal of Selection and Assessment*, **6**(1), 19–34.

Greguras, G. J., Robie, C., Schleicher, D. J. and Goff, M. (2003) A field study of the effects of rating purpose on the quality of multisource ratings. *Personnel Psychology*, **56**, 1–21.

Handy, L., Devine, M. and Heath, L. (1996) *Feedback: Unguided Missile or Powerful Weapon?* Berkhamsted, UK: Ashridge Management Research Group.

Iqbal, M. Z., Akbar, S. and Budhwar, P. (2014) Effectiveness of performance appraisal: An integrated framework. *International Journal of Management Reviews*, **17**(4), 510–533.

Jhun, S., Bae, Z-T. and Rhee, S-Y. (2012) Performance change of managers in two different uses of upward feedback: A longitudinal study in Korea. *The International Journal of Human Resource Management*, **23**(20), 4246–4264.

Jones, L. and Fletcher, C. (2002) Self assessment in a selection situation: An evaluation of different measurement approaches. *Journal of Occupational and Organizational Psychology*, **75**(2), 145–161.

Jones, L. and Fletcher, C. (2004) The impact of measurement conditions on the validity of self-assessment in a selection setting. *European Journal of Work and Organizational Psychology*, **13**, 101–111.

Kluger, A. N. and DeNisi, A. (1996) The effects of feedback interventions on performance: A historical review, a meta-analysis, and a preliminary feedback intervention theory. *Psychological Bulletin*, **119**(2), 254–284.

Latham, G. P., Almost, J., Mann, S. and Moore, C. (2005) New developments in performance management. *Organizational Dynamics*, **34**(1), 77–87.

Lefkowitz, J. (2000) The role of interpersonal affective regard in supervisory performance ratings: A literature review and proposed causal model. *Journal of Occupational and Organizational Pyschology*, **73**(1), 67–85.

London, M. and Mone, E. M. (2015) Designing feedback to achieve performance improvement. In K. Kraiger, J. Passmore, N. R. dos Santos and S. Malvezzi (Eds) *The Wiley Blackwell Handbook of the Psychology of Training, Development and Performance Improvement*. Chichester, UK: Wiley–Blackwell, pp. 462–485.

London, M. and Smither, J. W. (1995) Can multi-source feedback change self awareness and behavior? Theory-based applications and directions for research. *Personnel Psychology*, **48**, 803–839.

McDowall, A. and Kurtz, R. (2008) Effective integration of 360 degree feedback into the coaching process. *The Coaching Psychologist*, **4**(1), 7–19.

Mercer (2013) *Global Performance Management Survey Report*. Mercer Consulting Group. www.mercer.com/content/dam/mercer/attachments/global/Talent/Assess-BrochurePerfMgmt.pdf (accessed 17 January 2016).

Murphy, K. R. (2008) Explaining the weak relationship between job performance and ratings of job performance. *Industrial and Organizational Psychology*, **1**(2), 148–160.

Nowack, K. M. (2009) Leveraging multirater feedback to facilitate successful behavioral change. *Consulting Psychology Journal: Practice and Research*, **61**(4), 280–297.

Ostroff, C., Atwater, L. E. and Feinberg, B. J. (2004) Understanding self–other agreement: A look at rater and ratee characteristics, context and outcomes. *Personnel Psychology*, **57**(2), 333–376.

Pollack, D. M. and Pollack, L. J. (1996) Using 360 degree feedback in performance appraisal. *Public Personnel Management*, 25(4), 507–528.

Randall, R. and Sharples, D. (2012) The impact of rater agreeableness and rating context on the evaluation of poor performance. *Journal of Occuptional and Organizational Psychology*, **85**(1), 42–59.

Smither, J. W. and Walker, A. G. (2004) Are the characteristics of narrative comments related to improvement in multi-rater feedback ratings over time? *Journal of Applied Psychology*, **89**(3), 575–581.

Smither, J. W., London, M., Flautt, R., Vargas, Y. and Kucine, I. (2003) Can working with an executive coach improve multisource feedback ratings over time? A quasi-experimental field study. *Personnel Psychology*, **56**(1), 23–44.

Smither, J. W., London, M. and Reilly, R. R. (2005) Does performance improve following multi-source feedback? A theoretical model, meta-analysis, and review of empirical findings. *Personnel Psychology*, **58**(1), 33–66.

Tyson, S. and Ward, P. (2004) The use of 360 degree feedback technique in the evaluation of management learning. *Management Learning*, **35**(2), 205–223.

van Hooft, E. A. J., van der Flier, H. and Minne, M. R. (2006) Construct validity of multi-source performance ratings: An examination of the relationship of self-, supervisor- and peer-ratings with cognitive and personality measures. *International Journal of Selection and Assessment*, **14**(1), 67–81.

Vivekanandra-Schmidt, P., Mackillop, L., Cressley, J. and Wade, W. (2013) Do assessor comments on a multisource feedback instrument provide learner-centered feedback? *Medical Education*, **47**(11), 1080–1088.

Walker, A. G. and Smither, J. W. (1999) A five-year study of upward feedback: What managers do with their results matters. *Personnel Psychology*, **52**(2), 393–423.

Wilson, K. Y. (2010) An analysis of bias in supervisor narrative comments in performance appraisal. *Human Relations*, **63**(12), 1903–1933.

APPRAISAL WITH PROFESSIONALS, AND ACROSS DIFFERENT SECTORS

8

The attitudes and characteristics of professional and scientific staff are often so different from those of administrative and managerial staff that they represent a special case in appraisal – to the extent that they warrant a separate chapter. Much of what will be said here will be in the context of the public sector. This is because there is generally a higher proportion of professional staff in healthcare settings, the teaching profession, higher education and (to a lesser extent) local government than in the majority of commercial organisations; they might be said to be more knowledge-based organisations (Simmons and Iles, 2001). Nonetheless, a fair amount of what is said about the appraisal of professional groups is applicable to their employment in the private sector also. But before addressing the general and specific issues associated with the appraisal of such staff, we will review the evidence on such differences as have been found in relation to performance appraisal across different sectors, and within sectors.

APPRAISAL WITHIN AND ACROSS PUBLIC AND PRIVATE SECTORS

Research evidence on this theme does not produce an especially coherent account, other than to observe that there is a lot of commonality of practice – perhaps even when there should not be. For example, a survey by Towers Watson (Charman *et al.*, 2014) noted the striking degree of similarity of approaches to PM in UK organisations despite the drivers behind PM being different across companies. An international survey (Mercer, 2013) also noted that many design elements and practices in this field were consistent across industries, though it did note some differences; for example, the retail sector was the highest in reporting a culture of candid dialogue, whereas this was lowest in educational organisations. In the context of 360° feedback specifically, Brutus *et al.* (1998) found leniency in ratings to be high in educational settings, while inter-rater agreement was highest in education and manufacturing organisations and lowest in government agencies.

If we turn to just a broad comparison between the public and private sectors, accepting for the moment that talking in terms of the whole public sector or the whole private sector is lumping together a wide range of fairly disparate organisations, is there any real reason for expecting appraisal to be different between them? It could be argued that the vagaries of government policy and the way it affects the public sector are probably no greater than those of the marketplace and the City and their effects on the private sector. Large parts of the private sector are providing services, just as the public sector is. The types of organisational structure found in the two sectors have become more similar too.

But there are some important distinctions to be drawn. To list some of the main ones:

- Assessing the output and effectiveness of public-sector organisations is much more complex than with the private sector. How society should judge the effectiveness of an individual police officer and of a police service as a whole, or a social worker and the social services department of a local council, is generally seen as more debatable than how the effectiveness of managers and commercial companies is assessed. For example, in the USA, the question of whether and how teachers' performance should be measured and rewards linked to their effectiveness has been reported as being a contentious issue (Peretz and Fried, 2012).
- Much of the public sector has had to run appraisal on even more limited resource budgets than the private sector.
- More significantly, in many instances – teaching and higher education are notable examples – appraisal has been imposed directly as a result of government policy. This is certainly not a promising backdrop for setting up an appraisal scheme (Decramer *et al.*, 2012).
- In the health and educational fields (as we have already noted), there are large concentrations of professional staff organised in structures that have few hierarchical levels and where the concept of 'management' is somewhat alien.
- The values of those working in these organisations are sometimes different, and in some cases very strongly influential in why and how they are working there.

The thrust of these differences is that it is often more challenging to make appraisal work well in the public sector; much of what is said here also applies to the voluntary or not-for-profit sector. Despite these problems, as far as performance management schemes are concerned, there is some reason for believing that many public-sector organisations can be at least as advanced as those in the private sector (Audit Commission, 1995a, 1995b, 1995c). Perhaps one of the most interesting and potentially difficult areas for appraisal is its application to the medical profession; as Box 8.1 shows, however, this is an area of great progress on a number of fronts. Doctors are a prime example of the issues that arise in appraising professionals, and it is to that topic that we now turn.

BOX 8.1

DEVELOPMENTS IN THE APPRAISAL OF MEDICAL PRACTITIONERS

The old joke about doctors burying their mistakes has presumably worn thin, as it would be difficult to find a greater transition in application of appraisal practices than that currently occurring in the medical profession. From a situation where there was little or no formal appraisal, the performance of doctors is now coming under scrutiny from several different angles.

In the UK, performance appraisal has been mandatory for hospital consultants from April 2003. Government policy statements made it clear that revalidation, based on a portfolio of evidence collected over a five-year period, will be necessary for doctors to maintain their registration with the General Medical Council (GMC). Both appraisal records and multi-source feedback will be inputs to the revalidation process.

- The GMC framework for good medical practice (GMC, 2013) covers four domains:
  1. Knowledge, Skills and Performance
  2. Safety and Quality
  3. Communication, Partnership and Teamwork
  4. Maintaining Trust.

These domains, each of which represents a cluster of competencies, are used in both appraisal and the revalidation process. For more details on the GMC framework and its use in revalidation, see www.gmc-uk.org/doctors/ revalidation/revalidation_gmp_framework.asp.

- In North America, the Physician Achievement Review follows much the same pattern. Doctors are assessed on behaviourally anchored scales against five practice domains – consultation communication, patient interaction, professional self-management, clinical competence and psychosocial management of patients – leading to a confidential report focusing on achieving better practice (Sargeant *et al.*, 2011).

Similar developments can be found in a number of other countries, including Australia and New Zealand. Clearly, the appraisal of doctors in both hospitals and primary care settings is being taken very seriously.

One of the features of developing appraisal in the medical profession is that it has spawned its own literature on competencies (e.g. Patterson *et al.*, 2013), appraisal (e.g. Lyons *et al.*, 2006) and multi-source feedback (e.g. Violato *et al.*, 2008). Good as all this is, one sometimes gets the impression that in the process, the medical world is taking little notice of the accumulated research and experience in non-medical settings. To be sure there are some important differences between doctors and, say, middle managers, which have to be recognised and addressed. However, a reading of the medical appraisal literature quickly brings to light the similarity in the problems faced, such as reconciling the individual-level need for a developmentally orientated process and the organisational need for a more assessment-focused one.

This is an area that is developing quickly and with some thoroughness, for which the medical profession is to be congratulated and for which most patients should perhaps breathe a sigh of relief. Moreover, as we will see in Chapter 11, there is a tangible benefit of good appraisal practices in the most fundamental performance measure of all – mortality rates.

APPRAISAL ISSUES WITH PROFESSIONAL AND SCIENTIFIC STAFF

Decramer *et al.* (2012: 687), writing in a Flemish educational context, observe that "the management of academic employees in higher education institutions is challenging" and quote Harley *et al.* (2004) in pointing out that such staff tend to set their own priorities and goals according to criteria set by their disciplines rather than by the institutional needs dictated by employing organisations. Some writers (e.g. Smeenk *et al.*, 2009) claim that there is incompatibility between professional values and management values in higher education institutions. Much the same could be said of all professional and scientific groups, and probably in all countries. The key to understanding some of the potential difficulties in making appraisal work with such groups is to contrast the ethos of the professional with the ethos of organisations. The former is typified by:

- high levels of autonomy and independence of judgement;
- self-discipline and adherence to professional standards;

- the possession of specialised knowledge and skills;
- power and status based on expertise;
- operating, and being guided by, a code of ethics;
- being answerable to the governing professional body.

There are other attributes, but these are the main ones. Where professionals operate within the context of a private practice or some other small professional grouping, there is no serious problem, as all are working to the same model. Not so, however, when they work as part of a much larger and more general organisation. Listing the characteristics of the conventional organisational ethos immediately shows the conflict of value systems:

- hierarchical authority and direction from superiors;
- administrative rules and procedures to be followed;
- standards and goals defined by the organisation;
- primary loyalty demanded by the organisation;
- power based on legitimate organisational position.

Small wonder that professionals experience role conflict at times, with different expectations and demands from their profession and from their organisational employers. For example, doctors and university lecturers are apt to see their work as being determined by the needs of their patients or students respectively, and by their professional training, rather than by the pragmatic considerations that drive so many organisational decisions on how resources are allocated. Many professional groups do not take easily to the idea of being managed (Decramer *et al.*, 2012) and see appraisal as seeking to exercise excessive control over them. There are of course variations in the extent to which this is true – for example, engineers are perhaps more used to working within commercial organisational management structures than are some other professions.

Appraisal is likely to fall right into the centre of this 'ethos gap'. It represents an organisational procedure that is embedded within a hierarchical authority structure; it frequently implies that some external agent or process is necessary to motivate and guide the individual's work; and it is the mechanism whereby the organisation's goals are imposed at lower levels. The kinds of performance measures that enter into appraisal discussions may well reflect outcomes that are of primary importance at organisational level, but which seem misleading, crude or irrelevant to the professional. Thus, measures like the number of students enrolled, the number of patients seen or the number of social work cases covered are of limited importance to the professionals concerned without some meaningful check on how well quality has been maintained. It is perhaps not surprising that Decramer *et al.* (2015) found that in a sample of Belgian nurses, performance planning and goal-setting did not have quite the same pattern of positive effects it tends to have with non-professional groups. The professional's aspiration is, more often than not, to achieve the highest standard possible and to extend professional skills and expertise in doing so. The organisation's goals, on the other hand, tend to be more about cost-effectiveness and delivering a reasonable product or service rather than the best possible, with some lip service to quality.

On top of all this, the appraisers may or may not be fellow professionals. Where they are not, there is a serious danger of a communication mismatch between the two parties; they start from different positions and speak different languages. Where professionals appraise one another, this problem does not usually exist, but instead, the organisational agenda for appraisal may well be ignored. Also, it is often the case that the whole process is perceived as embarrassing, as being inappropriate or even distasteful by both parties – with the consequence that it is not treated seriously and is carried out in a superficial manner.

The result of the differences between professional ethos and organisational ethos is to make appraisal far more difficult to introduce and run successfully. It is simply no use to try to operate the appraisal of professional and scientific staff as if they were no different from any others. Quite apart from the points already made, it has to be remembered that this is a group who have usually been through an extended qualification process, and they have a far higher level of educational achievement than most. This alone might serve to make them a more challenging prospect as far as appraisal is concerned, but in addition, for many professionals, their qualifications make them more mobile and attractive in terms of employment prospects. If they don't like the way they are treated, they can very easily move elsewhere. We can look at the detailed implications of all this for how appraisal functions with members of professional and scientific groups later in the chapter. But for the moment, a more general point has to be made. If performance appraisal in one form or another is to be part of the way these staff groups work and are managed, then it would be better to face head-on the issues of the conflicting value systems outlined above before any practical appraisal arrangements are put in place. If both the professionals concerned and the non-professional elements of the organisational management can discuss their expectations and differences at the outset – in seminars, consultative sessions, organisational development workshops or whatever – many of the problems can be addressed and perhaps minimised. They may not be eliminated, but raising awareness of the differing expectations can help in achieving some of the compromises necessary between organisational and individual goals if the appraisal process is to be constructive. The general requirement for performance appraisal to recognise the needs and values of appraisees and appraisers, rather than just the organisation's aims, is even stronger with professional groups.

DESIGNING AND IMPLEMENTING APPRAISAL FOR PROFESSIONAL STAFF

Potentially, appraisal can serve the same functions for this group as for other employees. However, two points need to be kept in mind:

1. Professionals tend to be fairly high on self-motivation, and an overt emphasis on appraisal as a motivating device may cause it to be rejected as unnecessary.
2. Assessment against professional and personal standards is acceptable, but is usually perceived as being more relevant to development than to deciding on rewards.

The organisation will generally want appraisal to be a means of directing the efforts of professional staff in such a way that they are in line with the main organisational objectives and priorities. This is far from straightforward, as we have noted. What this means is that the *presentation* of the aims of appraisal becomes almost as important as the aims themselves.

Appraisal is more likely to be acceptable if it is seen as a means of facilitating effective cooperation in achieving common goals and as a mechanism for improving professional development than if it is perceived as a way of assessing and motivating professionals to drive organisational performance. In the final analysis, there may not be much difference between these two perspectives in what they actually entail, but there may be a world of difference in how they are thought of. The language and terminology are thus of some significance here. The word 'appraisal' seems to have more negative connotations with professionals than it has for most people, probably because it is seen as 'something to do with industry' and not relevant to their approach to work. Consequently, it may be wise to look for alternative terms. The most popular tend to be variations on a few themes:

- individual development interviews
- work planning and review sessions
- professional development interviews
- performance development sessions
- job progress reviews.

Any title that diminishes the implication that the session is about assessment is an improvement (of course, staff may still call it the appraisal anyway!).

So far, this discussion has treated all professional groups as being much the same. While their similarities might outweigh their differences, the latter do exist. It cannot be assumed that where there is more than one professional group, they will all react in the same way. This was illustrated in Chapter 5, when it was recounted how local government engineers and social workers had been found to have rather different styles and preferences in relation to appraisal. These differences, too, have to be addressed in the design process, by ensuring that all the professional groups concerned are represented in the consultation exercise, and that they are made aware of the differing views of their colleagues in other professions. This is particularly beneficial, as professionals do sometimes need reminding that their own particular profession does not have a monopoly on wisdom. The main point here, though, is that it may make the consultation and design stage of appraisal slower where professional groups are involved than would normally be the case. That slower progress should be built in to the planned timetable for introducing appraisal. Trying to rush into implementation by cutting the discussion process short is liable to leave a residue of problems. See Box 8.2 for a case study of a professional group which has, rather like doctors, been among the last to embrace the concept of appraisal – lawyers.

BOX 8.2

DEVELOPING A PERFORMANCE MANAGEMENT SYSTEM FOR CORPORATE LAWYERS

This case study relates to a request by the legal services division of a multinational oil company to help them develop a new performance management system. Some – but not all – of the most senior lawyers wanted a new form of appraisal that encouraged a more objectively based assessment of performance and one that could be used to assist in development. A team of external and internal consultants was commissioned to carry out this task. The first step was to develop an agreed competency framework, which was done by using a mixture of job analysis techniques, and then feeding back drafts of the output to focus groups to check validity. At the same time, the focus groups, representing various levels of legal staff and drawn from different operating companies and countries, were consulted about the existing appraisal arrangements and what they wanted from the new ones. This proved to be a long, slow process, as it takes time for such a diverse group of people to find something they can all agree on. It was of crucial importance to build the competency descriptions in the words and language that they could relate to – if there is any professional group likely to pore over the slightest ambiguity in meaning, it is lawyers!

Eventually, the competency descriptions were agreed and, after another round of focus groups held in two countries, so was the performance-management framework. It consisted of a two-part process, with an assessment of performance that linked in with pay and – at a separate point in the year – a developmentally orientated discussion based on the assessment. Training the senior lawyers in appraisal brought to light all the problems outlined in this chapter, and also some of the tensions within the managing group of lawyers themselves – some wanting the kind of system designed and some still hankering after something very much simpler; one said, "I only have 15 minutes to spend on performance management for each member of my staff!" The hope of many of his colleagues was that the new system would help drive a culture change that would make it difficult if not impossible for that kind of attitude to survive. One point about this example, though, is that it relates to professionals who are deeply embedded in a competitive commercial environment, and who are thus more familiar with management concepts and control mechanisms than some of their professional colleagues who operate in private practice.

It was noted earlier that the hierarchical authority structures of organisations do not always fit the professional's concept of control and discipline. This not only affects the aims of appraisal, but who should carry it out. The traditional notion of the immediate boss being the appraiser is called into question. If that boss is a member of the same profession as the appraisee, there is a considerable chance of them colluding to make it a non-event if they do not feel downward appraisal to be appropriate. Or it may focus exclusively on professional content – the appraisal may be seen as an opportunity to discuss arcane technical issues and to review career development, and may therefore neglect the less intrinsically congenial matter of meeting objectives. If the boss is not a fellow professional, then the situation may be even worse – the appraiser can be viewed by the appraisee as lacking the knowledge and skills to make a valid judgement about performance, as well as not being in a position to offer career development advice. An additional problem is that in some organisations dominated by professional staff there are very few layers of authority, and these are often ill-defined. The consequence is that where line-management responsibility can be defined, the number of appraisees to each appraiser may be rather high. So, the question of who the appraiser should be therefore requires careful consideration. There are several options:

1: Allow choice

The idea of people choosing their appraisers is found in both teacher and (some) university appraisal schemes. The virtue of letting people nominate their own appraisers is that they can pick those individuals who have the most relevant knowledge of their work and their professional specialism, and whom they respect. There are certainly occasions where it can be appropriate to follow such a route:

- where there is no obvious immediate superior who is in a position to appraise;
- where the person works in a very highly specialised field;
- where the numbers of staff to be appraised would be too great for the appraiser and some way has to be found to spread the load.

Unfortunately, there are many potential problems that limit the value of taking this approach more generally. The main one is that appraisees may choose appraisers on less desirable grounds – personal friendship, or the knowledge that X is a 'soft touch' – which result in a less than thorough or constructive discussion. Some comfort here is provided by evidence from the 360° feedback context which suggests that focal managers choose assessors on the basis of those who are familiar with their performance rather than those whom they simply like (Brutus *et al.*, 2005). Even where appraisers are chosen for legitimate reasons, they may not be in a position to give the broader perspective and support necessary to help the appraisee. There are also administrative difficulties that arise if this choice process is allowed on a widespread basis. So, the principle of allowing choice of appraiser is useful in some special circumstances, but has to be carefully controlled – the choice needs to be sanctioned by whoever has responsibility for the appraisal process.

2: Multi-level, multi-source appraisal

Some general points on multiple-source appraisal were discussed in Chapter 7; most of these apply in appraising professionals. Again, this approach has been used in various forms in teaching and university appraisal, and now increasingly with doctors, as indicated in Box 8.1. The attraction of multiple-source appraisal for professional staff rests mainly on self- and peer-review, both of which fit the professional ethos much better than appraisal by superiors. In universities and in the scientific community, the peer-review process has long been established and accepted as the best way of judging the merit of individual pieces of work and of assessing the suitability of people for promotion. However, it has to be noted that, in this context, the word 'peers' is often used to refer to members of the same professional group and specialism rather than necessarily to imply people of the same rank or level.

Input to appraisal from colleagues working in the same professional field is acceptable because they are knowledgeable about that field and the individual's contribution to it, not because they are in some sense senior or in a position of authority – their authority comes from expert power, not rank or seniority.

But the concept of multiple-source appraisal has wider implications for some professionals than it generally does for managers. It can include input from patients about the way they are dealt with by healthcare professionals, from students on the way they are taught by lecturers and so on (there are limits to this – criminals' views on their arresting officers may be a touch biased). Where such sources of information are mooted, they are sometimes questioned on their capacity to offer objective or useful evidence. However, to take the case of lecturers as an example, the evidence shows that student ratings of their teachers are sufficiently reliable and valid (for example, they correlate quite highly with ratings of teaching ability made by superiors, peers and classroom observers) to use in feedback aimed at performance improvement and in personnel decision making (Rushton and Murray, 1985).

The problem with appraisal input from consumers of professional services is that getting it is usually time-consuming and sometimes costly. But with the growing focus on quality considerations, this is something that may well play a larger part in appraisal in the future, and not just with professionals.

3: Split-role appraisal

Sometimes an alternative is to have a form of multiple-source appraisal, but in separate sessions – which might be called split-role appraisal. This is useful in addressing the problem of the appraisee having dual responsibilities and roles. On the one hand, there is the professional specialism and all that it entails, and on the other there is the administrative and managerial role the individual may fill in the organisation. It is quite possible to have different appraisers for each, a professional mentor for the professional role and a senior manager for the organisational role. There are some difficulties with this, mainly in connection with the areas of interface and overlap, and it is more costly in resource terms, but it can work well enough, provided that the appraisers consult each other where necessary before and after the session.

Appraisal training with professionals and scientific staff

The subject of appraisal training generally is dealt with in Chapter 10, but training can receive a somewhat different and very mixed reception amongst professionals and scientists. Some see no difference in kind between attending an appraisal training course and the prolonged training they have already received for their professional career. For other senior members of this fraternity, however, the idea of attending a skills-based appraisal course, with the attendant risk of being seen not to perform well (or, as they might think of it, making a fool of themselves) in front of others may not be very appealing. In view of these mixed reactions, the first step in setting up appraisal training for professionals is to gauge their attitude to the idea, and to assess how much help – and in what form – they feel they need.

The briefing sessions that introduce the appraisal system can be used as a vehicle for assessing the demand for training. Such sessions may also have the function of examining some of the professional–organisational ethos differences, if these have not been brought out in a prior consultation process. While it might be rather late in the day to raise these, it is better that they are made explicit and thought about rather than simply ignored. The briefing sessions can be extended to have a more direct training function by going over guidance notes on how to handle the interview, discussing ways of dealing with problem performers and so on. This in itself can be used to raise awareness of the need for training, and to demonstrate its potential value. Little is achieved by forcing people to undergo training that they do not want, so being able to offer training to those that would like it, without it being mandatory (at least, initially) is a reasonable approach. In addition, the use of e-learning is often especially appealing to professionals; they have become used to studying alone at their computers, and so software-based training packages of the sort mentioned in Chapter 10 are highly relevant for this group. For some professionals, after doing appraisals for the first time, there is a change of attitude and any resistance to the idea of attending a skills training course may decrease or disappear.

The actual content of appraisal training, where professional and scientific staff are involved, does not usually need to be any different from normal. However, there are some points to be aware of, and these are relevant to the briefing sessions too. Staff in HR who have been involved in appraisal training in organisations with large numbers of scientific staff will tell you that the latter tend to apply their normal perspective on the world to appraisal as well: they will take an evidence-based approach, and want some data to show that what is being presented to them achieves its objectives. This evidence can be examples of how the same approach is used successfully elsewhere, in similar organisations of sufficient status for them to respect; and/or it can be academic research demonstrating that the principles embedded in the appraisal scheme are effective in achieving the desired ends (in this context, see the research cited in Chapter 11). Any figures or statistics delivered in the course of this will be subject to careful scrutiny and evaluation. Concepts and assumptions will be examined in detail. All of this can make the delivery of appraisal training to groups of this kind fairly demanding for the trainers. They will need to be prepared to deal with questions of a rather different kind from such staff, who are more inclined to focus on underlying principles than is the average manager.

There is also a need for trainers to be sensitive to likely differences between professional groups in how they react to the subject of appraisal. Typically, the more technically based professionals are prone to emphasising content and procedural issues. They often feel quite happy and comfortable with rating scales and quantitative measures, with appraisal that revolves around clear procedures and the completion of report forms. In contrast, experience suggests that the 'soft' professions and disciplines, those that deal with human and social issues in the main, are much more likely to react negatively to the quantitative aspects of appraisal and assessment. Instead, they direct their attention to the process aspects of appraisal, and show more concern about handling the interaction with the appraisee in a sensitive and conflict-free manner. Perhaps this is the reason for the finding that more Arts faculty are given higher overall performance ratings than Science and Engineering faculty (Barr *et al.*, 2012).

It is the task of the trainer to organise the appraisal training to cater for these differences in outlook and style. Two basic approaches are possible. One is to make sure that, on any course, the participants are from a mixed group; the idea here is that they act as corrective influences on each other. The alternative is to try to make the course membership group-specific and to gently shape the training in such a way as to counterbalance the biases of that particular group. There is no hard and fast evidence to prove which is superior – much depends on the wider context of the organisation and the groups concerned.

APPRAISING PROMOTION POTENTIAL AMONG PROFESSIONAL STAFF

There are, broadly speaking, two different pathways open to professionals: one is to make progress in their own specialism and reach positions of responsibility within the profession; while the other is to branch out into more generalist roles, where their training may still play a part in their work, albeit a steadily diminishing one. In the early career stage, the promotability of an individual will often be based on both professional competence and development and on effectiveness in their organisational role. It is usually important for both of these to be assessed and taken account of in the promotion decision. Sometimes they go hand-in-hand, and there is no great problem. It is not always the case, though, and many organisations – for example, those operating in the advanced technology field – find that some of their staff are so good technically that they have to be given career advancement on this basis alone (if the company is to keep them), even if their more general personal skills are seriously deficient. For other individuals, the balance tilts in the opposite direction. If this is the situation, then the appraisal process has some role in identifying both to the individual and to the organisation what the future career pattern is likely to be, so that everyone concerned knows where they stand. It seems essential here that the appraisal does include inputs from both professional and organisational perspectives.

In some settings, the relationship between the professional and the organisational aspects of performance can become distorted by the reward system. A classic example of this is to be found in research-led universities, where young academic staff quickly learn that their promotion will very largely be determined by their personal research output and their capacity for winning external funding – with the result that many of them will seek to minimise their teaching hours and their share of administrative duties, though these are vital to the organisation and to their 'customers'. Going back to the discussion of different perspectives on the nature of performance in Chapter 3, these individuals would be showing some good aspects of task performance, but perhaps at the cost of some aspects of citizenship or contextual performance.

As with other staff groups, appraisal does not itself offer a very satisfactory mechanism for making decisions on longer-term promotion potential. The alternative methods, reviewed in Chapter 6, can all be applied with professional groups. Of these, though, the assessment (or development) centre is perhaps the most appropriate. Its flexibility makes it possible to devise AC exercises that are designed to assess potential for managing professionals or exercises that are designed to assess potential for generalist management. The latter can be quite useful in acting as a realistic job preview, giving candidates a taste of what such work might be like and allowing them to decide whether they would want to go down this route.

IN SUMMARY

The context in which performance appraisal operates is rather different in public-sector organisations, which can serve to make it a more challenging process to introduce and run. In particular, such organisations often have a high proportion of technical, scientific or professional staff, and the attitudes and ethos of these groups can sometimes work against the management aims of the organisation – not least because they may take a more independent viewpoint and not identify with some of the organisation's aims or policies. The design of an appraisal system for professional staff needs to address this, and in particular to encourage participation in the development of the process and to place emphasis on developmental aspects. Other features of the scheme – for example, in terms of who actually conducts the appraisal – may also need some tailoring. Finally, there are implications for how training is delivered to such groups and for the way promotability and potential are assessed.

DISCUSSION POINTS AND QUESTIONS

8.1 How are professionals likely to differ from general administrative or managerial staff in their attitude to appraisal, and why?

8.2 What are the main challenges to implementing performance appraisal with professional staff? What would you pay special attention to in doing performance appraisal training with them?

8.3 Select two of the following: police officers, teachers, doctors, social workers, nurses. How would you assess their performance – what do you think would be the most relevant performance criteria to judge them on? How would you measure them?

KEY REFERENCES

Charman, C., Rudbeck, S. and Powell, M. (2014) *Ticking All the Boxes: A Study of Performance Management Practices in the UK*. London: Towers Watson.

Decramer, A., Audenaert, M., Van Waeyenberg, T., Claeys, T., Claeys, C., Vandevelde, S., Loon, J. V. and Crucke, S. (2015) Does performance management affect nurses' well-being?, *Evaluation and Program Planning*, **49**, 98–105.

Decramer, A., Smolders, C., Vanderstraeten, A., Christiaens, J. and Desmidt, S. (2012) External pressures affecting the adoption of employee performance management in higher education institutions. *Personnel Review*, **41**(5–6), 686–704.

Simmons, J. and Iles, P. (2001) Performance appraisals in knowledge-based organisations: Implications for management education. *International Journal of Management Education*, **2**(1), 3–18.

REFERENCES

Audit Commission (1995a) *Paying the Piper: People and Pay Management in Local Government*. London: HMSO.

Audit Commission (1995b) *Calling the Tune: Performance Management in Local Government*. London: HMSO.

Audit Commission (1995c) *Management Handbook: Paying the Piper and Calling the Tune*. London: HMSO.

Barr, C., Docherty, F. and Ward, S. (2012) Benchmarking report: Performance and development review (P&DR) systems. Working Paper, University of Glasgow.

Brutus, S., Fleenor, J. and London, M. (1998) Does 360 degree feedback work in different industries? A between-industry comparison of the reliability and validity of multi-source performance ratings. *Journal of Management Development*, **17**(3), 177–190.

Brutus, S., Petosa, S. and Aucoin, E. (2005) Who will evaluate me? Rater selection in multi-source assessment contexts. *International Journal of Selection and Assessment*, **13**(2), 129–138.

Charman, C., Rudbeck, S. and Powell, M. (2014) *Ticking All the Boxes: A Study of Performance Management Practices in the UK*. London: Towers Watson.

Decramer, A., Audenaert, M., Van Waeyenberg, T., Claeys, T., Claeys, C., Vandevelde, S., Loon, J. V. and Crucke, S. (2015) Does performance management affect nurses' well-being?, *Evaluation and Program Planning*, **49**, 98–105.

Decramer, A., Smolders, C., Vanderstraeten, A., Christiaens, J. and Desmidt, S. (2012). External pressures affecting the adoption of employee performance management in higher education institutions. *Personnel Review*, **41**(5–6), 686–704.

GMC (2013) *Good Medical Practice*. London: GMC. http://www.gmc-uk.org/guidance/good_medical_practice.asp (accessed 18 January 2016).

Harley, S., Muller-Camen, M. and Collin, A. (2004) From academic community to managed organizations: The implications for academic careers in UK and German universities. *Journal of Vocational Behavior*, **64**(2), 329–345.

Lyons, N., Caesar, S. and McEwen, A. (2006) *The Appraiser's Handbook: A Guide for Doctors*. Oxford: Radcliffe Publishing.

Mercer (2013) *Global Performance Management Survey Report*. London: Mercer Consulting.

Patterson, F., Tavabie, A., Denney, D., Kerrin, M., Ashworth, V., Koczwara, A. and Macleod, S. (2013). A new competency model for general practice: Implications for selection, training and careers. *British Journal of General Practice*, **63**(610), 331–338.

Peretz, H. and Fried, Y. (2012) National cultures, performance appraisal practices, and organizational absenteeism and turnover: A study across 21 countries. *Journal of Applied Psychology*, **97**(2), 448–459.

Rushton, J. P. and Murray, H. G.. (1985) On the assessment of teaching effectiveness in British universities. *Bulletin of the British Psychological Society*, **38**, 361–365.

Sargeant, J., Macleod, R., Sinclair, D. and Power, M. (2011) How do physicians assess their family physician colleagues' performance? Creating a rubric to inform assessment and feedback. *Journal of Continuing Education in the Health Professions*, **31**(2), 87–94.

Simmons, J. and Iles, P. (2001) Performance appraisals in knowledge-based organisations: Implications for management education. *International Journal of Management Education*, **2**(1), 3–18.

Smeenk, S. C., Teelken, R., Eisinga, R. and Doorewaard, H. (2009) Managerialism, organizational commitment, and the quality of job performance among European university employees. *Research in Higher Education*, **50**(6), 589–607.

Violato, C., Lockyer, J. and Fidler, H. (2008) Changes in performance: A 5-year longitudinal study of participants in a multi-source feedback programme. *Medical Education*, **42**(10), 1007–1013.

CULTURAL CHALLENGES IN APPLYING PERFORMANCE APPRAISAL

9

Although numerous changes in appraisal have been charted and described elsewhere in this book – principally, the rise of 360° feedback and the increasing application of appraisal to professional groups – there is another development that has been only briefly mentioned previously in Chapter 6, but which will be addressed here. This is the impact of culture in the context of appraisal. With increasing freedom of movement of labour within the countries of the European Union, and the growing globalisation of business, the question arises as to the applicability of management concepts and approaches developed in one culture to people coming from a different one. How well do our ideas on how to structure and carry out performance appraisal – and on performance management more generally – travel? The vast majority of published research on PA/PM emanates from the developed countries of the West – in fact, most of it comes from the USA, with some additional input from Western Europe. The extent to which we can generalise the findings from this research to countries in the developing world looks very doubtful when one finds that differences arise even across similar cultures. For example, Earley and Stubblebine (1989) found that workers in the UK reacted differently to feedback compared to those in the United States.

Research has indeed found systematic differences in work-related values across countries and even different concepts about what performance is (Varma *et al.*, 2008). Thus, the question arises as to whether established appraisal methods, insofar as they do largely come from Western advanced economies, are appropriate or effective in other cultural settings? Addressing this issue is becoming more urgent because of the increasingly international nature of business referred to above. However, it is not simply a question of whether imposing Western appraisal philosophies on other countries will prove effective; it also relates to differences within countries. Kikoski (1999: 301), talking in an American context, observes that "the problems of face-to-face communication in an essentially monocultural work force may be insignificant compared to the interpersonal communication difficulties which may accompany the more culturally diverse work force that is forecast". While Kikoski was referring to the growing proportion of workers in the United States from Hispanic, Asian or African backgrounds, even the growing cultural diversity found in the USA is exceeded within the borders of the European Union.

To illustrate some of the potential problems that might be encountered, we can turn to the work of Hofstede (1980, 2001), whose research is the most frequently cited on the relationship between national culture and work-related values (Fernandez *et al.*, 1997). Hofstede identified a number of dimensions of cultural difference; these are described in Box 9.1. Here, we will focus on just two of them – Power Distance and Individualism/Collectivism – as there is more evidence in relation to these in the context of appraisal. Readers interested in a fuller treatment are referred to Bailey and Fletcher (2008) and to Peretz and Fried (2012).

BOX 9.1

HOFSTEDE'S DIMENSIONS FOR DESCRIBING CULTURAL DIFFERENCES

Hofstede (1980, 2001), working largely in the context of the multinational IBM, identified four major dimensions of cultural values difference. His model is used by the vast majority of theoretical and empirical investigations in this area, and it describes national cultures in terms of their position along these dimensions: Power Distance, Uncertainty Avoidance, Masculinity/Femininity and Individualism/Collectivism. Although all four are described below, more attention will be given to the first and last, as they generally are seen to be the most relevant in this context.

Power Distance (PD) concerns how less powerful organisational members accept and expect that power is distributed unequally. In high *PD* cultures there is acceptance of unequal distribution of power within a culture. Supervisors and subordinates consider themselves unequal and subordinates are more dependent on their supervisors – they may be afraid to express disagreement with their supervisors, while the latter tend to have an autocratic or paternalistic management style. High PD is also associated with greater centralisation of power in the organisation. In low *PD* cultures, relationships between individuals across hierarchical levels are closer and less formal in nature. They are marked by more limited dependence of subordinates on their supervisors and the use of and preference for a consultative or participatory style of management. In addition, when power distance is low, so too is emotional distance – resulting in subordinates possibly showing more willingness to approach and even contradict their supervisors.

Uncertainty Avoidance (UA): The degree to which people in a country prefer structured over unstructured situations. Low UA cultures are more risk-taking and tolerant of organisational ambiguity and change than high UA cultures.

Masculinity/Femininity (M/F): Masculine cultures are associated with values like assertiveness, performance, success and competition (associated with the male role in almost all societies). Feminine cultures are associated with values like quality of life, maintaining warm personal relationships, service, and care for the weak.

Individualism/Collectivism (I/C) reflects the extent to which the interests of the individual prevail over the interests of the group. *Individualistic* cultures value personal identity and choice – people act in their own interest and the relationship between the employee and employer is conceived of as a business relationship. Emphasis is often placed on personal freedom of choice and individual initiative -- and companies are not expected to get involved in the personal lives of their employees. *Collectivist* cultures emphasise group values over individual goals, and the welfare of the group over individual needs. Thus, the interests of the group prevail over the interests of the individual. Emphasis is given to reducing differences between members of the collective and to maintaining group harmony, loyalty, and preserving relationships and 'face'. Collectivist societies tend to be hierarchical and to value seniority. The relationship between the employer and employee typically involves protection in exchange for loyalty.

There is some evidence that Power Distance and Individualism are in fact correlated (Hofstede, 1980). But Hofstede's model has been hugely influential in our thinking on cultural differences and has been well supported. The individualism/collectivism dimension is increasingly being used as an explanatory concept in cross-cultural psychology and the power distance dimension has been found to correlate with theoretically similar factors in other studies of cross-cultural values. Hofstede's work has been further developed and built on by House *et al.* (2004).

To give some geography to Hofstede's descriptions as they relate to countries at the time he was writing – high Power Distance countries included France, Malaysia and Mexico; low Power Distance countries included the USA, the UK and (to a lesser extent) Germany. High Collectivist cultures can be found, for example, in Japan, Thailand and Singapore, while countries high on Individualism included the USA, Chile, France and Australia. It is not difficult to see how the differences outlined in this theory are likely to have an impact on appraisal schemes. According to Hofstede, Western cultures are high in Individualism, medium in levels of Power Distance and Uncertainty Avoidance and are Masculine more than Feminine. Within the appraisal setting, this manifests itself as a need for individual achievement and recognition, with individuals being encouraged to express assertive, challenging behaviours, and to be personally ambitious at the cost of group-orientated actions and nurturing behaviours. Consequently, appraisal systems are generally focused upon the individual (not the group), and have emphasised stereotypically masculine values over feminine ones. As a result, the appraisal system can be viewed as an opportunity for negotiation between the individual and the organisation.

Things look very different elsewhere, though. Snape *et al.* (1998) observed that in societies such as China, with a strong Collectivist orientation, a sense of hierarchy and acceptance of authority, the focus of 'Western' PA practices on individual performance, accountability and open confrontation is unlikely to be seen as appropriate. Huo and Von Glinow (1995) likewise found that Chinese managers were reluctant to engage in two-way communication or provide counselling in the performance appraisal process, because of the high PD values of Chinese culture. Thus, employees' participation in appraisal was low in comparison to Western countries, and peer evaluation was seldom encountered – because of the high Power Distance, only the immediate manager is regarded as sufficiently qualified to appraise subordinates' performance (but see below in relation to multi-source feedback). However, the rate of change and economic growth in China may call into question the future validity of these earlier findings. Cooke (2008) observes that appraisal in China is now more reward-driven and focuses on the individual worker and their performance with less emphasis than in Western countries on development and alignment of individual and organisational goals. This is quite surprising, given the level of state intervention there, which probably makes it more difficult to assess the extent to which performance outcomes are actually attributable to the individual. Notwithstanding the more Western trend in Chinese appraisal systems, as Campbell and Wiernik (2015) report, studies have found that some dimensions of work behaviour may be manifested in a different form there; for example, interpersonal aggression being expressed through indirect and political behaviour rather than through direct confrontation.

The picture presented by China illustrates a fundamental point about using the work of Hofstede and others to characterise different countries and their values. While presenting a useful framework for analysis, and leading to valid observations at the time, such research conclusions can quickly become outdated – the economic, social and political climate of countries and whole continents changes fast. Varma *et al.* (2008) see China moving to PM systems that have more in common with South Korea and, eventually, with Japan, where the approach to PM is reportedly more similar to that of Western countries. China is but one example; we are looking at a constantly shifting perspective in relation to many countries.

Another factor that relates to cultural values and which represents a significant difference in terms of underlying drivers of the approach taken to performance appraisal is the legal context in which the systems operate. Varma *et al.* (2008) note that equal opportunity legislation is a powerful influence for performance management systems not only in the USA but also in the UK, France, Germany (to name but three European nations) and Australia. While the details of the legislation differ between these countries, the effects are much the same – a concern about the assessment method (in particular a focus on ratings) and a need to have a formal process in place to deal with what Campbell and Wiernik (2015) call 'high stakes appraisal'; that is, where appraisal is used as a basis for decisions on dismissal, promotion, financial rewards and career progression. Without a formal appraisal system, the organisation is vulnerable to legal challenges to such decisions, which may turn out to be very costly indeed both financially and in terms of reputational damage. Thus, the legal context of appraisal has led to a heightened concern for the reliability and validity of performance measures used, for their transparency, and for their perceived organisational justice and equity.

There is not space here to detail the similarities and differences in approach to performance management across the full international spectrum, so, having said something about what has until recently been one of the two great growing powerhouses of the world economy – China – we can turn to another, namely India. In Hofstede's work, India is characterised by low Uncertainty Avoidance, high Power Distance and middle-level Collectivism and Masculinity. Here, though, there is a problem of disentangling the historical culture and beliefs; for example, the Indian concept of 'dharma', which reflects moral duty to others and is essentially collectivist, and the impact of British colonial influence, which is more individualistic. It is interesting to find that in earlier years, Indian government bodies used a confidential (i.e. not seen by or discussed with the employee concerned) annual report as the key element in appraisal, which was precisely the approach taken in the British Civil Service at that time. Looking at more recent practices, however, as with China, the picture is again one of rapid change. Sparrow and Budhwar (1997) reported that appraisal was relatively under-emphasised in managerial practices. But with massive foreign investment and economic growth, various writers (Amba-Rao *et al.*, 2000; Sharma *et al.*, 2008) reflect a different impression. There appears to be a variety of PM systems and approaches being adopted, depending on the nature of the organisation and its business, though this is perhaps less true of smaller (often family) businesses. Overall, though, the movement is increasingly towards more Western approaches, with the emphasis on employee development and productivity.

CULTURAL DIFFERENCES IN THE CONTEXT OF MULTI-SOURCE FEEDBACK

Multi-source feedback in particular, with its capacity to deliver critical assessments across hierarchical boundaries, may be susceptible to widely varying reactions according to the cultural background of the participants. Shipper *et al.* (2007) assessed the effectiveness of a 360° feedback process implemented within a large multinational organisation. Their study found varying levels of effectiveness across five different countries; for example, 360° feedback was related to declines in performance in Malaysia, but improvements in Ireland! The authors argued that the application of multi-source feedback in cultures with values that are inconsistent with those inherent in the process may be detrimental. Peretz and Fried (2012), in a study ranging over nearly 6,000 organisations across 21 countries, found multi-source feedback to be more acceptable in countries where the cultural make-up (in Hofstede's terms) was consistent with its use (see Box 9.1 for some indications of where a mismatch might occur). For example, they found that higher Power Distance was associated with less likelihood of use of multiple raters. These international differences are further reflected in a study which looked at the characteristics of such systems as they operated across six countries (Brutus *et al.*, 2006). To pick out just some of their findings:

- Argentina – had a high proportion of non-voluntary participation (80 per cent) and developmental use (90 per cent).
- China – had the highest input to appraisal (78 per cent), highest mandatory participation (89 per cent), raters were often chosen by a third party (67 per cent) and supervisors had access to the feedback report in 100 per cent of the cases encountered in the study.
- Slovakia – had mostly developmental use and voluntary participation in all cases (100 per cent).

- Spain – the line manager chose the focal managers' raters in two-thirds of cases.
- UK – it was more likely (86 per cent of cases) that raters would be chosen by the focal manager than in any of the other countries covered in the study.

There are some interesting variations here, but it comes as no surprise to find the rather top-down, somewhat hierarchical approach taken in China. Nonetheless, the fact that such systems are operating at all there perhaps indicates a significant shift – and it should be noted that China has only a very recent history of using them compared to the USA and Europe. The pattern in Argentina is also unusual: mainly a developmental focus, but with a hint of authoritarianism thrown in – you will be developed whether you like it or not! Despite the variations noted, Brutus *et al.* (2006) report that the suggested solutions to the problems and challenges posed in implementing multi-source feedback were surprisingly consistent across the countries sampled. For example, pre- and post-communication were seen as crucial to success: HR professionals and others responsible for introducing such processes in these countries commented at length on their communication efforts, prior to implementation, to attain required levels of trust and support from users. They also discussed the need for follow-up efforts in order for feedback to have an impact.

THE INTERPLAY OF ORGANISATIONAL AND NATIONAL CULTURES

Problems of cultural differences can, of course, also arise within a single organisation, when the feedback provider and feedback recipient are from different national cultures – a situation that is becoming increasingly common. Triandis and Brislin (1984) noted that when a supervisor from one culture appraises the performance of a subordinate from another, the accuracy of appraisal is likely to be lower, in part due to the fact that the appraiser is not aware of the norms in the other culture that govern certain behaviours. So let us look at how differences in Power Distance and in Individualism/ Collectivism might impact an appraisal session at an individual level; two examples will serve to illustrate some of the possible difficulties:

- *Situation 1.* An appraiser from a culture lower on Power Distance than an appraisee's seeks the latter's self-assessments and their views on how to solve job problems. The appraisee may feel reluctant to participate in the performance appraisal process in this manner and feel it is not their place to do so – they feel it is their superior's job to propose solutions.

Indeed, the appraisee may also view the appraiser's request for input of this kind as a sign of weakness. The appraiser, on the other hand, may be disappointed by the response and judge the appraisee as being uncooperative or simply devoid of ideas on how to deal with the problems identified.

• *Situation 2*. The appraiser is from a culture higher on Individualism than that of the appraisee, and focuses on the personal contribution of the individual, paying less attention to team issues. The appraisee, in contrast, wants to emphasise their role in the team and in consequence fails to highlight their personal achievements, leading to the appraiser assessing them less positively.

Clearly, there is scope for a host of problems and variations in such cross-cultural interactions, and in an organisation where this may be an issue it will be important – ideally – to take some account of it in designing the system, but more especially in the training delivered to both appraisers and appraisees (see Chapter 10, pages 203, 209). But the difficulties can also be over-played. The influence of *organisational* culture should not be underestimated. Multinational companies tend to build up a strong, identifiable and pervasive culture of their own, and this can to some extent ameliorate the impact of differences in the national cultures of their workforce over time. Because there is a set way of doing things in the organisation, it can become the accepted norm for everyone when they have become fully socialised into the organisation. Chiang and Birtch (2010) examined the influence of cultural differences on appraisal practices in a single industry (banking) across seven countries. While their findings demonstrated a relationship between cultural dimensions and the structure and purpose of appraisal in different countries, they concluded (2010: 1365) that the relationship was not straightforward and "should not be overstated". For example, they noted that the impact of appraisal directives coming from the head office situated in another country, or HR managers benchmarking their organisation's appraisal practices against those of local competitors, or globalisation leading to a convergence on appraisal purposes and mechanisms, could all play a role in influencing appraisal methods notwithstanding the potential effect of national culture.

Resorting to anecdotal evidence to illustrate this theme, when one of the authors was addressing a group from the Portuguese Association of People Management (APG) on the subject of multi-source feedback, some people in the audience felt that their national culture was not ready for such initiatives – but a representative of an international hotel chain operating there spoke up to point out that, in fact, they used 360° feedback and had experienced no problems at all, with staff being enthusiastic about it.

WHAT SHOULD WE CONCLUDE?

That differences in cultural values exist and that these can and do impact on appraisal and other HR practices is well supported in general terms (Harris, 2007; Chiang and Birtch, 2010; Peretz and Fried, 2012). However, although there has been quite a lot written about the effects of culture on appraisal, the amount of empirical work is still small, and more is needed to test out precisely how and to what extent these influences impact on the reality of appraisal in the workplace. There are also two other significant factors that have to be taken into account. The first is that cultural and economic conditions change; the emergence of multi-source feedback in the 1990s is an example of a phenomenon that was not widely acceptable prior to that in the UK culture – so we are looking at a dynamic situation, where conclusions drawn at one time point may be invalid a decade later (Fletcher, 2001). Another example of this is that some countries have been shown to have shifted their position on the Hofstede dimensions from the time of his original observations (Fernandez *et al.*, 1997). As noted earlier, the 'melting pot' of international business, not to mention the influence of the Internet, probably serves to reduce (but not eliminate) differences in approach and expectations over time.

The second factor comes down to the individual – someone who is never very far away in appraisal. Research tells us that there is considerable variation in cultural values *within* countries (Mishra and Roch, 2013). Indeed, not only are there within-country variations of this kind, but there are also individual differences – for example, in personality or cognitive ability – and their effects may swamp even those of the broader culture or subculture in which a person was raised; in other words, there will be an interplay between the culture and the individual's own disposition. Research on this intersection between culture and self has focused largely on variations in how individuals are "tuned in, sensitive to, orientated toward, focused on, or concerned with others" (Erez and Earley, 1993: 25). Such a perspective has given rise to the notion of self-construal, which defines the self along two broad types: an independent or individualistic self and an interdependent or collectivistic self (Earley and Gibson, 1998). Variations in self-construal are reflected in people's belief about the relationships between themselves and others and, more precisely, the extent to which they see themselves separate from others versus connected with others. Independent self-construal is characterised by the extent to which individuals construe an inherent separateness between themselves and others. In contrast, those high on interdependence or collectivism strive for connectedness; for these individuals, the imperative is to maintain one's position as a member of a larger social unit. In many respects, then, self-construal is a personality variable akin to the cultural dimension of Individualism/Collectivism. Brutus *et al.* (2009) found that this was related to attitudes to appraisal. As expected, people who think of themselves as independent of others were much more comfortable in making or communicating appraisal ratings, handling the discussion and so on – they had higher self-efficacy in relation to appraisal in general. This is supported by Mishra and Roch (2013), who found that rater self-construal had a significant effect on overall performance evaluations – in particular, raters with high interdependent self-construal showed a preference for ratees who had a similarly high level of interdependence, in contrast with raters high on independent self-construal, who did not.

This may be one particularly influential personality variable, but there are likely to be a whole host of other cognitive, personality and group differences, and one cannot assume a blanket effect of culture on an individual's reaction to appraisal – it is likely to result from a complex interaction between the nature of the scheme, the organisational context, the relationship with the appraiser, culture and individual differences. All of which points to the importance of making line managers aware, in their training, of the kinds of influences at work. At the end of the day, much depends on the sensitivity of the appraiser in understanding and taking account of these, and showing skill in conducting the appraisal interaction accordingly.

The present chapter has only signalled some of the kinds of cultural difference that may influence appraisal interaction and attitudes – there are certainly others (see House *et al.*, 2004). Organisations operating across national and cultural boundaries would be well advised to (a) read the literature available on this topic; (b) seek guidance from those external or internal to the organisation who have expertise and experience in dealing with cross-cultural issues; (c) consult the different cultural groups involved about their expectations in relation to appraisal processes – and then build the results into both the design of their appraisal systems and the training they offer. One size will *not* fit all.

IN SUMMARY

With the internationalisation of business, it becomes more important to understand how culture may influence responses to appraisal. Assumptions about performance appraisal based on experience and research in predominantly Western countries may not hold good when transferred to other cultures. For example, individuals from cultures high on Individualism and low on Power Distance (which typify the USA and some European nations) may have a very different attitude to appraisal compared to people who have been raised in Collectivist and high Power Distance cultures; such differences can impact on an individual's willingness to give feedback, to question feedback, to claim achievements for themselves rather than the team and so on. This is at least equally relevant for the use of multi-source feedback, and should thus be taken into account when devising systems – they need to be consistent with the cultural values in which they will be embedded. However, with an increasingly multinational workforce, there may be a wide range of cultural backgrounds represented within a single organisation, and both appraisers and appraisees need to be sensitised in appraisal training about some of the possible differences and resulting outcomes. That said, it is important not to make assumptions too quickly on the basis of national cultures, as individual differences and organisational culture may be equally influential in determining how any given individual responds in the appraisal situation.

DISCUSSION POINTS AND QUESTIONS

9.1 What might be the problems or issues in an appraisal discussion being held between a line manager who is from a culture that (in Hofstede's terms) is Masculine and marked by low Uncertainty Avoidance and an appraisee who is from a more Feminine culture and one that is high on Uncertainty Avoidance?

9.2 How and in what way do you think social, economic and political changes – including globalisation – in the world today will impact on existing cultural differences? What are the implications for your country and organisation?

9.3 What sort of elements would you include in appraisal training if there was likely to be a range of different cultural backgrounds represented in both the appraisers and the appraisees in your organisation?

KEY REFERENCES

Bailey, C. and Fletcher, C. (2008) Performance management and appraisal – an international perspective. In M. M. Harris (Ed.) *The Handbook of Research in International Human Resource Management*. Mahwah, NJ: Lawrence Erlbaum, pp. 125–144 (and indeed the whole book!).

Chiang, F. F. T. and Birtch, T. A. (2010) Appraising performance across borders: An empirical examination of the purposes and practices of performance appraisal in a multi-country context. *Journal of Management Studies*, **47**(7), 1365–1393.

Hofstede, G. (1980) *Culture's Consequences: International Differences in Work-related Values*. Beverley Hills, CA: Sage.

Varma, A., Budhwar, P. S. and DeNisi, A. (2008) *Performance Management Systems. A Global Perspective.* Abingdon, UK: Routledge, pp. 3–14 (and again, the whole book!).

REFERENCES

Amba-Rao, S., Petrick, J., Gupta, J. and Von der Embse, T. (2000). Comparative performance appraisal practices and management values among foreign and domestic firms in India. *International Journal of Human Resource Management,* **11**(1), 60–89.

Bailey, C. and Fletcher, C. (2008) Performance management and appraisal – an international perspective. In Harris M. M. (Ed.) *The Handbook of Research in International Human Resource Management.* Mahwah, NJ: Lawrence Erlbaum, pp. 125–144.

Brutus, S., Derayeh, M., Fletcher, C., Bailey, C., Velazquez, P., Shi, K., Simon, C. and Labath, V. (2006) Multisource feedback systems: A six-country comparative analysis. *International Journal of Human Resource Management,* **17**(11), 1888–1906.

Brutus, S., Fletcher, C. and Bailey, C. (2009) The influence of independent self-construal on rater self-efficacy in performance appraisal. *International Journal of Human Resource Management,* **19**, 999–2011.

Campbell, J. P. and Wiernik, B. M. (2015) The modeling and assessment of work performance. *Annual Review of Organisational Psychology and Organizational Behavior,* **2**(1), 47–74.

Chiang, F. F. T. and Birtch, T. A. (2010) Appraising performance across borders: An empirical examination of the purposes and practices of performance appraisal in a multi-country context. *Journal of Management Studies,* **47**(7), 1365–1393.

Cooke, F. L. (2008) Performance management in China. In A. Varma, P. S. Budhwar and A. DeNisi (Eds) *Performance Management Systems: A Global Perspective.* Abingdon, UK: Routledge, 193–209.

Earley, P. C. and Gibson, C. B. (1998) Taking stock in our progress on individualism–collectivism: 100 years of solidarity and community. *Journal of Management,* **24**(3), 265– 304.

Earley, P. C. and Stubblebine, P. (1989) Intercultural assessment of performance feedback. *Group and Organisation Studies,* **14**(2), 161–181.

Erez, M. and Earley, P. C. (1993) *Culture, Self-Identity, and Work.* Oxford: Oxford University Press.

Fernandez, D. R., Carlson, D. S., Stepina, L. P. and Nicholson, J. D. (1997) Hofstede's country classification 25 years later. *The Journal of Social Psychology,* **137**(1), 43–54.

Fletcher, C. (2001) Performance appraisal and performance management: The developing research agenda. *Journal of Occupational and Organizational Psychology,* **74**(4), 473–487.

Harris, M. M. (2007) *The Handbook of Research in International Human Resource Management.* Mahwah, NJ: Lawrence Erlbaum.

Hofstede, G. (1980) *Culture's Consequences: International Differences in Work Related Values*. Beverly Hills, CA: Sage.

Hofstede, G. (2001) *Culture's Consequences: Comparing Values, Behaviors, Institutions and Organizations across Nations*. Thousand Oaks, CA: Sage.

House, R. J., Hanges, P. J., Javidan, M., Dorfman, P. W. and Gupta, V. (2004) *Culture, Leadership and Organizations: The GLOBE study of 62 societies*. Thousand Oaks, CA: Sage.

Huo, Y. P. and Von Glinow, M. A. (1995) On transplanting human resource practices to China: A culture driven approach. *International Journal of Manpower*, **16**(9), 3–15.

Kikoski, J. F. (1999) Effective communication in the performance appraisal interview: Face-to-face communication for public managers in the culturally diverse workplace. *Public Personnel Management*, **28**, 301–323.

Mishra, V. and Roch, S. G. (2013) Cultural values and performance appraisal: Assessing the effects of rater self-construal on performance ratings. *The Journal of Psychology*, **147**(4), 325–344.

Peretz, H. and Fried, Y. (2012) National cultures, performance appraisal practices, and organizational absenteeism and turnover: A study across 21 countries. *Journal of Applied Psychology*, **97**(2), 448–459.

Sharma, T., Budhwar, P. S. and Varma, A. (2008) Performance management in India. In A. Varma, P. S. Budhwar and A. DeNisi (Eds) *Performance Management Systems: A Global Perspective*. Abingdon, UK: Routledge, pp. 180–192.

Shipper, F., Hoffman, R. C. and Rotondo, D. M. (2007) Does the 360 feedback process create actionable knowledge across cultures? *Academy of Management Learning and Education*, **6**(1), 33–50.

Snape, E., Thompson, D., Ka-ching Ya, F. and Redman, T. (1998) Performance appraisal and culture: Practice and attitudes in Hong Kong and Great Britain. *International Journal of Human Resource Management*, **9**(5), 841–861.

Sparrow, P. and Budhwar, P. (1997). Competition and change: Mapping the India HRM recipe against world-wide patterns. *Journal of World Business*, **32**(3), 224–243.

Triandis, H. C. and Brislin, R. W. (1984) Cross-cultural psychology. *American Psychologist*, **39**(9), 1006–1017.

Varma, A., Budhwar, P. S. and DeNisi, A. (2008) Performance management around the globe. In A. Varma, P. S. Budhwar and A. DeNisi (Eds) *Performance Management Systems: A Global Perspective*. Abingdon, UK: Routledge, pp. 3–14.

TRAINING, AND THE IMPLEMENTATION AND MAINTENANCE OF APPRAISAL

10

The role of training in determining the success of an appraisal scheme cannot be overestimated. This is not a new conclusion; Anstey *et al.* (1976) were able to show that organisations which had longer and more skills-based appraisal training produced more constructive outcomes from appraisal interviews than comparable organisations which had shorter courses that did not incorporate a skills training component. Surveys show that training is (allegedly) *offered* to appraisers by nearly 80 per cent of UK organisations (Industrial Society, 2001). Unfortunately, this does not mean either that the training was taken up by all appraisers or that the quality of what is offered is high. Thus, another survey, this time of line managers rather than of HR representatives, indicated that 30 per cent of them said they had not been trained (Strebler *et al.*, 2001). Indeed, the picture may be worse than this. In a survey of over 1,000 organisations across 55 countries, Mercer (2013) found that a third of line managers were judged to have only 'marginal' skills in handling the performance management dialogue with their staff, and only 5 per cent were assessed as highly skilled in this respect. Another survey (Charman *et al.*, 2014) of more than 100 UK organisations reported that only 17 per cent of managers had 'in person' training (i.e. actually attending for a course).

So, on both these criteria – take-up and quality of training – there is great room for improvement. One of the main failings of appraisal training in the past has been the emphasis on the procedure and paperwork rather than on the process and the skills needed to carry out appraisal in a sensitive and constructive manner. It is, of course, important that everyone knows what the scheme consists of and how it is to be operated, but this is really the easy part. Because it has a high 'comfort factor', there is a tendency to focus on the appraisal forms, etc. as if they were the main purpose of the exercise, which they are not – in fact, they often just get in the way of holding a meaningful discussion of performance (Hirsh, 2006). Nonetheless, it is important to offer training that enhances the formal assessment element of appraisal – which usually means helping appraisers to make more accurate judgements of performance and to express these effectively in the ratings they make. Accordingly, the first part of this section on training will deal with this aspect.

DIFFERENT APPROACHES TO TRAINING RATERS

The use of performance ratings and the difficulties that arise from them were outlined in Chapter 4. The question is how to assist appraisers in using them, almost irrespective of what form they take. The four main approaches used are:

- rater error training
- performance dimension training
- behavioural observation training
- frame-of-reference training.

The notion behind the first of these is to make appraisers aware of the classic rating errors that arise, such as the 'halo effect' or a tendency to be overly lenient in one's assessments (see Chapter 4, Box 4.3 for a list of such errors). The hope is that by sensitising appraisers to such biases and distortion in the assessment process, they will subsequently avoid them. The second approach, performance dimension training, focuses, as the name implies, on deepening the appraisers' understanding of the assessment dimensions they are using. This involves familiarising appraisers with the rating scales and what each one means in terms of the qualities and behaviour relating to it. One way of doing this is to involve the raters in the scale construction: doing this, of course, would entail the appraisers' involvement in setting up the appraisal system at an early stage in its development – we set out a participative approach to design in Chapter 5. Turning to behavioural observation training (BOT), this is chiefly about training appraisers to identify what aspects of their subordinates' behaviour they should concentrate their attention on – what they should observe – and to differentiate these from those that are not relevant to the assessment task. The idea is that, in so doing, appraisers will not only recognise the important behaviours and incidents, but will also remember them better and make them less susceptible to rating errors. Finally, frame-of-reference training (FOR) has some similarities with BOT, but goes further and is a more integrated approach. It is a cognitively orientated training method that is intended to provide a theory of performance for appraisers, helping them understand not only the assessment dimensions, but also how these integrate with each other and how they express the ideas about performance that are held by the organisation concerned. It makes them better at correctly interpreting what appraised behaviours reflect which levels of performance. There is an extensive literature on FOR (Roch *et al.*, 2012). While all these methods have something to offer, the weight of evidence is clearly coming down on the side of FOR. Meta-analyses (Woehr and Huffcutt, 1994; Roch *et al.*, 2012) indicate that this kind of training can lead to significant improvements in rating accuracy.

A somewhat different 'spin' on rater training is provided by Selden *et al.* (2012), with an approach rooted in cognitive neuroscience. Managers were randomly assigned to either a control group, which had the traditional training focused on assessing performance by reference to a set of dimensions, or an experimental group, which had both this traditional approach but also training that put them through a series of exercises designed to help them access global impressions (or person schemas) of their appraisees. The former, traditional approach is in brain terms a characteristically left-hemisphere activity, whereas the person schema approach should entail right-hemisphere activity – and since the experimental group had both kinds of training, they should exemplify a 'whole brain' approach. Pre- and post-appraisal evaluations indicated that appraisees of the experimental group perceived their appraisals as being more useful. While this was a fairly small-scale study, it is an interesting example of seeking to use neuroscience as a basis for appraisal training.

Rater training is important. However, it is not nearly enough. Giving appraisers a full understanding and appreciation of the assessment dimensions they are using, and perhaps also encouraging them to take a holistic approach, is desirable – but it leaves aside the question of their *willingness* to put accuracy of assessment at the top of their agenda, and it also only goes so far in helping them manage the performance discussion in appraisal, on which the success or otherwise of appraisal schemes stands or falls. It is to this wider view of appraisal training that we now turn.

BEYOND RATING SCALES: TRAINING IN HANDLING APPRAISAL

Most of what follows is rather atheoretical and will concentrate on the severely practical issue of how the behavioural skills needed in appraisal can be imparted; some further guidance on training, specifically in the context of professional groups, has been given in Chapter 8. We will also consider what training for appraisal needs to be provided for appraisees – hugely important, but usually neglected.

Before deciding on what form appraisal training might take, it is worth addressing the issue of where it should start. The conventional wisdom seems to be right – to introduce appraisal at the top and to work down, on the basis that (a) top management have to be seen to be taking it seriously; and (b) it is a salutary experience for someone to have been appraised before they themselves appraise anyone else. There is some evidence to support the first contention. A review study by Rodgers and Hunter (1991) has demonstrated the importance of senior management involvement, though in the context of management by objectives (MBO) schemes rather than appraisal as such. It found that organisations introducing MBO with a high level of senior management commitment achieved average productivity gains of over 56 per cent, compared to average gains of just over 6 per cent in the case of organisations where such commitment was lacking. By analogy, since more appraisal schemes now take in director-level staff, there is reason to hope that the commitment will be present.

Background briefing and documentation

This element of appraisal training can be run as part of the appraisers' skills course or as a separate preliminary session. If the latter, it will most likely be delivered online. Its purpose is to tell all the appraisers what the thinking is behind the appraisal scheme, what it is trying to achieve, how it is structured and implemented, and to introduce and explain the forms and paperwork. If there has been a good consultation process in developing the scheme, then all this will be that much easier to put across. Without it, the briefing element will probably take longer, not least because some mechanism – such as a helpline – will be needed to deal with questions or issues that may arise. In some respects, the briefing session is doubling as a commitment-gaining exercise. The aim is not just to inform, but to sell the scheme to the appraisers. As Latham and Latham (2000) point out, appraisers must take the appraisal process seriously.

Briefing should normally be given fairly shortly before the appraisal training courses (if these are separate) and the first round of appraisals. It is often helpful to include a short description of the recent history of appraisal in the organisation, and why there has been a need to change and/or to develop the new scheme. The aims of the new scheme and how it is to be operated can then be outlined. As part of this, some of the issues mentioned above in relation to training in rating performance may be included – for example, explaining the origin and rationale of the performance dimensions to be rated. Some organisations present quotes at some point during the briefing, indicating that there is top management support of the appraisal scheme, to emphasise high-level commitment to it and to stress that it is a worthwhile activity.

Training the appraisers

What follows is mainly about training in relation to handling the performance discussion. Though training in use of the rating scales using one or other of the methods described earlier will be important, perhaps the biggest problem in training line managers in appraisal is overcoming their own psychological concerns. Many managers do not have a great deal of confidence in their ability to handle appraisal interviews effectively, and so tend to cling to the paperwork and to the rating scales. This focus on the administrative side of the process – not least just getting the forms off the desk and into HR on time is sometimes reinforced by the HR function itself (Hirsh *et al.*, 2011). Some managers have an exaggerated idea of what appraisal involves and what it demands of them (this is especially true if they have little or no experience of it). They see the appraisal as being akin to professional counselling, and feel ill-equipped to take it on. In particular, they may worry about generating conflict over the assessments they make and then having to handle it; as Brutus *et al.* (2013) point out, training needs to raise their level of self-efficacy in coping with this. Other managers try to reduce their anxieties by minimising the importance of appraisal, seeking to make it sound trivial or unnecessary. This usually gives rise to the kinds of comment every trainer who has run an appraisal course has heard umpteen times: "This is only what I do on a day-to-day basis anyway", "Good managers (i.e. those like me) don't need appraisal", etc. The implication is that appraisal is a superfluous and redundant addition to the dialogue that is already taking place. However, both research (e.g. Nathan *et al.*, 1991) and experience suggest very strongly that this is not true. It is precisely those managers who have frequent communications with their staff who have the most productive appraisals.

The extent of the appraisers' concerns about their ability to conduct the appraisal will depend on its content and aims, and how much say they have had in them. But even where they have participated fully in the design stage, there will still be a fair number who need to have their confidence built up through the training process. Training here is as much about giving that confidence as it is about teaching specific skills. For this reason, it is vital that

- the training is organised so as to ensure that there is enough time for participants to see that they are capable of doing a good job. If there is time for just one practice session, the appraiser often does not handle it well and then has no opportunity to learn from the feedback and improve both performance and confidence;
- the training is delivered as close as possible to the time of the first appraisals.

Neither of these is very easy to arrange. The ratio of participants to trainers on any one course should not really rise above 4:1 if there is to be a supervised practical element and effective feedback. Unless the organisation has a lot of trainers (somewhat unlikely), this means that it will take some time to train everyone. So those going through on the first courses might have some time to wait before conducting their appraisals, if the organisation is working on a common starting date and the principle that no one will appraise unless trained to do so. In addition, the time commitment needed for good skills training makes it rather costly.

The time problem is particularly acute for senior managers, as it is difficult, if not impossible, to get them away from their desks for 2 days. There are three main options open to cope with this. First, run shorter courses for more senior and (in theory) more experienced people. The problem here is that they give the lead, and if they do not demonstrate their belief in the importance of the scheme by making time for training and being competent in handling appraisals themselves, the message will get through to those below them. Also, being more senior and more experienced does not mean being more competent in handling appraisal. As has been observed on many occasions, 20 years' experience can often be 1 year's experience repeated 20 times. A better, second option, if at all possible, is to try to break up the training for senior managers so that they can attend on a couple of separate sessions. There is another difficulty in delivering training to the most senior levels, though. Top managers are not noted for their willingness to expose any of their real or imagined failings in front of peers. As a result, skills training conducted by in-house trainers is often politically unacceptable at these higher levels. One way round this is to find suitable externally run, open courses pitched at senior management level. However, there is another option available, which is to make available to appraisers a training package which is delivered through their PC and which they can work through in their own time. E-learning of this kind allows self-pacing and gets round the problem of senior managers feeling exposed in a training situation. Moreover, it allows the user not only to revisit aspects of appraisal where they feel they need to reinforce their learning, but also to ensure that the learning is fresh in their minds by doing so immediately prior to actually holding the appraisal sessions. There are a number of such software programs available. Ideally, of course, this kind of approach would supplement conventional skills training.

Appraisal interview training

Carrying out the appraisal interview calls for the appraiser to draw on a range of knowledge and skills. For example, an understanding of motivation is important in this context, and later in this chapter we will return to this theme.

The appraiser may well need to make use of coaching skills too – again, this is a theme to which we return in this chapter. Especially important, of course, are the skills of giving feedback (see below). And it is the giving of feedback that can be the greatest source of apprehension for appraisers (as is receiving it for appraisees). To be sure, there may from time to time be occasions when managers will have to have difficult conversations. Dealing with this topic is beyond the scope of this book, but there is no shortage of helpful advice – for example, ACAS in the UK has published a short guidance booklet that covers the ground well (Advisory, Conciliation and Arbitration Service, 2014).

More often than not any sense of apprehension (by either party) is likely to be misplaced – whether it is called a conversation (Gordon and Stewart, 2009; see also Gordon and Miller, 2014), dialogue (Hirsh, 2006), or discussion (Heneman, 1991), the appraisal interview is likely to be pretty much a straightforward event. Accompanying these shifts of terminology, there has been much advocacy of making the discussion a joint, problem-solving event (e.g. Beer, 1987; Tourish, 2006). The skills required (by both parties) are learnable but this needs to be done in a hands-on fashion; here we will focus on the kind of training necessary to impart process skills relevant to appraisers – training for appraisees will be covered later in the chapter.

Many courses include a video or training film, either produced in-house or obtained from external sources to illustrate teaching points. Some of these are very useful, not least in promoting discussion amongst the course members. However, they do need to be professionally made and presented to be really effective – amateurish efforts simply give the more sceptical amongst the audience further ammunition to ridicule the appraisal scheme. There is little doubt, though, that appraisal interview training can best be tackled through practical exercises where the participants get feedback on their performance from trainers and fellow course members. One of the most commonly used techniques is the role-play interview. Typically, this involves one course member appraising another on the basis of a written brief that describes the situation and their different perspectives. An alternative is to ask the individual playing the role of the appraisee to base it on a real problem case known to them. However, this kind of exercise exacerbates the inevitable artificiality of the training situation, and allows the favourite escape clause of "Well, of course, I would not have handled it that way in real life."

A much better approach, and one that generates a higher level of realism and course member involvement, is to get the participants to perform a task that they are then appraised on by their fellow course members. There are a number of ways of doing this. They may work on a group project – often akin to an assessment centre group decision-making task – and then appraise one another on their individual contribution and performance. Depending on the numbers involved and the time available, they may all be given a turn at leading the rest of their syndicate in a task (building structures from LEGO bricks, etc.) and then be appraised on that. A third variation is to get one course member to give a short presentation on a topic, have a second one appraise them on that, the third participant appraises the second on the handling of the appraisal and so on. There are as many permutations on the exercise theme as the trainers' imagination permits.

The point about exercises of this kind is that, while they only allow the appraisal of performance in one isolated event, they do offer an opportunity to practise appraisal skills on genuine behavioural examples. The course members are ego-involved to the extent that they find it a demanding task, with the minimum of artificiality. True, the nature of the task that they are appraised on is not specifically and directly job-relevant, but this is not a disadvantage – a task that is very complex or involved in the work of the organisation runs the risk of focusing too much attention on content and detracting from the real point of the exercise, which is about process.

The usual format in running such exercises is for the syndicate tutor to ask the appraiser and then the appraisee for their feelings and observations on how the practice interview was conducted, followed by feedback from the tutor and the other syndicate members. The latter may have been given a behavioural checklist to guide their observations, and the tutor may divide the monitoring and feedback between them so that they individually concentrate on different aspects of the way the appraiser handled the session. Whichever way this is done, however, it provides another valuable opportunity to practise much the same feedback skills as are needed in an appraisal situation. This needs to be pointed out before the practice interviews commence, and some guidance given to course members on how to go about giving feedback to one another. Box 10.1 presents some general guidance on giving feedback in this context (and, indeed, on conducting an appraisal interview itself). You will find a full and helpful treatment of feedback in London (2015): more detailed guidance on feedback skills, and exercises to develop them, can be found in Cardy and Leonard (2011), and Egan (2014) is a key source on helping skills more broadly. The value of having a course which permits each participant the chance of doing at least two practice interviews is that they have a chance to learn from the first and to improve their skill and confidence in the second.

BOX 10.1

SOME GENERAL POINTS ON GIVING FEEDBACK

The purpose of feedback is to help the person to whom it is directed. To this end, it should be given in such a way that the person (a) understands it, (b) accepts it and (c) can do something about it. How can this be achieved? There are some general rules to follow that can help here:

- *Be tentative* – seldom are things so clear-cut that observations take on the mantle of indisputable fact, to be conveyed as such.
- *Be willing to listen* – individuals may well have observations to make that throw new light on the problems under discussion. They should be encouraged to put forward their views. Even where their reaction is more emotional than 'reasoned', it is probably better to let people get it off their chests rather than try to cut them short.
- *Be concrete* – discuss specific behaviours and examples to illustrate and support the points being made.
- *Be respectful* – try to communicate acceptance and understanding of the individual; you are talking about their performance of a task, not discussing their personality and values.
- *Identify both the positive and the negative aspects of performance* – resist the temptation to harp on about the deficiencies alone.
- *Be constructive* – offer suggestions as to how the situation might have been tackled differently and how problems might be tackled in the future.
- *Do not try to make too many critical points* – apart from the danger of generating defensive reactions, people can only take in and deal with just so much at one time.
- *Concentrate your observations on the aspects of performance that the individual can do something about* – there is little sense in focusing on deficiencies that will be impossible for the person to remedy.
- *Make sure your value judgements are identified as such* – and not presented as facts.

Exercises of the kind described give the opportunity for practising skills in collecting information. The appraiser should be asking the right kind of questions to find out why the appraisee approached the task in the way they did and so on. Skills can also be practised in giving feedback and, to an extent, in coaching on how to improve. The exercises may be a vehicle for demonstrating skill in problem solving, though this will not necessarily be the case unless some deliberate effort has been made to build this in from the inception. Perhaps the one area in which they do not give adequate opportunity to develop skills is that of motivation. This is such a neglected topic in appraisal training that a separate section is devoted to it later in this chapter.

The practical component of an appraisal course needs to be supported with some written notes for guidance to reinforce the message conveyed in the training. These can be provided online and referred to by the appraisers to refresh their memories before they do their appraisals. Apart from going over the basic points again, guidance notes can deal with issues that there may not be time for on the training course; for example, how to deal with special problem cases. There is an understandable desire on the part of some people attending appraisal courses to be told how to deal with every conceivable reaction and problem. Clearly, it is not possible to provide answers to this; the aim of the training is usually to impart generic skills and techniques that can be adapted and applied to a range of situations and needs. Course exercises normally focus on examples of typical appraisal content and interaction, since this is what most appraisers have to deal with most of the time. But there are extreme cases that occasionally arise – appraisees becoming overly emotional, or aggressive, or seeking to be manipulative, for example. The appraisers' concerns about these make them loom larger in their minds than the probability or frequency of them happening actually warrants. But they cannot be ignored. Even if they are the exception rather than the rule, when they *do* occur, they can cause the appraiser a disproportionate amount of trouble. If the time available for practical exercises is too limited to deal with them, then the alternatives are (a) to include some advice on the handling of problem cases that the individual appraiser can consult online; (b) provide a 'helpline' that appraisers can ring to seek advice, usually from the HR department.

One last point on the training of appraisers: it is valuable if they can be offered the opportunity to attend some kind of follow-up session run by training and/or personnel department staff. This might be in the nature of an 'appraisal clinic', where they bring back for discussion specific problems or issues that they have encountered in carrying out their interviews. It could also take the form of a review group made up of the original course membership convened at the end of the appraisal cycle, where (for an hour or so) they can raise any particular difficulties and seek advice. Both of these serve a further purpose in acting as monitoring devices for the appraisal scheme as a whole.

TRAINING IN COACHING

There is little point in holding appraisal interviews and giving feedback if the appraisees are not to be supported in their efforts to develop and enhance their performance. As we saw in Chapter 3, Box 3.4, one of the basic leadership performance factors identified by Campbell (2012) has to do with training and coaching. And, according to the 2015 learning and development survey carried out by the Chartered Institute of Personnel and Development (2015a), coaching (and mentoring) by line managers and/or co-workers is widely offered by organisations. But how widely is developmental support experienced by employees? The *Employee Outlook, Spring 2015* survey carried out by the Chartered Institute of Personnel and Development (2015b) paints a somewhat more encouraging picture of coaching than for training and development more broadly. Just under 40 per cent of survey respondents said that their manager always or usually discussed training and development with them; for coaching, the incidence was a little below 60 per cent.

As we've noted at several points in this book, changes in organisational structures and the like have made various aspects of line managers' jobs more difficult. We noted also in Chapter 1 that the failure of PM systems not uncommonly is attributed to 'deficiencies' on the part of line managers and we queried whether this is in part a selection problem, in part a training problem. Though survey evidence indicates that coaching is quite widespread, the picture when it comes to training in how to coach is less clear. How many managers get training in how to coach others? We suspect that all too often this is left to learning by experience, perhaps through the example set by the individual manager's own bosses previously. Unfortunately, these examples and experiences may not be at all good. Very focused training on handling the appraisal process is all well and good, but even more important is the acquisition of wider coaching skills that are relevant not only to the appraisal situation, but also to the development of staff more generally. A discussion on training in coaching generally is beyond the scope of this book, but many helpful sources are available. For example, Passmore (2005) shows how the GROW model may be used by managers. For fuller treatments of a range of approaches to coaching (and mentoring), take a look at Cox *et al.* (2010) or Passmore *et al.* (2013). And for concise, helpful advice on what managers should be doing as developers of others, there is guidance from the Institute for Employment Studies (2004).

TRAINING APPRAISEES

Research tells us that when those appraised put more time into preparing for their appraisal, the appraisal session lasts longer, and that longer appraisal sessions are associated with more positive outcomes (Fletcher, 2010). But do appraisees know how to prepare? Providing training for them is far from commonplace; a survey (Industrial Society, 2001) showed that 62 per cent of UK organisations gave appraisees details of the mechanics of the appraisal scheme, 40 per cent offered formal training (how much training or how positively the offer was made we know not) and 25 per cent did nothing for them at all. This is probably a major flaw in appraisal provision. If appraisal systems ask appraisees to make a self-assessment prior to the appraisal, and to think about their objectives (as most of them do), why should the appraisees not be given training to help them in this? Arguably, they should need it more than their more senior appraisers. If the appraisees are to have a significant input into the appraisal process, then they should be given some help in making it effective. Of course, many appraisers are, in their turn, appraised by their own bosses. For them, the appraiser training will probably fulfil most of their needs from the appraisee perspective, though a short session specifically focusing on this could be included in the appraisal interview course. It is no bad thing to give appraisers an opportunity to put themselves on the other side of the desk and see how things look from there.

Frequently, appraisee courses are simply briefing sessions, with no real practical component – they can easily be delivered online. They sometimes take place within the broader context of induction courses, and in contrast with appraiser courses, there is seldom any pressure to attend. One county council in the UK reported that the take-up rate of places on appraisee courses was so low that they eventually withdrew them. This is rather disappointing and fairly unusual, perhaps caused by a lack of understanding of what was on offer. The content of appraisee training to some extent mirrors that of the appraisers. It can include the following:

- *Background briefing*. At the very least, they need to know what the aims of the scheme are and how it is to run.
- *How to prepare*. This may be simply providing an agenda, or giving a preparation form, or it may include how to complete a self-appraisal form that is an integral part of the process.
- *Guidance on objectives*. This should encourage the appraisee to think in advance about what these might be for the year ahead, and give some training on how objectives should be framed. (See Chapter 5, Box 5.4 for questions the appraisee might ask about goals and goal-setting.)
- *Discussion of self-assessment*. This should look at the strengths and weaknesses of self-assessment, and review its place in appraisal.
- *How to respond to criticism*. One of the concerns uppermost in appraisees' minds is the prospect of criticism and how they will

react – talking through the issues here can help them respond more constructively and confidently if and when it happens.

- *Assertiveness training.* Some basic guidance can be given to help appraisees put their own point of view across to their boss without being unduly emotional or defensive.
- *How to get action.* The appraisees can be encouraged to take the initiative in following up action recommendations to ensure that they are implemented.

Many of these can be presented in the form of discussion topics, though there is plenty of scope for practical exercises if desired. Training appraisees is something that can add a significant impetus to the effective running of an appraisal scheme, in that if they are empowered to drive it from their side, the appraisers will find it hard to do anything but respond with their best efforts. As things stand at present, this lack of focus and effort on preparing appraisees to get the most out of performance reviews is probably one of the major weaknesses of how such systems are applied, and a reason why they are often less than successful.

OTHER ISSUES IN APPRAISAL TRAINING

Appraising diversity

As we have already seen in Chapter 9, where appraisees and appraisers are from different cultural or ethnic groups, there can be the potential for misunderstanding and poor communication. A business services organisation found evidence of this and did all they could to make sure that their new appraisal documentation was framed in language that was understandable to all. Piloting it with representatives of all the groups involved will help here. It is worth sensitising appraisers to this issue in training if they are likely to appraise staff of very diverse cultural backgrounds (or, indeed, educational levels). The different styles of interpersonal communication and self-presentation that have been found to characterise different cultures were discussed in Chapter 9 and so will not be repeated here.

Another aspect of having a diverse workforce is that it can produce the bias and prejudice that give rise to unfair discrimination, on the grounds of ethnicity or gender (or other non-performance-related grounds). While there is a need to monitor the output of appraisal schemes for this, there is also a need to tackle it from the other end, the input. Bias does not always show itself in the form of ratings or the assessment of target achievement (if the latter is as objective as it is supposed to be, then it is to be hoped there is less opportunity for this to happen). It can be more subtle than that, but just as damaging. Going back to the concept of attributional error (Chapter 4, Box 4.3), Garland and Price (1977) found that successful performance in female managers was attributed by prejudiced male managers either to luck or to the task being an easy one, whereas unprejudiced managers put it down to high ability and hard work. Similar distortions in the explanation of good or poor performance can arise where the appraisees are members of ethnic minorities and the appraisers are racially prejudiced.

This kind of bias can be illustrated in various ways. One approach is through assessment exercises – for example, appraisers can be given written descriptions of individuals and their performance and asked to react to them in some way (e.g. by rating the people described or explaining their likely motives for behaving the way they did). Half the appraisers can be given the description containing a female principal character and the other half are given the same one but with a male character. Comparing the ratings and accounts of the two groups – without identifying individuals – often brings out into the open the kinds of stereotypes and assumptions that are part and parcel of bias. Needless to say, though, this requires especially sensitive handling on the part of the trainers.

Finally, one other mistake that male appraisers, in particular, need to be alerted to was identified by HR staff in a large UK local authority. This was a tendency to equate working late in the office with quality of work and commitment, which was then reflected in PRP recommendations. The most frequent losers from this were women who, having worked the full day, then went home to their families.

Diversity is a broad issue, and the reader who wishes to go into it further is referred to King and Gilrane (2015) for an introduction to other sources. In Chapter 4, Box 4.3 on bias also is relevant to this topic.

Training to motivate

Many, perhaps most appraisal schemes pay at least lip service to the aim of motivating those who are appraised. For some of them, it is one of their main purposes. Yet if you look at the content of appraisal training courses, you seldom find any mention of the word 'motivation'. There seems to be an assumption that simply doing the appraisal is enough to motivate the appraisee, and if that is not the case, then it is down to the performance-related pay to do the job. What does motivate people at work, and how can this knowledge be built into appraisal courses?

There is no single, universally accepted theory of motivation that explains the differences between people in the effort and commitment they put into their work (for a good general introduction to this field, the reader is directed to Latham, 2012). We have already referred to goal-setting theory (Chapter 3) and expectancy theory (Chapter 2), the former being more readily applicable than the latter, as we have already discussed. The application of goal-setting in appraisal is widespread, and training in how to do it should be provided for both appraisers and appraisees. The training should also cover the limitations of goal-setting. We noted earlier (in considering performance-related pay), that expectancy theory is concerned with what employees regard as valued outcomes and the need for performers to be able to see a clear and positive relationship between the effort they put in, the resulting performance, and how that leads to the valued outcome. An increase in pay may be a valued outcome for a great many employees, but bear in mind the point we made in the earlier discussion of merit pay – the amount of additional pay on offer has to be seen as worthwhile; too little, and a motivating effect is unlikely.

Bear in mind, too, that people vary greatly in what motivates them, and that different things are important to the same person at different career stages. The appraiser needs to be aware of this, and to know what, in expectancy theory terms, are the outcomes the individual values. If the organisation runs an appraisal scheme that allows managers some latitude in dispensing rewards – and the emphasis here is at least as much on the non-financial variety as the financial – and the manager knows the appraisees well enough, then the appraisal process can be successful in motivating performance improvement. Appraisal training, then, can facilitate this by directing course members' attention to the nature of individual differences in this respect. Brainstorming some ideas about what rewards both the appraisees *and* the appraisers themselves value can be a useful course exercise that provides a basis for more creative thinking about appraisal as a motivational tool.

Such an exercise is likely to bring to the surface the distinction between extrinsic and intrinsic motivation. With respect to the latter, it is valuable to recognise the power of the job itself as a source of motivation. Research at Ashridge Management College (Holton et al., 2009) into what managers find to be motivating pointed to the importance of intrinsic factors:

> When asked to describe what motivates them – although financial rewards are mentioned – it is often the intrinsic aspects of motivation which managers talk about. The desire for autonomy and freedom in carrying out their work is a key theme; having the freedom to take decisions, and

having the power and authority to deliver their task in the way that they think is right, is important to them. It's also about being trusted and given space to 'get on with the job' without being micro-managed.

(Holton *et al.*, 2009: 1)

There is much that we know from research on job design/work organisation about important design principles – the characteristics that 'good' jobs, that is, jobs that will motivate, should possess. Training for appraisers should cover this ground, given that they often are in a position to shape the content of jobs and the way in which work is organised. A number of theories have been important in helping us to understand the properties of jobs that are likely to be motivating – these are characteristics that need to be designed *in* to jobs. The Job Characteristics Model (JCM) set out by Hackman and Oldham (1980) sets out five such properties of motivating jobs:

*   skill variety – good jobs require the use of a range of skills;
*   task identity – doing a 'whole' job, seeing it through from the beginning to the outcome at the end;
*   task significance – the job has a meaningful impact on the lives of others (inside the organisation or elsewhere);
*   autonomy – over the way in which the work gets done;
*   feedback from the job – knowledge of results that comes from the job itself.

The idea is that the stronger these characteristics are within jobs, then the more motivating the job will be, so leading to better performance. Though the research on the Hackman and Oldham model has not supported the theory in every particular, the importance of the five characteristics has been endorsed, particularly with respect to their links to psychological outcomes such as job satisfaction and intrinsic motivation, but less so to behavioural outcomes such as job performance (Jayewardene and Clegg, 2014). And this probably is because the relationship is not as simple a matter as more = better. Take autonomy, for example. Latham (2012: 179) makes the point that "Autonomy should not be granted to employees who do not value it or who lack the knowledge or ability to perform interdependent tasks that are too complex for them." So, once again, it is important to remember that people differ in what they find motivating. Also, though influential, the JCM has been criticised on the grounds that it failed to include a sufficiently wide range of job characteristics – in particular, the social and interpersonal aspects of jobs did not feature. Co-workers, customers, clients and others with whom the performer interacts are included here, but the role of the supervisor is especially important given their responsibilities for agreeing performance requirements/expectations, giving feedback, etc. Appraisal training, therefore, ought not to ignore managers' broader people-management responsibilities. Organisations may have captured these in a competency framework. If you don't already have one, there's no shortage of them. For example, there are the National Occupational Standards for Management and Leadership (NOS, 2008), there are the dimensions of leadership/managerial performance that we referred to in Chapter 3 (Box 3.4), or you might want to consider using the management competencies for enhancing employee engagement developed by the Chartered Institute of Personnel and Development (2011).

Who does the training?

This used to be a fairly straightforward matter, and probably remains so for many organisations where appraisal falls directly into the lap of the HR and training departments. There is also increased reliance on self-development, with the provision of online resources for managers to use as and when they need. Things are less simple, though, where appraisal is part of a wider PM system and is owned by line management. If the latter have had some part – possibly a major one – in designing it, then they may also have some role in the training. The problem is that they may not be very good at training! Rather than abdicate this role to the line, the best solution may be for the HR department to work in collaboration with line representatives to tailor and deliver the training required by local circumstances. This can be through jointly designed and presented courses, or through a system of cascaded training, where HR staff train a cadre of line managers (self-nominated and/or nominated by local management) to go out and train their colleagues, providing them with the necessary back-up materials (Powerpoint presentations, handouts and so forth). This group of managers can then adapt the basic package to the way appraisal operates in their own divisions. One of the advantages of this approach reported by organisations that use it is that these line managers – if they are well-chosen – have a high level of credibility with their colleagues, and are the most effective representatives for the appraisal scheme. The initial training provided for them by HR has to be of the highest standard, though; they have to go away convinced of the value of what they are doing if they are to gain the commitment of their colleagues.

On a rather different theme there is the relative virtue of in-house versus bought-in training. At very senior levels, for reasons given earlier, it is often necessary to go outside the organisation to arrange suitable courses. For the rest, much depends on the training resources available. If there is no expertise in-house, then getting external help is the only option. This does not necessarily mean buying places on courses; it can be much better to hire a consultant to work with the organisation and run courses specifically for it. In fact, buying places on externally run public courses is probably the least attractive and least effective form of training. Such courses can be of a high professional standard and put over generic appraisal skills in a competent way, but what they cannot do is to cater for the unique characteristics of the organisation and the way appraisal operates there. They therefore tend to be seen as rather remote and lacking in relevance to the appraisers' context.

MONITORING AND MAINTENANCE: KEEPING APPRAISAL ON THE RIGHT LINES

Training is part of the implementation of appraisal; now it is appropriate to turn to the other end of the process – post-appraisal evaluation and its role in maintaining an effective appraisal system.

The HR director of an organisation employing more than 50,000 people which had introduced comprehensive performance management and appraisal policies, when asked what he would do differently if he were to start again, replied that he would lay more emphasis on the importance of maintaining them. He was putting his finger on one of the eternal problems of appraisal – how to keep it alive and well. Great effort is often expended on setting it up in the first place, with very little thought given to the follow-through action needed once it is up and running. Yet the frequency with which organisations encounter difficulties with their appraisal schemes should give ample warning of how essential it is to monitor them from the outset, and to modify and correct any deficiencies at the earliest possible stage. If problems do arise, they have to be caught quickly, or the whole appraisal scheme rapidly generates scepticism and disillusionment that is hard to dispel – and which can make any effort to modify the scheme an uphill struggle.

Much of what follows here implies a central role for the HR department, despite the emphasis elsewhere in the book on moving away from monolithic, centrally driven appraisal schemes. It is certainly desirable, as ever, to evaluate appraisal in a manner that involves line management and others. But the complexities of the exercise and the need, in many respects, for a broader perspective indicate that this is an area where HR have to act as the driving force and prime facilitators.

Performance indicators for performance appraisal

How do we recognise excellence in an appraisal scheme? What are the criteria by which an appraisal scheme might be judged successful or unsuccessful?

These can be broken down into short-term and long-term criteria, with the former being much easier to define than the latter.

Short-/Medium-term criteria

As far as monitoring the effectiveness of the appraisal scheme in its first year or so of operation is concerned, it is obviously the short-/medium-term criteria that are relevant. These include:

Completion rate

The most basic measure of all is whether the appraisals are actually carried out. Research over the years has shown just how often appraisals are not done, and how far managers will go to avoid them; a survey by the Industrial Society (1997) showed that less than one-third of UK organisations achieved a two-thirds completion rate – and there is no evidence to suggest things have improved since. If the appraisal scheme has been well designed, with a good level of consultation, this should not happen. Where all appraisal forms go to central HR (usually electronically), it is relatively easy to check on completion. Contemporary trends in appraisal, however, mean that it is less often the case that HR are automatically sent copies of appraisal documents. These tend to reside with the appraisee and appraiser as working documents to be referred to when, say, objectives are subject to interim review or development needs are discussed. There is a lot to be said for this practice, as it makes appraisal reports live documents rather than just file fodder. But it need not preclude the emailing of a simple action sheet to HR indicating what action recommendations, if any, have been agreed. This can serve the triple function of notifying HR that the appraisal has been done, informing them if there are some action recommendations that fall within their sphere of responsibility, and providing them with a means of checking on the subsequent implementation of action recommendations.

There will always be a few appraisals that are not done for one good reason or another, but any sizeable shortfall should set alarm bells ringing. The MD of one business services organisation decided to give further encouragement to the prompt and full completion of appraisals; he made it a pre-condition for considering promotion applications from the appraisers! That said, however, a high completion rate is by no means a guarantee of an effective appraisal system; as in most things, quantity does not imply quality. Good completion rates mean little if productive outcomes are not achieved.

Action generated

Another useful indicator of how things are going is the extent and type of action recommendations generated by the appraisal. If appraisal produces few agreed action points, then something is not quite right, the more so if there is any indication of development needs – how are they going to be dealt with? The nature of the action recommended is as important as the quantity. If the bulk of the action is to be taken outside the immediate job context – such as external training courses – then it may be an indication that the appraiser and appraisee are not looking hard enough at what they can do together to improve performance. Indeed, if most of the recommendations coming forward relate just to appraisers or to appraisees, the question needs to be asked whether the system is working as intended. It is reasonable for the majority of action following appraisals to be for implementation by the appraisees (overall, that is – clearly there will be individual cases where this is not so), but not all of it. If appraisers are taking responsibility for nearly all the post-appraisal action, then the suspicion arises that they are not getting their appraisees sufficiently involved in the process – though it would be encouraging in the sense that it could indicate that they are taking their coaching role seriously.

Quality of written reports

Where the appraisal scheme entails the completion of a formal written report, the content of this can give some indication of how the process is operating. At its simplest, the issue is whether the report is being completed in the manner required. More searchingly, the written content can be evaluated in terms of how much is recorded, whether there are any inconsistencies or deficiencies (e.g. weaknesses being identified but no remedial action mentioned), and the frequency and nature of the dissenting comments recorded by appraises (where there is scope for this on the form). Analysing all written reports, especially in a systematic way, is usually far too time-consuming to be worthwhile, though there are now software packages available that analyse textual material. It is more realistic to do it on a sampling basis, or to rely on the corrective input from other appraisers where more than one manager is involved (e.g. where the appraisal is done by the appraisee's immediate boss, but also seen by the boss two levels up) – though in the latter case, this function needs to be emphasised in training as part of the second appraiser's role.

Attitudes and the perceived value of appraisal

From action to reaction – how appraisers and appraisees feel about the scheme once they have been through a round of appraisals, what they see as the benefits and outcomes, what they see as the problems are all important indicators of how the scheme is working. Depending on when they are collected, these reactions can be short- or long-term criteria. If the participants feel positive about the scheme and see it as leading to useful developments (e.g. performance improvement, knowing where they stand, greater role clarity), then there is some cause for optimism. Although these might be subjective responses, they are as important as any hard data; the commitment of the participants rests on them. Any reported difficulties in the way the appraisals were conducted (too much emphasis on objectives, insufficient recognition of work done well, avoidance of giving feedback on the part of appraisers and so on) from the perspective of either appraisers or appraisees can be investigated and remedial action taken.

Equity

The concept of equity in relation to monitoring performance appraisal has two main aspects. One is the way reward decisions are made and the spread of assessments that give rise to them. Do certain sections of the organisation fare significantly better than others in terms of assessments and rewards, and, if so, is it justifiable? Are they really better? The other aspect concerns equal opportunities and unfair discrimination. Are the distributions of assessments, and the content of appraisals generally, similar for both genders, across ethnic groups, and for the other groups for which the law makes equality provisions? Inequity in these domains is likely to pose severe problems for the organisation and its appraisal scheme – see Chapter 4, Box 4.2 for some examples of rating distributions. Appraisals not only have to be fair, but they have to be seen to be fair (see Appendix B for advice on survey questions about fairness perceptions). For a more academic perspective, attention given by management writers to organisational justice theory bears directly on the question of equity in appraisal (e.g. Erdogan *et al.*, 2001; McDowell and Fletcher, 2004; Latham, 2012).

Long-term criteria

It could be argued that there should not be any long-term criteria for the effectiveness of an appraisal scheme, because no scheme should continue in the same form for a long period if it is to remain relevant to the changing circumstances of the organisation. But given that there is likely to be some continuity in the appraisal arrangements – most changes in appraisal schemes are more in the nature of evolution than revolution – it does seem reasonable to look at the longer-term benefits that the appraisal and related processes have produced. In fact, it is probably worth considering what the long-term criteria might be even if there is no intention to actually try to measure them. The rationale for this is simply that it often clarifies the organisation's thinking about appraisal to formally identify what the long-term success of an appraisal scheme might look like. It is, of course, possible that such a process will bring to light the fact that the organisation sees appraisal as an activity that has only short-term pay-offs. For those – it is hoped, the majority – who do see appraisal as having a strategic contribution to make, four broad criteria that might guide their evaluation are outlined below. None of them is determined solely by the effectiveness of appraisal, but in each case, the appraisal scheme has a role to play and can reasonably be assessed in that context.

Organisational performance

There are obviously many factors that influence the basic indices of organisational performance, and some of them (such as government policy or the state of the economy in general) are more potent in their effect than appraisal can ever be. Nonetheless, appraisal policies – particularly within a broader PM framework – should have some effect; we will see in Chapter 11 that evidence supports this contention. Perhaps the clearest indicator of their impact on organisational performance in the broadest sense is the extent to which the targets set for individuals are seen as being achieved. If they are, and if those targets relate in a systematic way to the business plan, then the appraisal process might fairly be judged to be making an effective contribution.

Quality of staff

One of the main functions of appraisal is, or should be, the development of talent. If it is successful in that, then the organisation will find either that it has enough trained employees to meet its normal requirements at any given time or that it can readily identify where gaps are likely to occur (which might arise through problems in recruitment) and take remedial action. In other words, one of the criteria that can be used is whether the promotion vacancies or new posts can be filled from within the organisation by the talent pool it has developed.

Retention of staff

Appraisal is a communication device, and in the process of discussing performance and meeting development needs, problems that might cause individuals to leave the organisation can be detected and (sometimes) dealt with. If the appraisal scheme is an effective vehicle for motivating people and raising job involvement and job satisfaction, it can help to minimise the wastage rate and boost staff retention, so saving the money that might otherwise be used in recruiting and training new staff.

Levels of engagement and well-being

As implied by the last point, an effective appraisal system should eventually – not overnight – lead to more positive attitudes to the job and to the organisation, which in turn should impact on well-being at work more generally. Thus, levels of job involvement, job satisfaction, organisational commitment, engagement and well-being are all indicators that are relevant to judging how well an appraisal system is operating and the kind of impact it is making in the long term (relevant measures will be discussed shortly).

METHODS AND SOURCES OF EVALUATION

To say what the evaluation criteria might be is one thing, but how to actually collect the data is quite another. The methods of evaluation are implicit in most of the criteria outlined above. However, more needs to be said about evaluating three of them: attitudes and perceived value, equity and levels of engagement.

Measuring attitudes to appraisal and its perceived value

There are three main methods available here – interviews, focus groups and questionnaires – and all three can be targeted on appraisers and appraisees alike. Interviews produce richer data – the interviewers can ask probing questions and follow up on interesting observations, and will be able to grasp the nuances of the appraisal process and its context for the people they are interviewing. The three drawbacks of this approach are: (a) it is time-consuming, and this inevitably limits the sample size; (b) it is sometimes difficult to analyse and summarise this kind of qualitative data; and (c) it does not give the respondents anonymity, which may inhibit their frankness. Bringing together focus (or feedback) groups has all the same advantages and disadvantages of the interview, bar one – it allows data collection from a much larger sample for much the same time investment.

The pros and cons of the questionnaire method are just the opposite. On the positive side, it allows for larger samples, quantitative analysis, and can afford anonymity to the respondents. The cost of this is that it does not yield the richness and detail of observations that come from interviews. Also, not all organisations have the resources or expertise to run questionnaire surveys, or can afford to commission them from outside consultants. (A cheaper alternative to the latter is to approach an occupational psychology department or a business school in a university and ask if any students would care to run an evaluation study as a project – the disadvantage here being that the company loses some control over the evaluation process.)

The core content of the evaluation is much the same whichever method is used. The areas to be covered are likely to be:

- background details of the respondent (age, gender, job/grade);
- what was discussed in the appraisal;
- perceptions of the effectiveness, fairness and outcomes;
- overall attitudes to the appraisal scheme;
- broader attitudes and feelings about the organisation.

The exact content and framing of questions will depend on the nature of the appraisal system and the level of the respondents. As most organisations have a lot more experience of interviewing than of mounting questionnaire surveys, the basic steps involved in the latter are described in Box 10.2. Developments in IT have made it much easier to mount web-based surveys, and indeed where elements of the appraisal process itself are delivered this way, it becomes possible to capture much more data on the distribution of ratings, etc. and to check for biases (see the subsection on equity, above).

BOX 10.2

RUNNING A QUESTIONNAIRE-BASED EVALUATION STUDY

It is not as difficult to run questionnaire surveys as might be imagined; most medium or large organisations should be able to cope with them. The sequence to follow is this:

1. The aim of the survey and when it is to be carried out are the first things to consider, as the two questions are linked. If the chief objective is to find out what went on in the interview and whether the appraisers followed the training guidelines they had been given, then the survey has to be done as soon as possible after the interviews have taken place (otherwise, people simply forget and do not report accurately). If, on the other hand, the main concern is the effects and outcomes of the appraisal process, then the questionnaires have to go out long enough after the appraisal for some effects to have been

observed – perhaps 3–6 months at least. Ideally, both types of information are sought. This means either having two separate surveys or staggering the distribution of the questionnaires, some going out immediately after the appraisals and some rather later. The latter is probably the more economical approach, but care has to be taken that the time elapsed since the appraisal is taken account of in analysing the data and interpreting the findings.

2. Decide on the sample. To a large extent this depends on the size of the organisation and the resources available. In small companies, it should be possible to cover all appraisees and appraisers (though a decision has to be taken about whether staff who find themselves in both roles are to be burdened with completing two questionnaires, one as appraisee and one as appraiser). In larger organisations, some kind of sampling will probably be necessary. The sampling can be done on a random basis from personnel records, or various divisions can be chosen and all staff in them covered. The main thing is to ensure that the sample is (a) as representative as possible in terms of age, gender, level, function and geographical area; and (b) large enough to give worthwhile information – it is important to remember that the response rate may be as low as 50 per cent, though it is to be hoped that it will be more like 75 per cent.

3. Develop a pool of questions on the basis of what you want to ask about the appraisals and what effects they have had. One set of items will be for appraisers, and the other set – on a separate questionnaire – will be for appraisees. Keep in mind the length of the questionnaire and the time it takes to complete; most people will not spend more than around 20 minutes on it at best.

4. Put the items together in questionnaire format, paying particular attention to the instructions (on how to complete the questionnaire) and the wording of the items. In the case of the instructions, are they clear and appropriate to the kind of response format (e.g. ticking one of a series of response alternatives)? And in relation to the item wording, avoid asking two questions in one, e.g. 'Did the appraisal lead to an increase in your job satisfaction and performance?' (Whatever the answer, you will not know if the respondent was referring to satisfaction, performance or both.)

5. Pilot the draft questionnaires by giving them to a small group of staff at the target levels. When they have completed them, discuss the content and format of the questionnaire with the pilot sample. Were the instructions and the questions clear? Was any item especially difficult to answer or did it pose problems in some way? Was anything omitted that they felt was important? Did they have a common

understanding of what the items meant? How long did it take to complete?

6. Redraft the questionnaire in the light of this feedback, and send it out (either electronically or on paper) to the sample with a suitable covering letter. The latter should:

- make clear the purpose of the exercise;
- say who will receive the output from it and how it will be used;
- if possible, guarantee anonymity for the respondent;
- state who has authorised the evaluation study;
- explain how the sample has been chosen;
- ask for the cooperation of the person receiving the questionnaire and give an indication of the (short) time it takes to answer it;
- indicate how to return it on completion. In the case of large samples, the data can be analysed using any one of a variety of statistical packages available.

For smaller sample sizes, it is possible to do the analysis manually. Often, simple percentage response breakdowns on each question will provide the information necessary, though further analysis using simple statistics like chi-square will help bring out any significant differences between the various staff groups (i.e. analysing the data by gender, age, function and so on).

In any evaluation study aimed at investigating attitudes and perceptions, whether by interview or questionnaire, the quality of the information obtained will, in part, depend on the degree to which the respondents cooperate. If members of trade unions or staff associations are involved, then these bodies should be consulted on the evaluation exercise and asked for their suggestions on its content. This will not only help to gain their support for the study, and so encourage their members to participate, but will also increase their interest in the findings and in implementing changes as a result of them. Senior management involvement and backing should be sought for the same reasons. After all this support is gained, employees can be informed of the impending study, told that it has been sanctioned by the various interested parties, and asked for their cooperation through the medium of in-house publications (newsletters, blogs, etc.) or departmental meetings.

When it comes to interpreting evaluation data of this kind, a number of issues arise. It has to be recognised that the observations collected are subjective, although they represent the reality for the people concerned and will determine their reactions to the appraisal process. But there will be some inconsistencies, not least between appraisers and appraisees. The objective truth, such as it is, usually lies somewhere between the two. More difficult is to ascertain what constitutes a satisfactory set of results. For example, is it good to have 30 per cent of appraisees feeling that the appraisal helped improve their performance, or is that rather low? Can we realistically expect a 100 per cent positive response? The best way to answer questions of this kind is to have some 'norms' – a picture of what average results look like – so that the organisation can compare their results against them and see if they were higher, lower or the same. Data collected by the authors in evaluation studies across seven organisations of varying size in the public and private sectors go some way towards providing this basis for comparison. The figures given in Box 10.3 below are based on responses from 5,940 appraisees and 1,332 appraisers (the response rates in the studies were generally high, 75–95 per cent). The quality of the appraisal systems and the adequacy of the training offered varied a good deal from one organisation to another, and it can be seen that even with the better ones, there was still room for improvement in several respects.

BOX 10.3

COMPARISON OF EVALUATION DATA FROM STUDIES IN VARIOUS ORGANISATIONS

% of cases in which –	Best result achieved	Average result achieved	Worst result achieved
The appraisee was given some notice beforehand	99	91	67
The appraisee did some preparation beforehand	83	62	16
The appraiser spent an average of not less than half an hour preparing for the interview	95	69	34
Weaker aspects of performance were discussed in the appraisal	81	54	40
Training needs were discussed in the appraisal	70	47	21
The appraisee reported their job satisfaction as being higher after the interview	40	30	15
The appraisee felt their performance had improved (or was likely to) as a result of the appraisal	54	40	20

Once the evaluation results are in and have been analysed, their implications for the way the appraisal scheme is operating and how it might be modified have to be considered. The general principle of encouraging ownership and participation in appraisal can be followed through here by arranging group feedback sessions in which small groups of appraisers (and possibly, in separate sessions, appraisees) are presented with the main findings of the evaluation and invited to discuss them and their implications. This both provides feedback and acts as a vehicle for generating improvement. If problems in the way the appraisal scheme is running have been identified, some action has to be taken – there is not much point doing the evaluation if the will to act on the findings is lacking. This may entail additional training (possibly targeted at certain groups or particular skills), clarification of the written guidance, or changes to the nature of the scheme itself. The most important thing is that something should be seen to be done, and done quickly.

Measuring levels of engagement, satisfaction and well-being

If introducing or revising performance appraisal is a significant organisational development intervention, then it should have broader and longer-term effects on communication, staff attitudes to the organisation and their levels of involvement in their work. All these and more can be tapped by a questionnaire survey, but there is a basic problem. To be meaningful as an evaluation of the changes brought about by appraisal, or any other intervention, there has to be a baseline measure against which to project those changes. In other words, you need a before-and-after measurement strategy.

Rather than constructing questionnaires from scratch, an alternative is to use one or more of the standard measures of job satisfaction, organisational commitment, engagement and similar variables. This saves time and effort and, more importantly, has the advantage of offering the opportunity to compare the organisation's scores on these measures with those published from other organisations. This makes it possible to look at the changes that have taken place within the organisation *and* at whether the levels of job satisfaction, etc. are higher or lower than elsewhere. Research (Fletcher and Williams, 1992, 1996) on performance management using this approach demonstrated how the differing quality of PM schemes was reflected in the scores on such variables. This has been extended and replicated by the Audit Commission in their very comprehensive research on PM in UK local government (Audit Commission, 1995a, 1995b). Acquiring these kinds of measures is not very difficult. They are readily available in the occupational psychology literature and can, in most cases, be used without having to purchase them. Some specific measures that are relevant and the references for them are listed in Appendix B. However, it may be wise to get some guidance from an occupational psychologist who is registered with the UK Health and Care Professions Council (HCPC) if the organisation is contemplating incorporating measures of this type in its long-term evaluation of appraisal.

Many large organisations conduct staff surveys on a regular basis, and these may provide a vehicle for evaluating the impact of appraisal either directly (by including specific questions on appraisal in the survey questionnaire) or indirectly. In relation to the latter, questions on how people feel they are being managed or led may partly reflect their experience of appraisal, and if (as is often the case) surveys are repeated on an annual basis, then they may offer an opportunity to track any changes in the pattern of responses that may result from the introduction of a new appraisal or multi-source feedback scheme. Examples of such staff surveys can readily be found online; for example, reports of surveys run by the UK National Health Service (www. nhsstaffsurvey.com) and by the UK Civil Service (simply type 'Civil Service People Survey' into your browser and you will find several years' worth of survey results!).

Assessing equity: the fairness of the distribution

The basic task here is to collect all the relevant data from the appraisal documentation and recommendations. This is usually done by the central HR department, monitoring the distributions of ratings and pay recommendations and checking to see that there are no unfair variations between staff groups. Public-sector organisations in the UK undertake diversity/equality monitoring of their HR procedures. Box 4.2 (Chapter 4) showed some illustrative appraisal ratings for some UK Government departments: follow the links in Box 4.2 for more examples.

If differences in the distribution of assessments are found, it may be that they are entirely justifiable. However, if a group of workers from a particular ethnic background does less well on performance ratings than do the majority of appraisees, the question is whether this genuinely reflects attributes of the appraisees or whether it is due to biased perceptions on the part of the appraisers. If there is evidence that this group of appraisees have less experience or lower educational levels, this could be the reason for the lower performance levels. On the other hand, if no such differences between them and the rest are observable, and no development action for them (or less than for the majority) was recommended by the appraisers, there would be cause for suspicion and concern. Monitoring appraisal assessments, and checking to see if there are unexplained variations in them, is a key part of the evaluation process. Neglecting to do so can cost the organisation dear in more ways than one.

Reward decisions represent an instance, frequently encountered, where justifiable inequities can arise. It is probably unrealistic to assume that all parts of the organisation are performing effectively, and this will be represented in the PRP recommendations. The problem is one of determining whether the higher levels of PRP awards being put forward by managers do reflect superior performance or just excessive leniency in assessment. The best way of sorting this out is to leave it to the line managers themselves to justify their pay recommendations to their peers, with HR providing any statistical information that is relevant (e.g. changes in divisional output, expenditure, and so on over the year).

While variations in appraisal data may be a function of gender, race, division, etc. and have to be investigated, there is a broader level of evaluation and monitoring that needs to be done. This is checking to see if the *overall* distributions of ratings and merit pay increases look right, which implies that there is some idea at the outset of what they should be. This is clearly essential if pay costs – and employee career expectations – are to be kept under control. The case of a major UK bank illustrates this. It started out with the expectation that 10–15 per cent of staff would be assessed as having exceeded their targets, 60–70 per cent as having met their targets, and 10–20 per cent as having fallen short of their targets. They did not get quite this kind of distribution, as the actual proportion of staff in each category was 22 per cent, 69 per cent and 9 per cent. This is not far off what they wanted, but the impact on the pay bill is worth pointing up. The top group, which contained 7–12 per cent more staff than anticipated, got a 10 per cent bonus, while the bottom group, which had 1–11 per cent fewer staff in it than anticipated got a 2.5 per cent bonus. If the distribution had departed much further from what was expected and desired, the consequences could have been fairly serious.

Sometimes the overall distribution produces quite a different problem. The overall performance rating for 6,000 middle-range administrative staff in a large UK county council after one year of a new appraisal and PRP scheme looked like this:

Highest Rating	1	2	3	4	5	Lowest Rating
% Staff	0.01	5.2	93.1	1.0	0.01	

The problem here is one of almost everyone being rated in the middle. Given that the rating is a basis for PRP decisions, this is very unhelpful, as it fails to discriminate effectively between different performance levels (unless one makes the unlikely assumption that there were virtually no differences amongst 6,000 staff). The fact that PRP was new in this organisation may have contributed to the excessive caution of the appraisers. In cases of this kind, those who have responsibility for appraisal within the organisation have to take some corrective action. Again, the best way to do this is by group feedback sessions backed up by written guidance.

The general point then, is that it is helpful (essential in the case of PRP systems) to have some idea of what the rating distributions should be overall, and to communicate this to the appraisers – and probably to the appraisees (as a restraint on expectations) as well. However, this does *not* mean applying a forced distribution of ratings; for example, 10 per cent get the top rating, 20 per cent the next to top, 40 per cent the middle, 20 per cent the one below the middle, and 10 per cent the lowest rating. The use of forced distributions may serve the purpose of making appraisers differentiate between appraisees, but it is a false and artificial differentiation that comes at a cost. The appraisers may feel alienated by a system that prescribes so heavily what they do. They, and the appraisees, may perceive some unfairness, quite possibly justifiably, if some divisions have genuinely higher-performing staff, yet have to apply the same distribution as lower-performing divisions. Interesting reflections on forced ranking from an evidence-based perspective are to be found in Pfeffer and Sutton (2006).

Why is there so often a lack of evaluation?

It is not easy to carry out evaluation exercises, and one is often struck by the contrast between organisations' willingness to commit considerable human and financial resources to setting up HR systems – be they psychometric tests in selection, assessment centres, appraisal schemes or whatever – and their extreme reluctance to commit a fraction of those resources to seeing if they are getting their money's worth. It may be the difficulty of doing evaluation work, it may be that the organisation does not think it has the expertise, but the suspicion is that, in quite a few cases, it comes down to not wanting to know. Some managers responsible for designing systems have an understandable resistance to finding that what they have done is not actually working very well, with all the implications that has for their self-esteem, their standing with the organisation and the subsequent effort they have to put in to get things right. Small wonder that they show little enthusiasm for evaluation, with the risks that it may carry for them personally. To overcome this, it needs to be publicly recognised from the outset (the design stage) – by everyone involved – that it is the exception rather than the rule for appraisal schemes to run perfectly from Day 1, and that evaluation and further improvement are a normal expectation.

Training makes a substantial impact on the quality of appraisal – indeed, it is crucial. It should start with briefing sessions to help those involved understand the appraisal scheme and its aims, before moving on to actual skills training. The latter will include both making an accurate assessment (and here the frame-of-reference approach seems to be the most effective) and holding an appraisal interview. It is also desirable to help line managers who are going to appraise their staff to understand their motivations and to be sensitive to differences between one person and another in what they are likely to respond to. There are many different elements in training that may be relevant, including the use of e-learning solutions, and these have to be chosen and adapted to meet the level and needs of the appraisers. While training efforts have traditionally been centred on the appraisers, there is good reason (and evidence) for thinking that much more should be done to help appraisees prepare for the session and to get the most out of it. One of the most important considerations in delivering training is to ensure that it addresses the issue of diversity, raising awareness of the kinds of biases and misunderstandings that can arise in the appraisal context.

At the other end of the process from training is evaluation. When things go wrong with an appraisal system, it usually happens quite early on, and it is important to identify them quickly. There are various evaluation strategies and methods available to assess the short-, medium- and long-term outcomes from PA. A vital aspect of evaluation is its role in monitoring the equity of the assessments made, and ensuring that there is no evidence of systematic bias against any particular group.

DISCUSSION POINTS AND QUESTIONS

10.1 How would you adapt appraisal training to the needs and context of management groups at different levels in an organisation?

10.2 What steps can we take to identify and eliminate bias and unfair discrimination in performance appraisal? How can we assess whether an appraisal system supports diversity? What sort of data do we need to collect?

10.3 If you were devising a training programme to help staff who were going to be appraised to get the most out of the experience, what elements would you include and why?

KEY REFERENCES

Egan, G. (2014) *The Skilled Helper. A Client-Centred Approach*. EMEA edn. London: Cengage Learning.

Fletcher, C. and Williams, R. (1996) Performance management, job satisfaction and organizational commitment. *British Journal of Management*, **7**(2), 169–179.

Latham, G. P. (2012) *Work Motivation: History, Theory, Research, and Practice*. 2nd edn. Thousand Oaks, CA: Sage.

Roch, S. G., Woehr, D. J., Mishra, V. and Kieszczynska, U. (2012) Rater training revisited: An updated meta-analytic review of frame of reference training. *Journal of Occupational and Organizational Psychology*, **85**(2), 370–395.

REFERENCES

Advisory, Conciliation and Arbitration Service (2014) *Challenging Conversations and how to Handle them*. London: ACAS.

Anstey, E., Fletcher, C. and Walker, J. (1976) *Staff Appraisal and Development*. London: George Allen & Unwin Ltd.

Audit Commission (1995a) *Paying the Piper: People and Pay Management in Local Government*. London: HMSO.

Audit Commission (1995b) *Calling the Tune: Performance Management in Local Government*. London: HMSO.

Beer, M. (1987) Performance appraisal. In J. W. Lorsch (Ed.) *Handbook of Organizational Behaviour*. Englewood Cliffs, NJ: Prentice Hall, pp. 286–300.

Brutus, S., Donia, M. B. and Ronen, S. (2013) Can business students learn to evaluate better? Evidence from repeated exposure to a peer evaluation system. *Academy of Management Learning and Education*, **12**(1), 18–31.

Campbell, J. P. (2012) Behaviour, performance, and effectiveness in the twenty-first century. In S. W. J. Kozlowski (Ed.) *The Oxford Handbook of Organizational Psychology. Vol. 1*. New York: Oxford University Press, pp. 159–194.

Cardy, R. L. and Leonard, B. (2011) *Performance Management: Concepts, Skills, and Exercises*. 2nd edn. New York: M. E. Sharpe.

Charman, C., Rudbeck, S. and Powell, M. (2014) *Ticking All the Boxes: A Study of Performance Management Practices in the UK*. London: Towers Watson.

Chartered Institute of Personnel and Development (2011) *Management Competencies for Enhancing Employee Engagement*. London: Chartered Institute of Personnel and Development.

Chartered Institute of Personnel and Development (2015a) *Learning and Development 2015. Annual Survey Report*. London: Chartered Institute of Personnel and Development.

Chartered Institute of Personnel and Development (2015b) *Employee Outlook, Spring 2015. Employee Views on Working Life*. London: Chartered Institute of Personnel and Development.

Cox, E., Bachkirova, T. and Clutterbuck, D. (2010) *The Complete Handbook of Coaching*. London: Sage.

Egan, G. (2014) *The Skilled Helper: A Client-Centred Approach*. EMEA edn. London: Cengage Learning.

Erdogan, B., Kraimer, M. L. and Liden, R. C. (2001) Procedural justice as a two-dimensional construct: An examination in the performance appraisal context. *Journal of Applied Behavioral Science*, **37**(2), 205–222.

Fletcher, C. (2010) Performance appraisal – what the research tells us about getting it right. Keynote address, '*In Search of Performance Management' Conference, School of Social Profit and Public Management*, University College of Ghent, November, Ghent, Belgium.

Fletcher, C. and Williams, R. (1992) *Performance Appraisal and Career Development*. 2nd edn. London: Stanley Thornes.

Fletcher, C. and Williams, R. (1996) Performance management, job satisfaction and organizational commitment. *British Journal of Management*, **7**(2), 169–179.

Garland, H. and Price, K. H. (1977) Attitudes towards women in management, and attributions of their success and failure in managerial positions. *Journal of Applied Psychology*, **62**(1), 29–33.

Gordon, M. E. and Miller, V. D. (2014) The appraisal interview: Finding the right words. In V. D. Miller and M. E. Gordon (Eds) *Meeting the Challenge of Human Resource Management: A Communication Perspective*. New York: Routledge, pp. 109–120.

Gordon, M. E. and Stewart, L. P. (2009) Conversing about performance: Discursive resources for the appraisal interview. *Management Communication Quarterly*, **22**(3), 473–501.

Hackman, J. R. and Oldham, G. R. (1980) Motivation through the design of work: Test of a theory. *Organisational Behaviour and Human Performance*, **16**(2), 250–279.

Heneman, H. H. (1991) A solution to the performance appraisal feedback enigma. *The Academy of Management Executive*, **5**(1), 68–76.

Hirsh, W. (2006) *Improving Performance through Appraisal Dialogues*. London: Corporate Research Forum.

Hirsh, W., Brown, D., Chubb, C. and Reilly, P. (2011) *Performance Management: The Implementation Challenge*. Brighton, UK: Institute of Employment Studies.

Holton, V., Dent, F. and Rabbetts, J. (2009) *Motivation and Employee Engagement in the 21st Century: A Survey of Management Views*. Berkhamsted, UK: Ashridge Management College.

Industrial Society (1997) *Appraisal Report No. 37*. London: The Industrial Society.

Industrial Society (2001) *Managing Performance: Managing Best Practice series, No. 86*. London: The Industrial Society.

Institute for Employment Studies (2004) *Managers as Developers of Others: A Practical Framework for Managers*. Brighton, UK: Institute for Employment Studies.

Jayewardene, D. and Clegg, C. W. (2014) Job design. In C. L. Cooper (Ed.) *Wiley Encyclopedia of Management*. Chichester, UK: Wiley, section 11, pp. 1–4.

King, E. and Gilrane, V. (2015) *Social Science Strategies for Managing Diversity: Industrial and Organizational Opportunities to Enhance Inclusion*. Bowling Green,

OH: Society for Human Resource Management and Society for Industrial and Organizational Psychology.

Latham, G. P. (2012) *Work Motivation: History, Theory, Research, and Practice.* 2nd edn. Thousand Oaks, CA: Sage.

Latham, G. P. and Latham, S. D. (2000) Overlooking theory and research in performance appraisal at one's peril: Much done, more to do. In C. Cooper and E. A. Locke (Eds) *International Review of Industrial and Organizational Psychology*. Chichester, UK: John Wiley & Sons, pp. 199–215.

London, M. (2015) *The Power of Feedback: Giving, Seeking, and Using Feedback for Performance Improvement*. New York: Routledge.

McDowell, A. and Fletcher, C. (2004) Employee development – an organizational justice perspective. *Personnel Review*, **33**, 8–29.

Mercer (2013) *Global Performance Management Survey Report*. London: Mercer Consulting Group.

Nathan, B. R., Mohrman, A. M. and Milliman, J. (1991) Interpersonal relations as a context for the effects of appraisal interviews on performance and satisfaction: A longitudinal study. *Academy of Management Journal*, **34**, 352–369.

NOS (2008) *National Occupational Standards for Management and Leadership*. www.management-standards.org/standards/full-list-2008-national-occupational-standards (accessed 18 January 2016).

Passmore, J. (2005) The heart of coaching: A coaching model for managers. *The Coaching Psychologist*, **1**(2), 6–9.

Passmore, J., Peterson, D. B. and Freire, T. (2013) *The Wiley–Blackwell Handbook of the Psychology of Coaching and Mentoring*. Chichester, UK: Wiley–Blackwell.

Pfeffer, J. and Sutton, R. I. (2006) Evidence-based management. *Harvard Business Review*, **84**(1), 62–74, 133.

Roch, S. G., Woehr, D. J., Mishra, V. and Kieszczynska, U. (2012) Rater training revisited: An updated meta-analytic review of frame of reference training. *Journal of Occupational and Organizational Psychology*, **85**(2), 370–395.

Rodgers, R. and Hunter, J. E. (1991) Impact of management by objectives on organizational productivity. *Journal of Applied Psychology*, **76**(2), 322–335.

Selden, S., Sherrier, T. and Wooters, R. (2012) Experimental study comparing a traditional approach to performance appraisal to a whole-brain training method at CB Fleet Laboratories. *Human Resource Development Quarterly*, **23**(1), 9–34.

Strebler, M., Robinson, D. and Bevan, S. (2001) *Performance Review: Balancing Objectives and Content*. Brighton, UK: Institute for Employment Studies.

Tourish, D. (2006) The appraisal interview reappraised. In O. Hargie (Ed.) *The Handbook of Communication Skills*. 3rd edn. London: Routledge, pp. 505–530.

Woehr, D. J. and Huffcutt, A. I. (1994) Rater training for performance appraisal: A quantitative review. *Journal of Occupational and Organizational Psychology*, **67**(3), 189–205.

PERFORMANCE APPRAISAL
BEST PRACTICE, BEST RESULTS

11

The changes in organisations and the context within which they have to operate now have been mentioned many times throughout this book. The pace of change is likely only to increase in the years ahead, though. Today's leaders have to operate in an environment that is increasingly political (Hartley and Fletcher, 2008), one that paradoxically is both more competitive but also demands greater collaboration, because so often their organisations now have to form partnerships or strategic alliances to achieve their goals. In addition, they have to cope with a huge increase in the speed and volume of communications, through formal and informal (social) media, face scrutiny from 24/7 news media and (in some cases) deal with increasing regulation. With the continuing globalisation of business, line managers find themselves in a very different relationship with their staff than would have been the case for their predecessors a decade or more ago, frequently leading virtual teams with whom they have much less face-to-face contact.

Has PA, even set in a wider PM framework, any relevance or future within such a radically changed setting? We believe the answer to this is very definitely 'Yes' – providing it changes to reflect the needs of the current situation. The deconstruction of traditional approaches to appraisal we referred to in the Preface (see page xiii) – the annual, one-size-fits-all, bureaucratic-forms-driven type of exercise – is long, long overdue. Quite apart from anything else, such approaches have consistently failed to deliver on almost every count – as we have seen (Chapter 1), they satisfy the needs neither of the organisations nor the participants. Also, as noted in the Preface (page xii), at the time of writing, there is much reporting in the media of a number of large companies in different fields abandoning their approach to PA or to PM as a whole (Pulakos *et al.*, 2015). Mostly, the systems operated by these organisations seem to represent the outdated assessment-rankings-driven approaches mentioned above, so their desire to shed them is to be welcomed (though perhaps not everyone would agree – see Smither, 2015).

Unfortunately, this has led some journalists and commentators to write banner headlines such as "Appraisals are finished. What next?" and "No, please, not the performance review", often accompanied by much throwing of the baby out with the bath water and lots of simplistic statements like "We should just appoint good managers; then we would not need appraisal" (Question – how does one know who are the good managers? Answer – probably by some kind of appraisal process!).

One academic (Culbert, 2012: item 1) is quoted as saying, "There isn't a scintilla of evidence that performance reviews do a company, or an employee, any good at all." So let's start with the evidence, rather than sweeping assertions. As is usually the case when one gets down to facts, the truth is rather more complicated than simply saying whether PA or PM is effective or ineffective. We noted in Chapter 7 (page 160) that when seeking to evaluate multi-source feedback systems, a range of criteria of differing perspective and duration might be relevant. The same is true across the whole domain. We may look at the evidence in relation to PA specifically, or to PM more broadly in which PA is but one part, or to wider HRM strategy of which PM is just one element. Indeed, evaluation research studies have taken all these perspectives. And within them they have collected data on participant attitudes to appraisal in particular, on employee commitment and engagement, on the quality and fairness of ratings distributions, and on objective measures of organisational performance and effectiveness. Thus, there is much evidence, and of various kinds, available to us.

We'll start with the research that has taken the broader perspectives on the impact of HRM policies and of PM within them. In Chapter 1 (page 6), we noted that many – but not all – studies have failed to show a strong association between HRM practices and organisational-level performance measures. This is deeply unsurprising, as so many other factors impact on organisational performance – the state of the national and world economies and their impact on demand, government policies, innovation and change, unemployment levels and the availability of skilled labour, commodity prices, even the weather! So at this strategic level, the wonder is, as Paauwe (2009: 133) concludes, that "HR practices, be it individually or bundled in a system, are at least weakly related to firm performance." Even when we delve below the strategic level, the picture is complicated by the many intervening or moderating variables that may influence the relationship between features of PA or PM systems and what they achieve. So, for example, in Chapter 1 (page 8) we quoted research showing that the way employees viewed the nature and purpose of a PM system can influence how readily they seek to operate it in the way HR intended. There are numerous studies along similar lines. Dewettinck and Vroonen (2013) found that implementation of a PM system was positively related to employee levels of engagement and job satisfaction. Dewettinck and van Dijk (2013) found that the perceived fairness of a PM system mediated its outcomes, and similarly, Farndale (2010) reported the importance of employees' perceptions of organisational justice in mediating their response to PM.

Should we just throw up our hands in the face of all these complexities and give up on seeking to find clear-cut evidence of anything positive achieved by PA or PM? No, but we should be mindful of the difficulties and perhaps not be too quick to jump on the bandwagon that says PA is a waste of time and that PM is "more broken than ever" (Pulakos *et al.*, 2015: 51). Even at the simplest level – whether appraisers and appraisees feel they get something useful from these systems – we get mixed findings. There is no shortage of surveys showing that people find giving and receiving performance feedback difficult, and that they often feel negative about the whole process (though it should be noted that feedback is not something that is only supposed to occur in the context of appraisal!). One survey suggested that 15 per cent of US managers would prefer to go to the dentist rather than carry out an appraisal. However, Kirton (2015) reports that two-thirds of employees in PricewaterhouseCoopers (PwC) said that their appraisals helped them understand how their performance 'shaped up', and 48 per cent said they helped them to think about their wider career. In Chapter 10 (Box 10.3), we presented some findings from questionnaire evaluation studies done in the UK which show that many appraisees reported positive outcomes – though this varied according to how well the appraisal system had been introduced and run.

Quite apart from this kind of evidence on perceived value by participants, there are also studies (interestingly, largely from the UK) showing that PA and PM can make a big difference to attitudes. In a study covering 860 staff, Fletcher and Williams (1996) found that better PM practices accounted for a substantial proportion of the variance in both job satisfaction and organisational commitment across nine public- and private-sector organisations. In a similar vein, an exceptionally thorough study of local government organisations in the UK demonstrated a high correlation between staff attitudes and the quality of the PM system, and between the latter and indices of organisational effectiveness in service delivery (Audit Commission, 1995).

And finally, despite all the methodological problems of research alluded to earlier, there have been some studies (e.g. Patterson *et al.*, 1998) demonstrating that good HR practices, and especially effective implementation of appraisal, show a close association with organisational performance indicators – though the relationship is complex (Guest *et al.*, 2003). Perhaps the most striking example of this is the study by West and Johnson (2002) which looked at the relationship of HR practices and procedures to various performance indicators across 61 hospitals in the UK National Health Service. Among the findings, the strongest correlation to emerge was between the quality of appraisals and patient mortality rates, with the former accounting for 25 per cent of the variance in the latter – even after many other factors such as doctor/patient ratios and size of hospital were controlled for. The researchers concluded that a significant number of lives could be saved by better HR systems, and in particular, better appraisal. So, it seems that appraisal is not just important; in some settings, it is a life-or-death matter.

To conclude this discussion of effectiveness – PA clearly can be successful in delivering some positive outcomes, but only if it is applied in a coherent and evidence-based way. The great variation in results from one study to another is readily understood when one considers the very wide range not only of organisational context, but of practice in terms of how PA and PM are resourced, designed and implemented. It would be amazing if we did not find differing and conflicting findings. Appraisal can contribute more when integrated into the framework of a PM system, and in these circumstances looks likely to achieve more from the organisation's point of view than it ever would by itself. But it needs more than that, or there would not be so many examples of PA systems failing to achieve the goals set for them. So what are the key parameters that enable PA to make a constructive contribution?

BEST PRACTICE IN DESIGNING AND IMPLEMENTING PA

There is no 'one best way' of doing PA (Hunt, 2015). What works best will vary according to the organisation, its background of HR practices, the kind of sector or industry it operates in, the cultural mix of its workforce and numerous other factors. However, from the academic research findings and the lessons learned from both more and less successful experiences of PA, we can distil clear criteria that give us the basis for some general best-practice guidelines:

* Analyse clearly what is desired from the PA system at the outset – what are the priorities? Resist loading too many functions and purposes onto a single event or process.
* Separate assessment and development functions of PA into different sessions (see below on the wisdom of adopting split roles in the

structuring of appraisal) and place the emphasis on development and motivation. Avoid using forced distributions of ratings.

- Keep immediate financial reward links to a minimum and, as indicated above, ideally position any discussion of them at a different time and session from the discussion of development.
- Facilitate a high level of participation in the development of the system by representative groups of those who will appraise and those who will be appraised, and through this win their buy-in. Consult with Trade Unions/ staff association where relevant. Conduct a trial run of the system with a small group of staff to ensure it is coherent and user-friendly.
- Competencies or other performance dimensions which are the focus for assessment or development must be appropriate and arrived at through a process of systematic analysis. Avoid making them too numerous and complex! Maintain a common core to what is appraised and how, but also allow for some variation to take account of local context and demands.
- Make links to other HR systems clear (e.g. promotion), but place more reliance on other methods (e.g. assessment or development centres) in the assessment of longer-term potential.
- Provide briefing and training for all appraisers, including skills training in giving feedback and in handling performance discussions. Emphasise fairness and raise awareness of potential sources of bias and faulty attributions.
- Provide training for appraisees in self-appraisal and goal-setting, in how to play their part in the performance discussion and in how to use the appraisal session for their development.
- Keep documentation and form-filling – online or otherwise – to a minimum. Deliver as much of the system online as is feasible to enable quicker completion and turnaround.
- Provide adequate resources to deal with development recommendations arising out of appraisal and make appraisers aware of them.
- Evaluate the system as soon as possible – especially in terms of monitoring the fairness and equity of assessments made, and the amount and nature of development action generated. Get feedback from appraisers and appraisees and address any problems identified quickly.

The above are criteria for best practice – though some may feel they represent ideal, rather than best, practice. But evidence and experience indicate that cheap fixes do not work. As in most things, one does not get something for nothing. Expecting PA and PM to deliver all the burdens placed on them without commensurate care, attention and resourcing will simply produce another in a long series of examples of failed systems. However, the above criteria do not tell us everything. In particular, they do not of themselves fully spell out how the delivery of PA and PM functions is best organised, and it is to that we now turn.

STRUCTURING PA: RE-LEARNING OLD LESSONS

It was noted in Chapter 1 and at various points subsequently that far too much has landed on the shoulders of a single, all-encompassing PA system. It was realised back in the late 1950s and 1960s that using a single session to assess, reward and develop an individual set up a potential conflict situation, where the appraiser was trying to be both judge and counsellor, and where an appraisee might 'switch off' after hearing any critical feedback and not respond to subsequent development suggestions. The solution advocated for this was to split the PA process into different components. This message (e.g. Maier, 1958; Meyer *et al.*, 1965) was largely ignored, but this is a case where 'back to the future' seems an appropriate description, as that approach is even more relevant today. The only way for practice in this field to make any progress is to break down the domain and purposes of PA into a series of linked processes, the main ones being:

1. *A performance planning session* that involves reviewing achievement of objectives over the period in question and setting objectives for the period ahead. If PRP has to come into the picture – and we believe that, in the case of merit pay, it would be better if it did not – this is what it is related to.
2. *A development review*, probably based on competencies or skill dimensions, that looks at the training and development needs of the individual, and which can feed into the assessment of potential (where the latter is done by other, more effective methods). If a competency approach has been used, then those competencies can be reflected in selection, appraisal, training and in assessing potential.

For an example of splitting the main functions of appraisal into two processes, see Box 11.1; this organisation adopts a slightly different approach to spreading the appraisal load across different sessions, and perhaps in contrast to some companies, prefers to use the word 'development' in reference to the session built around objective-setting and review, while the word 'performance' relates to the session on assessment against competencies. However, this simply illustrates how organisations may find their own solutions and terminology to meet their own requirements while still following the general principle of separating out different functions of appraisal.

BOX 11.1

AN EXAMPLE OF A MULTI-PROCESS PERFORMANCE APPRAISAL AND MANAGEMENT SYSTEM IN A UK ORGANISATION DEALING WITH ESTABLISHING STANDARDS ACROSS A RANGE OF ACTIVITIES

This system was built around the organisation's Core Success Factors, which were developed through a process that included consultation and discussion with all divisions of the organisation. These factors are:

- Delivery
- Customer focus
- Teamwork
- Self-management
- Adaptability
- Ownership.

The annual performance review process is called 'Focus on Performance'. The manager and the person reviewed independently complete a draft copy of the review form. Performance is reviewed against a four-point rating, from 'Consistently exceeds the expectations of the job role' to 'Consistently fails to meet the expectations of the job role'. An interesting feature of the system is that the form records both the manager's ratings and the appraisee's self-assessed rating. Also notable is the way it is kept simple – a single page – allowing both parties to focus on content rather than procedure. The form is reviewed by a more senior manager subsequently.

The second element in the review process is called 'Developing Success' and is an annual performance objective-setting and development-planning session. It is carried out separately from the 'Focus on Performance' session, though it obviously links in with it, and has a strong forward-looking emphasis. The manager and the person reviewed together agree performance objectives for the next 6–12 months, and record these, along with a reference to the wider relevant business objectives they relate to. They then go on to assess the areas where some development activity is necessary to achieve the objectives. These are framed in terms of the Core Success Factors. Following this, both parties consider the reviewee's development successes attained over the last review period, and also discuss career aspirations. On the basis of all of this, a Development Plan is recorded on the form. Again, the paperwork is kept as brief and simple as possible, with the Developing Success form running to just two pages.

This fragmentation of appraisal into different components does not necessarily imply that there should be only two occasions during a year when feedback is given, or when performance is discussed, or when development plans are made. We know that feedback has its greatest effect when delivered as close as possible in time to the event to which it relates (Latham and Marchbank, 1994; Kluger and DeNisi, 1996), so clearly it should not be 'stored up' and delivered in some kind of avalanche of comment at a particular time of the year. Moreover, with the faster pace of change and organisational life generally, it makes no sense for review of objectives to wait for a single occasion – this must be an ongoing activity. So, discussion of performance and development should be a continuous process operating at both formal and informal levels (Cardy, 2015) – but there is still virtue in holding specific review sessions to take a wider and longer-term perspective, such as career discussions, for example (Hirsh et al., 2001). Without these, there is the danger that excessively short-term and possibly knee-jerk responses to specific incidents may carry undue weight in both judgement and action.

In addition to the elements of appraisal described in items 1 and 2 above, other elements may be added:

3. *Multi-source feedback*, which should feed into the developmental session, but which could nonetheless be an element of the ongoing appraisal of the individual, focused on some (not all) of the key competencies.
4. *Use of assessment and development centres, and possibly psychometrics* in the assessment of potential.

Both of these elements are already widespread in their application, and increasing even more. The important thing is to make sure that they are properly integrated with performance and development reviews rather than happening as potentially confusing parallel processes. What one calls this overall approach is another issue. Referring to it as 'appraisal' does it less than justice, and even the overall term 'performance management' smacks of being overly organisation-centred in perspective. Perhaps something along the lines of 'feedback and development process' would be more appropriate, but organisations will find their own language for it.

Performance appraisal centred on performance improvement and development, and on wider, more objective evidence, along the lines of the linked processes described above, is likely to be more successful – and perhaps even essential for organisational growth. In recent years, the emphasis on bottom-line considerations has been so strong, and the changes in organisations so great, that an atmosphere of considerable uncertainty and a focus on short-term objectives have prevailed. These are conditions that erode the psychological security necessary for individuals to be willing to take the risks involved in innovation (King and Anderson, 2002). Yet the need for organisations to foster innovation has never been stronger and is recognised right up to government levels. A more developmentally and future-focused appraisal system can contribute to creating the right conditions for innovation.

As noted earlier, some of these ideas about splitting the functions of appraisal have been around for a while and have been put into practice by a number of organisations. But in many organisations they have not. How can companies be persuaded that they are wasting their time and resources in following approaches to PA that have repeatedly been shown to be bankrupt? It is usually down to the HR department, and/or external consultants, to bring the message home. There are a number of strategies that can be used, individually or in concert, to effect change in this area:

- The use of questionnaire surveys of attitudes to management, to communications, to reward systems and to the current appraisal arrangements is often a powerful way of highlighting problems and the need to take action (see Chapter 10 and Appendix B).
- The use of external examples is something that tends to hold senior management attention. Knowing what other high-performing and respected companies are doing can have a salutary effect. No board of directors likes to feel that the company is looking dated and backward in its approach, and that (in particular) the competition is stealing a march on them. The HR department can be judicious in picking its examples for comparison.
- Using research findings (as above) on appraisal from studies done elsewhere can be quite useful in presenting a case in the more science- and technology-based companies. This can be done through written briefings, but is usually more effective if embedded within a presentation by consultants and outside experts. Such people can make boardroom presentations about what is going on in appraisal and what the latest thinking is. They will often, and probably quite unjustifiably, be listened to more closely than would the organisation's own HR staff.
- Running a pilot study of a new appraisal scheme in one department can be an effective way of demonstrating the value of the approach and the principles it embodies. Being shown it can work within the organisation is reassuring and persuasive to senior management.
- Getting senior management to participate in any kind of strategic analysis – where the organisation is going, what it will look like in a few years' time, what sort of staff it will need and so on – should inevitably lead to a reconsideration of how people are selected, appraised and

developed. This kind of exercise may be facilitated by the HR department, with or without external consultants, and can be presented as part of organisational development as a whole (which it is) rather than as simply a mechanism for reviewing appraisal.

- The adoption of PM within the organisation can act as a vehicle for the review of appraisal arrangements – indeed, it has to, as appraisal in one form or another is the pivotal mechanism of performance management.

The HR professionals are always the key facilitators in bringing about changes in appraisal. Making appraisal a line-led activity actually strengthens their hand. They are in the position to guide and support, rather than being in the invidious role of demanding and enforcing. They will have access to much wider knowledge and expertise in the area than will the line managers, and they can use this to great effect in shaping what is set up and how it runs. By involving the line managers in setting the agenda for appraisal and in determining how it will run, the HR department is able to work alongside them in a more cooperative and positive relationship than is the case where appraisal is seen as an activity imposed by HR and for HR.

BEYOND PA: A BROADER PERSPECTIVE

Even in their more modern forms, PA and PM sometimes cannot deliver all that is asked of them. Part of the problem is that the level of understanding of what motivates people at work is not all that it might be. Giving greater emphasis to understanding motivation in appraisal training will help, but more research is also needed to improve our basic knowledge. Part of that effort needs to be directed at the appraisal interview itself. We are closer to getting the processes and procedures right, but in doing so have perhaps lost sight of making them user-friendly and relevant to the participants and their needs, as was noted in Chapter 5. A deeper understanding of the dynamics of the appraisal interview, and how to conduct it on both sides so as to make it a more motivating and satisfying experience – and putting this across in training – would be a big step forward. However, PA does not exist in some kind of vacuum – it takes place against the backdrop of the relationship of a manager with his or her team. Performance appraisal is no panacea for poor management, and should not be expected to be – managers who have good communication generally with their team will have the most productive appraisal sessions, but if a line manager does not take the time and trouble to get to know the team and to communicate with them on a regular basis, then he or she is likely to suffer a credibility gap when it comes to carrying out performance or development review sessions.

The lessening of central control in organisations and the empowerment of employees places more responsibility than ever on the shoulders of the individual. There is a danger here that the pressures can get out of proportion, and it is no coincidence that all the social and organisational changes referred to in this book have been accompanied by a burgeoning concern – backed up by evidence – about the continuing high levels of work stress: in 2014/15, the number of working days lost through work-related stress, depression or anxiety was 9.9 million, with stress accounting for over a third of all work-related cases of ill health and 43 per cent of all working days that were lost because of ill health (Health and Safety Executive, 2015). Better performance does not come from simply setting goals, giving a small amount of extra financial reward and exhorting people to go for improved quality and customer care. It comes from a better and more even relationship, or contract, between organisations and individuals, one that recognises individual differences in needs and capacities, and which accepts that, beyond certain levels, asking more of people is actually counterproductive. So, alongside the performance culture and the learning organisation, we have to put something else – the caring organisation (Newell, 2002). Only within that kind of environment will appraisal realise its full potential for offering routes to improved performance.

DISCUSSION POINTS AND QUESTIONS

11.1 How would you rate your organisation's PA system against the best-practice criteria outlined here?

11.2 How would you apply appraisal as a set of linked processes in your organisation? What would you have to change to bring this about and make it work?

11.3 How would you 'sell' the need for this new approach to top management and others in your organisation?

11.4 Why is it so difficult to make an overall assessment of the effectiveness of PA or PM systems?

KEY REFERENCES

Fletcher, C. and Williams, R. (1996) Performance management, job satisfaction and organizational commitment. *British Journal of Management*, **7**(2), 169–179.

Patterson, M., West, M., Lawthom, R. and Nickell, S. (1998) *Issues in People Management*. IPM Report No. 22. London: Institute of Personnel Management (now CIPD).

West, M. and Johnson, R. (2002) A matter of life and death. *People Management*, 21 February, pp. 30–36.

REFERENCES

Audit Commission (1995) *Calling the Tune: Performance Management in Local Government*. London: HMSO.

Cardy, R. L. (2015) Informal and formal performance management: Both are needed. *Industrial and Organizational Psychology*, **8**(1), 108–111.

Culbert, S. (2012) 10 reasons to get rid of performance reviews. *HuffPost Business*, The Blog, posted 18 December. www.huffingtonpost.com/samuel-culbert/performance-reviews (accessed 21 January 2016).

Dewettinck, K. and van Dijk, H. (2013) Linking Belgian employee performance management system characteristics with performance management system effectiveness: Exploring the mediating role of fairness. *International Journal of Human Resource Management*, **24**(4), 806–825.

Dewettinck, K. and Vroonen, W. (2013) Antecedents and consequences of performance management enactment by front line managers. Working Paper in Human Resource Management 2013/02. Vlerick Business School, Leuven, Belgium. https://public.vlerick.com/Publications/e6b61499-e7d7-e211-a8b9-005056a635ed.pdf (accessed 13 January 2016).

Farndale, E. (2010) High commitment performance management: The roles of justice and trust. *Personnel Review*, **40**(1), 5–23.

Fletcher, C. and Williams, R. (1996) Performance management, job satisfaction and organizational commitment. *British Journal of Management*, **7**(2), 169–179.

Guest, D. E., Michie, J., Conway, N. and Sheehan, M. (2003) Human resource management and corporate performance in the UK. *British Journal of Industrial Relations*, **41**(2), 291–314.

Hartley, J. and Fletcher, C. (2008) Leading with political awareness: Leadership across diverse interests inside and outside the organization. In K. T. James and J. Collins (Eds) *Leadership Perspectives: Knowledge into Action*. London: Palgrave, pp. 163–176.

Health and Safety Executive (2015) *Stress-related and Psychological Disorders in Great Britain 2014*. Bootle, UK: Health and Safety Executive. www.hse.gov.uk/statistics/causdis/stress/stress.pdf (accessed 15 January 2016).

Hirsh, W., Jackson, C. and Kidd, J. (2001) Straight talking: Effective career discussions at work. NICEC Briefing, National Institute for Careers Education and Counselling/Careers Research and Advisory Centre. www.nicec.org/nicec_straight_talking.pdf (accessed 15 January 2016).

Hunt, S. J. (2015) There is no single way to fix performance management: What works well in one company can fail miserably in another. *Industrial and Organizational Psychology*, **8**, 130–139.

King, N. and Anderson, N. (2002) *Managing Innovation and Change: A Critical Guide for Organizations*. London: Thomson Learning (Psychology@Work Series).

Kirton, H. (2015) Appraisals are finished: What next? CIPD Web Blog, posted 20 August 2015. www.cipd.co.uk/pm/peoplemanagement/b/weblog/archive/2015/08/20/appraisals-are-finished-what-next.aspx (accessed 19 January 2016).

Kluger, A. N. and DeNisi, A. (1996) The effects of feedback interventions on performance: An historical review, a meta-analysis, and a preliminary feedback intervention theory. *Psychological Bulletin*, **119**(2), 254–284.

Latham, C. and Marchbank, T. (1994) Feedback techniques. In G. Lee and D. Beard (Eds) *Development Centres*. Maidenhead, UK: McGraw-Hill, pp. 156–179.

Maier, N. R. F. (1958) Three types of appraisal interview. *Personnel*, March/April, 27–40.

Meyer, H. H., Kay, E. and French, J. R. P. (1965) Split roles in performance appraisal. *Harvard Business Review*, **43**(1), 123–129.

Newell, S. (2002) *Creating the Healthy Organization: Well-Being, Diversity and Ethics at Work*. London: Thomson Learning (Psychology@Work Series).

Paauwe, J. (2009) HRM and performance: Achievements, methodological issues and prospects. *Journal of Management Studies*, **46**(1), 129–142.

Patterson, M., West, M., Lawthom, R. and Nickell, S. (1998) *Issues in People Management*. IPM Report No. 22. London: Institute for Personnel and Development (now CIPD).

Pulakos, E. D., Hansen, R. M., Arad, S. and Moye, N. (2015) Performance management can be fixed: An on-the job experiential learning approach for complex behavior change. *Industrial and Organizational Psychology*, **8**(1),51–76.

Smither, J. W. (2015) The fate of performance ratings: Don't write the obituary yet. *Industrial and Organizational Psychology*, **8**(1), 77–80.

West, M. and Johnson, R. (2002) A matter of life and death. *People Management*, 21 February, pp. 30–36.

APPENDIX A

JOB AND WORK ANALYSIS AND COMPETENCY MODELLING

Long advocated as a foundation stone of good HR practice is job analysis. You are developing a new selection system to appoint junior entry scientists and engineers or are designing a development centre to assess management potential: you will need to know what skills and abilities to assess. You want to develop a customised 360° appraisal questionnaire to support your leadership development activities: you will need to identify the important dimensions of performance to assess. You want to include means (process performance) as well as ends (output performance) in your appraisal arrangements: again, which are the important dimensions? Though it is all too easy to sit around a meeting table and dream up lists of skills, abilities or competencies, job or work analysis traditionally has been (and remains) the good-practice approach to adopt.

As a field of practice, job/work analysis has by no means stood still; in addition, competency modelling has come along, although this has been found wanting when compared with job/work analysis. For example, a Job Analysis and Competency Modeling Task Force, set up by the Society for Industrial and Organizational Psychology in the USA (Schippmann *et al.*, 2000; Schippmann, 2010) compared competency modelling with traditional job analysis across two sets of variables, one set having to do with rigour of analysis. Variables included the methods used for data collection, such as level of detail, and assessment of reliability of results. Sackett and Laczo (2003: 29) note that the Task Force concluded that "Job analysis was seen as demonstrating more rigor on every evaluative criterion, with the exception of establishing a link to business goals and strategies." So, though competency modelling may have more to gain from job analysis than vice versa, bringing the two closer together has merit.

A wide range of analysis and modelling techniques is available and we can't possibly cover them all. Rather, we will focus on just a few illustrative examples of methods that are relatively straightforward to use and which bring a measure of the rigour that is necessary if you are to have confidence in your end product. But there is no shortage of further reading available. If you are looking for a comprehensive source, then the *Handbook of Work Analysis* edited by Wilson *et al.* (2012) will fit the bill. Briefer treatments (but which none the less extend what we present here) are Pearlman and Sanchez (2010), Brannick *et al.* (2012) or Rothman and Cooper (2015).

The Critical Incident Technique (Flanagan, 1949, 1954) goes back to the 1940s and has been advocated as having particular relevance for performance appraisal, as it can be used to identify effective and ineffective work behaviours (Latham and Wexley, 1994). It offers a lot of flexibility in application – for example, interviews (face-to-face or telephone) or structured forms, one-to-one or in groups. A common approach is to get job experts – incumbents, their managers or others who can give an informed view – to describe incidents that illustrate particularly good/exemplary/effective performance and incidents showing particularly poor/unsatisfactory/ineffective work performance for a given job (or job family). When being carried out as an interview, there is likely to be some scene-setting preamble about why the work is being carried out (reiterating what was said to interviewees when their involvement was solicited) before moving on to an initial request, e.g: "I'd like you to think back across the past 12 months and recall a situation or an occasion when you experienced particularly effective leadership."

Follow-up questions will be needed to stimulate thinking and generate fuller, more detailed responses so as to ensure that the following points are covered:

- the facts of the situation, the context, the circumstances that led up to the situation, the background;
- what specifically the individual did that was effective/ineffective – the focus here is on behaviour;
- what the outcome was of that action.

This process should be repeated a number of times, covering effective and ineffective incidents. How many incidents are covered will depend on the time available and the insight of the person being interviewed. The resulting behaviours from all of the participants can then be content-analysed to identify themes – in this example, dimensions of leadership – and accompanying behavioural indicators of effectiveness and ineffectiveness. The material generated by this method can also be used to generate situations (and associated scoring keys) that can be used in behavioural forms of interview, such as the situational interviews we described in Chapter 6.

The Repertory Grid Technique, originally developed by George A. Kelly (1955, 1963), like the Critical Incident Technique, allows the individuals interviewed to identify what they think is important in their own words; it does not force them into using some preconceived dimensions that the investigator has in mind. It, likewise, is flexible, so the approach we outline here should not be regarded as the only way to go. The procedure is followed on a one-to-one basis with a manager who is one or two levels up from the job(s) being looked at, though job incumbents can also be included.

1. Ask the individual to think of six managers in the level or role under consideration. They need to be people the respondent has known well, who have worked in the organisation for two or three years, and who differ in effectiveness. Ideally, three would be above-average or outstanding performers, while three would be below-average or poor performers. The respondent does not have to name these people to the interviewer, but to facilitate remembering who they are, the respondent is asked to write down some way of identifying each one of them (e.g. their initials) on a set of six cards. The better performers can be designated A, B, C and the other three as D, E, F.

2. The individual is asked to focus on cards/people A, C and E and to say – with their work behaviour in mind – which two seem more alike and different from the third. They are then asked to specify one aspect of work behaviour that reflects this. It is important (a) that they keep this to one aspect of behaviour; and (b) that their description has a verb in it – in other words, it is behavioural and not just a vague adjectival description. When they have done that, they also have to describe how the behaviour of the third person differs in this respect. The responses are recorded by the interviewer, who will ask follow-up questions to probe the replies in order to refine and clarify the nature of the behaviour being described. In RepGrid terminology, the dimension so elicited is called a Construct.

3. The procedure is repeated, this time with another triad – B, D and F. The same questions are posed, with the request that this should cover an aspect of behaviour that is *different* from that for the first triad.

4. This is continued with further combinations of the six cases, making sure that none are repeated. It may be that the respondent will not be able to go through all the permutations without running out of new behavioural differentiations.

5. The interviewer may record the responses on a sheet as the session progresses, something like this:
    Pair Alike: A, E – These two plan ahead; they take time to prepare in some detail.

Single Different: C – Always leaves things to the last minute. Does not think ahead – everything comes as a surprise to him.

The dimension here looks as if it centres on planning, but the exact nature of it does not matter too much at this stage, as the interviewer will want to administer the grid to several more respondents to get a good-sized and representative sample of views.

6. The grid can be analysed in a number of ways, and it is at this point that expertise and experience with the method is most needed. The simplest way is to label the dimensions that have come out in each respondent's grid, and then to go through them all, weeding out the ones that have not consistently been perceived as differentiating between high and low performers. Also, some of those dimensions that look a little different from one another (either within one person's grid or comparing across grids) will, on closer inspection, turn out to be the same thing in slightly different words. Alternatively, and much more ambitiously, each triad differentiation can be put on a separate sheet of paper, and all of them mixed up so that they are no longer 'attached' to the respondent they were elicited from. Then the interviewer reads through all of them, sorting them into piles, each one of which is made up of replies that seem to reflect the same kind of dimension. When this is done, each group of statements is looked at again, and the precise nature of the dimension and the behaviours relating to it are defined.

Try it for yourself! Either think of people you work with, or just friends, family or acquaintances.

These two approaches both have the potential to yield rich behavioural descriptions that, with further scrutiny, can be used for a range of purposes over and above appraisal. The main limiting factor, in terms of quantity and quality of output, is the ability of participants to think of sufficient incidents, enough cases of good and poor performers, or (for the RepGrid) their having such simple views on the world that they have only two or three constructs by which they differentiate people.

Though both these methods are quite straightforward, neither is especially quick. This tends to be true of job analysis generally, the more so as it would be ill-advised to rely on just one method or just one source (Koch *et al.*, 2012) – so, for example, draw on incumbents and their managers (and possibly others) rather than just one manager. Also, again like job analysis generally, both approaches are backward-looking – at best, they consider jobs as they are today. But suppose you are interested in the future? What do you do? One approach to tackling this problem has been labelled strategic job analysis (Schneider and Konz, 1989) and is outlined in Box A.1.

The first two steps illustrate conventional approaches to job analysis; the third outlines one possible way of anticipating the future. Another illustration of a forward-looking approach is given in Box A.2.

STRATEGIC JOB ANALYSIS

Task analysis

Carried out by means of observation, group discussion/interviews with job incumbents and their supervisors in order to establish "(1) the goals of the job and (2) the tasks that need to be accomplished for the goals to be met" (Schneider and Schechter, 1991: 221). From this a task survey is developed and used to gather quantitative data from incumbents about the criticality/ importance of the tasks and the relative amount of time spent on each.

Personal attributes analysis

Another round of interviews/group discussions, again with incumbents/ supervisors, is used to determine the competencies required to perform the tasks that have been identified. These are incorporated in a questionnaire administered to supervisors to establish, amongst other things, the importance of each competency for effective performance.

Envisioning the future

> To incorporate strategic issues . . . we first gather information about the kinds of issue in the job, the company, and/or the larger environment that may affect the job in the future. This is accomplished in a workshop composed of subject matter experts (e.g., job incumbents, supervisors, managers, human resource staff, strategic planners) and job analysts. The participants might also include experts in a relevant technical field, economists, demographers, and so forth, depending on the specific job of interest.
>
> (Schneider and Konz, 1989: 53)

> This process may lead to the identification of new tasks and/or revisions to the existing task list and list of competencies. The new task are then re-rated in terms of importance and time spent. Likewise, the new competencies are rated again in terms of their importance, difficult of learning, and when they will be learned.
>
> Source: Based on Schneider and Konz (1989);
> Schneider and Schechter (1991)

FORECASTING FUTURE COMPETENCY REQUIREMENTS

This is an approach that used multiple methods and multiple sources to determine competencies expected to be required by design engineers ten years in the future.

Selecting the future time horizon

One criticism of much competency modelling is that it is vague about the future time horizon. In this example, the investigators adopted a tangible time horizon in the hope of increasing the likelihood of more accurate predictions of competencies. Robinson *et al.* (2005) describe the rationale:

> The company under study primarily manufactures aerospace products with an average timescale of four years from initial design to initial production. Furthermore, the company had a relatively full order book and it was therefore relatively financially stable for the short-term future. It was therefore felt that a five-year horizon would be too short. Looking 20 years ahead was considered too speculative. Consequently, a 10-year future time horizon was selected as most appropriate.
>
> (Robinson *et al.*, 2005: 69)

Developing the competency profile

This proceeded through three phases.

Phase 1: Preliminary interviews. An initial round of interviews was carried out with senior managers and directors able to give diverse, informed views of the design engineer role as it might be in the future. These interviews "focused on identifying (a) future scenarios predicted to impact upon the design role during the forthcoming decade, and (b) which of the company's six design stages to focus on" in the subsequent phases (Robinson *et al.*, 2005: 71). The future scenarios that were identified and the selected design stages then were explored in more depth in a second round of interviews with another set of managers and directors.

Phase 2: Questionnaire survey. Drawing on materials already in use within the company, a list of 49 competencies (with accompanying definitions) was drawn up. This was a mix of generic and design-engineering-specific competencies. The questionnaire asked respondents (design engineers at several seniority levels) "to rate the importance, to their current job, of each of the 49 competencies, in two ways: (a) in their job as it is currently, and (b) in the same job as they think it will be in 10 years' time" (Robinson *et al.*, 2005: 73)

Phase 3: Critical Incident Technique (CIT) interviews. The ten competencies identified as most important for the future were used as the basis for these interviews, which were carried out with good-performing design engineers. This example illustrates a different way of using the CIT from that described earlier. In this instance the competencies were the starting point. "For each of the 10 competencies, interviewees were first read the definition that had appeared on the original questionnaire. Next, they were asked to describe a situation where either themselves, or a colleague, had successfully demonstrated the competency" (Robinson *et al.*, 2005: 77).

Transcripts of the CIT interviews then were subjected to content analysis to elicit indicators of effective performance for each competency. This generated 90 sets of indicators which the investigators were able to cluster into a smaller number of competencies. Based on the proportion of interviewees who had mentioned each indicator, the relative criticality of the competencies was established. A subsequent workshop, comprising a small group of senior managers with relevant expertise, validated the resulting competency framework. This comprised 42 individual competencies that clustered into six groups:

- Personal attributes, e.g. 'Is self-confident'
- Project management, e.g. 'Plans work'
- Cognitive strategies, e.g. 'Judges importance'
- Cognitive abilities, e.g. 'Makes effective decisions'
- Technical ability, e.g., 'Uses effective learning methods'
- Communication, e.g. 'Uses appropriate communication formats'

    As is typical with competencies, each one has a number of indicators as, for example, with 'Judges importance':

- Evaluates the relative importance of activites, using official procedures and with reference to business objectives where applicable, and prioritises them accordingly
- Accurately gauges, and compares, the importance and relevance of different factors, thereby realising which are critical
- Evaluates the advantages and disadvantages of alternative actions.

(Robinson *et al.*, 2005: 82)

Source: Summarised from Robinson *et al.*, (2005, 2007)

One of the advantages claimed for competency modelling is the attention it gives to the future, but on the debit side, the quality and validity of competency research have been called into question, such as when the senior team divines some list of competencies that it believes to be necessary for some imagined future dreamed up at an away day. Clearly, the future cannot be known, but the two examples that we have given show that it is possible to bring a degree of rigour to forecasting what future competency requirements might be.

If you have a particular interest in this area, we refer you to an excellent paper by Campion *et al.* (2011) entitled 'Doing competencies well: Best practices in competency modeling'. Acknowledging that there's little evidence about the practice of competency modelling, they present their guidelines as primarily experience-based. And they are best viewed as guidelines, rather than prescriptions – a set of issues to be considered or questions to be asked. Examples of their 20 best practices include:

- Consider organisational context.
- Use rigorous job analysis methods.
- Consider future-orientated job requirements.
- Use organisational language.
- Include cross-job and job-specific competencies.

Taken together, the best practices make clear the true complexity of competency modelling.

One of the attractions of competencies is that they can be used for several HR applications. But this does not necessarily mean that a single competency model can do duty across all those purposes. For example, there may be a need to identify generic competencies that apply across jobs and other sets of competencies that apply to a particular function (e.g. HR), or role (the example of design engineers in Box A.2), or job family (managers). And then the descriptions of the competencies may need different levels of detail for different HR purposes and there may be a need to specify different levels of proficiency.

Many organisations simply won't have the resources (expertise, money) to engage in job analysis/competency modelling. Buying a framework from a consultancy may be an option, but this is not without risks. Satisfy yourself that the model has validity, that it is the result of a rigorous development process – is there a technical manual that explains what was done? Professional bodies may have developed competency models that it would be appropriate to use. For management and leadership roles, the established body of research may be a rich source to guide you – for example, the factors in Chapter 3, Box 3.4. And the Competency Model Clearinghouse that we referred to in Chapter 5 is very definitely worth a look.

KEY REFERENCES

Brannick, M. T., Cadle, A. and Levine, E. L. (2012) Job analysis for knowledge, skills, abilities, and other characteristics, predictor measures, and performance outcomes. In N. Schmitt (Ed.) *The Oxford Handbook of Personnel Selection and Assessment.* New York: Oxford University Press, pp. 119–146.

Campion, M. A., Fink, A. A., Ruggeberg, B. J., Carr, L., Phillips, G. M. and Odman, R. B. (2011) Doing competencies well: Best practices in competency modeling. *Personnel Psychology,* **64**(1), 225–262.

Flanagan, J. C. (1949) Critical requirements: A new approach to employee evaluation. *Personnel Psychology,* **2**(4), 419–425.

Flanagan, J. C. (1954) The critical incident technique. *Psychological Bulletin,* **51**(4), 327–358.

Kelly, G. A. (1955) *The Psychology of Personal Constructs. Vols I and II.* New York: W. W. Norton & Company.

Kelly, G. A. (1963) *A Theory of Personality. The Psychology of Personal Constructs.* New York: W. W. Norton & Company.

Koch, A., Strobel, A., Miller, R., Garten, A., Cimander, C. and Westhoff, K. (2012) Never use one when two will do: The effects of a multi-perspective approach on the outcome of job analyses using the critical incident technique. *Journal of Psychology,* **11**(2), 95–102.

Latham, G. P. and Wexley, K. N. (1994) *Increasing Productivity through Performance Appraisal.* 2nd edn. Reading, MA: Addison-Wesley.

Pearlman, K. and Sanchez, J. I. (2010) Work analysis. In J. L. Farr and N. T. Tippins (Eds) *Handbook of Employee Selection.* New York: Routledge, pp. 73–98.

Robinson, M. A., Sparrow, P. R., Clegg, C. and Birdi, K. (2005) Design engineering competencies: Future requirements and predicted changes in the forthcoming decade. *Design Studies,* **26**(2), 123–153.

Robinson, M. A., Sparrow, P. R., Clegg, C. and Birdi, K. (2007) Forecasting future competency requirements: A three-phase methodology. *Personnel Review,* **36**(1), 65–90.

Rothman, I. and Cooper, C. L. (2015) *Work and Organizational Psychology.* 2nd edn. London: Routledge.

Sackett, P. R. and Laczo, R. M. (2003) Job and work analysis. In W. C. Borman, D. R. Ilgen and R. J. Klimoski (Eds) *Handbook of Psychology: Industrial and Organizational Psychology. Vol. 12.* Hoboken, NJ: Wiley, pp. 21–37.

Schippmann, J. R. (2010) Competencies, job analysis, and the next generation of modeling. In J. C. Scott and D. H. Reynolds (Eds) *Handbook of Workplace Assessment.* San Francisco: Jossey-Bass, pp. 197–231.

Schippmann, J. R., Ash, R. A., Battista, M., Carr, L., Eyde, L. D., Hesketh, B., Kehoe, J., Pearlman, K., Prien, E. P. and Sanchez, J. I. (2000) The practice of competency modeling. *Personnel Psychology*, **53**, 703–740.

Schneider, B. and Konz, A. M. (1989) Strategic job analysis. *Human Resource Management*, **28**(1), 51–85.

Schneider, B. and Schechter, D. (1991) Development of a personnel selection system for service jobs. In S. W. Brown, E. Gummesson, B. Edvardsson and B. Gustavsson (Eds) *Service Quality*. Lexington, MA: Lexington Books, pp. 217–235.

Wilson, M. A., Bennett, W., Gibson, S. G. and Alliger, G. M. (Eds) (2012) *The Handbook of Work Analysis*. New York: Routledge.

APPENDIX B

MEASURES FOR EVALUATING THE EFFECTS AND IMPACT OF PERFORMANCE APPRAISAL

If you are going to undertake monitoring and evaluation of your appraisal process you're likely to be interested in at least two sets of things – how the process is experienced and the impact it has on employee attitudes. Very often it will be possible to draw on established questionnaires as a source of questions to use: we provide some illustrative sources.

EXPERIENCE OF THE APPRAISAL PROCESS

It is worth asking about both the forward-looking and backward-looking aspects of appraisal. Forward-looking aspects might be covered by asking about such matters as performance expectations and the goal-setting process, for example:

- employee involvement in setting their work goals
- clarity and specificity of their goals
- perceptions of goal difficulty/challenge
- understanding of the rationale for their goals
- goal conflict
- clarity of performance expectations
- follow-up actions to develop skills and performance.

A particularly comprehensive questionnaire dealing with goal-setting has been tested by Lee *et al.* (1991).

As to the backward-looking aspects, you probably will want to ask questions about feedback and fairness perceptions, such as:

- My supervisor is generally familiar with my performance on the job.
- My supervisor is fair when evaluating my job performance.

- My supervisor gives me useful feedback about my job performance.
- My supervisor is supportive when giving me feedback about my job performance.
- My supervisor generally lets me know when I do a good job at work.
- On those occasions when my job performance falls below what is expected, my supervisor lets me know.

The above items are found in the feedback environment scale (Steelman *et al.*. 2004: 16–18). To tap into fairness perceptions you would need to cover both distributive justice (that is, reactions to the assessment) and procedural justice, including such aspects as sufficiency of the notice given of the appraisal interview, the 'voice' or say afforded to the performer and the extent to which factors outside the performer's control were taken into account. Colquitt (2001) has developed a set of adaptable items that can be used to measure perceptions of the different aspects of organisational justice. Illustrative items (adapted for appraisal) are shown below:

- Have you been able to express your views and feelings during your appraisal?
- Does your appraisal reflect the effort you have put into your work?
- Does your appraisal reflect what you have contributed to the organisation?
- Has your appraiser treated you in a polite manner?
- Has your appraiser been candid in (his/her) communications with you?

Also, there's no shortage of appraisal-specific questionnaire items that have been developed over the years (e.g. Tang and Sarsfield-Baldwin, 1996; Thurston and McNall, 2010):

- How much do you feel your last performance rating truly represented how well you have performed in your job?
- How fair do you feel your last performance appraisal was?
- How much input does your supervisor ask for during the appraisal process?
- How much opportunity are you given to express your feelings when your performance is evaluated?
- The appraisal I get reflects how much work I do.
- The appraisal I get reflects how well I do my work.
- The appraisal I get reflects the many things I do that help at work.
- The appraisal I get reflects the many things I am responsible for at work.
- The appraisal I get reflects the effort I put forth at work.
- My rater frequently lets me know how I am doing.
- My rater gives me information I can use to improve my performance.

- My rater routinely gives me feedback relevant to the things I do at work.
- My rater reviews with me my progress towards my goals.
- My rater lets me know how I can improve my performance.
- My rater helps me to understand the process used to evaluate my performance.
- My rater takes time to explain decisions that concern me.
- My rater lets me ask him or her questions about my performance appraisal.
- My rater gives me real examples to justify his or her appraisal of my work.
- My rater's explanations help to clarify for me what to do to improve my performance.

ATTITUDE MEASURES

There are a number of questionnaire measures that are both relevant to assessing broad employee attitudes and are readily available. Questionnaires developed in the UK include:

- The Organisational Commitment Scale produced by Cook and Wall (1980). This breaks down into three components: organisational loyalty, organisational identification and organisational involvement.
- The Job Satisfaction Scale (Warr *et al.*, 1979). This taps satisfaction with 15 different aspects of work, broadly grouped into intrinsic and extrinsic job satisfaction.

Both of the above, and several others (covering factors such as goal clarity), were used in Part 2 of the (former) Institute of Personnel Management study on performance management, and the reader can find the questionnaire items and various other details given there by Fletcher and Williams (Institute of Personnel Management, 1992). They report data about a number of private- and public-sector organisations that should facilitate making comparisons for other companies using the scales.

These days you might be interested in assessing the impact of appraisal on employee engagement. But be careful about the items you use to measure engagement. For example, do you want to use items such as the following?

- I am quite proud to be able to tell people who it is I work for.
- In my work I like to feel I am making some effort, not just for myself but for the organisation as well.
- I feel myself to be part of the organisation.

Well, these items come from the Cook and Wall (1980) organisational commitment questionnaire. To measure engagement you need to use different sorts of items. However, a major problem at the moment with employee engagement is that there is no consensus about the construct, so here's a selection of illustrative questionnaires.

The Utrecht Work Engagement Scale is probably the most thoroughly developed and tested questionnaire that is available. There are short and long versions. For full information, see Schaufeli and Bakker (2004).

The NHS (2013) used nine items reflecting three facets of what it terms *staff engagement*:

- Staff ability to contribute towards improvement at work
    - I am able to make suggestions to improve the work of my team/ department.
    - There are frequent opportunities for me to show initiative in my role.
    - I am able to make improvements happen in my area of work.
- Staff recommendation of the trust as a place to work or receive treatment
    - Care of patients/service users is my trust's top priority.
    - I would recommend my trust as a place to work.
    - If a friend of relative needed treatment, I would be happy with the standard of care provided by this trust.
- Staff motivation at work
    - I look forward to going to work.
    - I am enthusiastic when I am working.
    - Time passes quickly when I am working.

A paper by William Kahn (1990) is often cited as the paper that instigated much of the interest taken by academics in the engagement concept. Kahn used the term *personal engagement* and his model has been used as the basis for questionnaires. For example, one questionnaire was developed by May *et al.* (2004) and another by Rich *et al.* (2010). Both measured the three facets of Kahn's model. Illustrative items from these questionnaires are shown below. The May *et al.* questionnaire was used for the Chartered Institute of Personnel and Development's (2006) survey *How Engaged Are British Employees?* Note that asking about work engagement doesn't mean that you can't ask questions about pride, if that is something important in your organisation. But you should recognise that if you adopt a commitment model, then your referent is likely to be the organisation (as in the example above), whereas in Table B.1 below, the referent is the job. This is an important difference. And if you decide you want to measure work engagement, think hard about the sorts of items you will use to measure *physical engagement*. What signal might you be sending if you use items like 'I take work home to do'?

Table B. 1 Measures of personal engagement

	May et al. (2004)	Rich et al. (2010)
Physical engagement	• I exert a lot of energy performing my job. • I stay until the job is done. • I take work home to do.	• I work with intensity on my job. • I try my hardest to perform well on my job.
Emotional engagement	• I really put my heart into my job. • I get excited when I perform well on my job.	• I am enthusiastic in my job. • I am proud of my job
Cognitive engagement	• Performing my job is so absorbing that I forget about everything else. • I am rarely distracted when performing my job.	• At work, my mind is focused on my job. • At work, I am absorbed by my job.

Source: May *et al.* (2004); Rich *et al.* (2010).

REFERENCES

Chartered Institute of Personnel and Development (2006) *How Engaged Are British Employees?* London: Chartered Institute of Personnel and Development.

Colquitt, J. (2001) On the dimensionality of organizational justice: A construct validation of a measure. *Journal of Applied Psychology*, **86**(3), 386–400.

Cook, J. D. and Wall, T. D. (1980) New work attitude measures of trust, organizational commitment, and personal need non-fulfilment. *Journal of Occupational Psychology*, **53**(1), 39–52.

Institute of Personnel Management (1992) *Performance Management in the UK: An Analysis of the Issues.* London: Institute of Personnel Management.

Kahn, W. A. (1990) Psychological conditions of personal engagement and disengagement at work. *Academy of Management Journal*, **33**(4), 692–724.

Lee, C., Bobko, P., Earley, P. C. and Locke, E. A. (1991) An empirical analysis of a goal setting questionnaire. *Journal of Organizational Behavior*, **12**(6), 467–482.

May, D. R., Gilson, R. L. and Harter, L. M. (2004) The psychological conditions of meaningfulness, safety and availability and the engagement of the human spirit at work. *Journal of Occupational and Organizational Psychology*, **77**(1), 11–37.

NHS (2013) *Making Sense of your Staff Survey Data.* NHS Staff Survey Co-ordination Centre. www.nhsstaffsurveys.com/Caches/Files/ST13.%20MAKING%20 SENSE%20OF%20YOUR%20STAFF%20SURVEY%20DATA_FINAL.pdf (accessed 7 January 2016).

Rich, B. L., LePine, J. A. and Crawford, E. R. (2010) Job engagement: Antecedents and effects on job performance. *Academy of Management Journal*, **53**(3), 617–635.

Schaufeli, W. and Bakker, A. (2004) *Utrecht Work Engagement Scale: Preliminary Manual*. www.wilmarschaufeli.nl/publications/Schaufeli/Test%20Manuals/Test_manual_UWES_English.pdf (accessed 15 January 2016).

Steelman, L. A., Levy, P. E. and Snell, A. F. (2004) The feedback environment scale: Construct definition, measurement, and validation. *Educational and Psychological Measurement*, **64**(1), 165–184.

Tang, T. L-P. and Sarsfield-Baldwin, L. J. (1996) Distributive and procedural justice as related to satisfaction and commitment. *S.A.M. Advanced Management Journal*, **61**(3), 25–31.

Thurston, P. W. and McNall, L. (2010) Justice perceptions of performance appraisal practices. *Journal of Managerial Psychology*, **25**(3) 201–228.

Warr, P. B., Cook, J. and Wall, T. D. (1979) Scales for the measurement of some work attitudes and aspects of psychological well-being. *Journal of Occupational Psychology*, **52**(2), 129–148.

INDEX